D1497160

A FUTURE OF FAITH

This Large Print Book carries the
Seal of Approval of N.A.V.H.

A FUTURE OF FAITH

THE PATH OF CHANGE IN
POLITICS AND SOCIETY

POPE FRANCIS

with Dominique Wolton

THORNDIKE PRESS
A part of Gale, a Cengage Company

GALE
A Cengage Company

Farmington Hills, Mich • San Francisco • New York • Waterville, Maine
Meriden, Conn • Mason, Ohio • Chicago

Copyright© 2018 by Éditions de l'Observatoire/Humensis and Libreria Editrice Vaticana.
Translation copyright© 2018 by Shaun Whiteside.
Thorndike Press, a part of Gale, a Cengage Company.

ALL RIGHTS RESERVED
Thorndike Press® Large Print Popular and Narrative Nonfiction.
The text of this Large Print edition is unabridged.
Other aspects of the book may vary from the original edition.
Set in 16 pt. Plantin.

LIBRARY OF CONGRESS CIP DATA ON FILE.
CATALOGUING IN PUBLICATION FOR THIS BOOK
IS AVAILABLE FROM THE LIBRARY OF CONGRESS

ISBN-13: 978-1-4328-5585-7 (hardcover)

Published in 2018 by arrangement with Macmillan Publishing Group, LLC/St. Martin's Press

Printed in Mexico
1 2 3 4 5 6 7 22 21 20 19 18

CONTENTS

5

Recently I said and now I repeat, we are going through World War Three but in installments. There are economic systems that must make war in order to survive. Accordingly, arms are manufactured and sold and, with that, the balance sheets of economies that sacrifice man at the feet of the idol of money are clearly rendered healthy. And no thought is given to hungry children in refugee camps; no thought is given to the forcibly displaced; no thought is given to destroyed homes; no thought is given, finally, to so many destroyed lives. How much suffering, how much destruction, how much grief. Today, dear brothers and sisters, in all parts of the earth, in all nations, in every heart and in grassroots movements, the cry wells up for peace: War no more![1]

— POPE FRANCIS, OCTOBER 28, 2014

I dream of a Europe that is young, still capable of being a mother: a mother who has life because she respects life and offers hope for life. I dream of a Europe that cares for children, that offers fraternal help to the poor and those newcomers seeking acceptance because they have lost everything and need shelter. I dream of a Europe that is attentive to and concerned for the infirm and the elderly, lest they be simply set aside as useless. I dream of a Europe where being a migrant is not a crime but a summons to greater commitment on behalf of the dignity of every human being. I dream of a Europe where young people breathe the pure air of honesty, where they love the beauty of a culture and a simple life undefiled by the insatiable needs of consumerism, where getting married and having children is a responsibility and a great joy, not a problem due to the lack of stable employment. I dream of a Europe of families, with truly effective policies concentrated on faces rather than numbers, on birth rates more than rates of consumption. I dream of a Europe that promotes and protects the rights of everyone, without neglecting its duties toward all. I dream of a Europe of which it will not be said that its commitment to human rights was its last utopia.[2]

— POPE FRANCIS, MAY 6, 2016

INTRODUCTION:
"NOT EASY . . ."

The Project

There are individual destinies that intersect with history. This is true of Pope Francis who, coming from Latin America, brings a different identity to the Catholic Church. His personality, his journey, his deeds all question an era dominated by the economy but also by a search for meaning, authenticity and often spiritual values. It is this encounter between one man and history that lies at the heart of our discussions, between a man of the cloth and a French intellectual, a layman, a specialist in communication, who has worked for many years on issues of globalization, cultural diversity and otherness.

Why a dialogue? Because it allows us to open ourselves up to one another, to an argument, and to the presence of the reader. Dialogue gives meaning to human communication beyond questions of performance and limits of technology.

The angle I have chosen for this book has a bearing on one of the recurrent questions in the history of the Church: what is the nature of its social and political engagement? How does its approach differ from that of a politician? Questions constantly posed when each reading of the Gospel, each rereading of the Church Fathers and the Pope's encyclicals encourages a critical engagement and an action intended for the poor, the downtrodden, the excluded . . . Those who have stood up for centuries to denounce injustice and inequality have often established a direct connection between the political message and spirituality. The conflicted debate concerning liberation theology is one of the last great examples of this. How to conceive and distinguish the spiritual dimension of the political action of the Church? How far can we go, and where should we not go? The idea is to encourage a reflection on what unites and what separates spirituality and political action. This reflection becomes particularly important at a time when we can clearly observe a return of the spiritual question and a time when, simultaneously and through the globalization of information, inequality is more visible, increasing the urgency of commitment

16

to action, but sometimes also simplifying arguments and often increasing the desire to reduce everything to a political approach. How can we avoid, in the name of "modernity," reducing the critical engagement of the Church to that of a global politician, a close cousin of the UN? The Jesuits, through their history, and Latin America for the history of the Pope, are shining examples of this debate, of the need to preserve a distinction between these two logics, and the difficulty of doing so.

The Encounter

You don't master an encounter, it assumes a shape of its own. Here it was free, nonconformist, trusting, full of humor. There was a mutual sympathy. The Pope was very much present, he was listening, modest, inhabited by history, with no illusions about humanity. I meet him outside of any institutional context, at his home, but that doesn't fully account for his ability to listen, his freedom and his availability. There was very, very little double-talk.

Sometimes I get dizzy when I think of the crushing responsibilities that weigh on his shoulders. How can he choose, think, amidst so many obligations and requests? How can he listen and act, not only on behalf of the

Church, but also many global afairs? How does he do it? Yes, he is perhaps in real terms the *first Pope of globalization,* between Latin America and Europe. At once human, modest and at the same time so determined, with both feet planted firmly in history, his role has nothing to do with that of the world's great political leaders, and yet he is always confronted with politics.

Perhaps the most intense phrase that he said quite naturally, in the middle of our exchanges, was: "Nothing scares me." And at the same time there was that other phrase that he uttered gently in the doorway, as he left me one evening, and which I will never forget, so symbolic is it of his humanity, his apostolate: "Not easy, not easy . . . ." What can one say beyond such modesty, solitude, lucidity and intelligence?

The difficulty was to find the best possible level for this dialogue, when there are so many differences between us and at the same time a desire to try to understand one another, to "knock down walls" and admit failures of communication. If someone already expresses himself very well and with great simplicity, it's "not easy" to persuade him to speak, particularly since religious discourse already has an answer to everything, and everything has already been said . . . "Not easy" to avoid repetition of things already familiar from summaries of his speeches, to part company with religious and official vocabulary, seek the truth, assume inevitable failures of communication when they arise. We stayed more on the level of history, of politics, of human beings, than on spiritual matters.

This dialogue between the religious man and the layman might continue indefinitely, as rich in its convergences as in its differences. I was neither a stooge nor a critic, just a scientist, a man of good faith trying to engage in dialogue with one of the most exceptional intellectual and religious personalities in the world. This *freedom*, which I felt throughout the discussions, is profoundly his. It is neither conventional nor conformist. Besides, one need only see how he lived, spoke and acted in Argentina and Latin America to realize that. A radical difference from Europe.

Empirically, and without always being aware of it, I used the same method as I did for my dialogue with Raymond Aron (1981), Cardinal Jean-Marie Lustiger (1987) and the President of the European Commission, Jacques Delors (1994). Philosophy, religion, politics. Three areas which all crop up here as well. Without a doubt this position is best illustrated by the attitude of the researcher, a kind of spokesperson for the universal citizen, invisible, but indispensable when it comes to reflecting on global history. Speaking, engaging in dialogue, in order to shrink unbridgeable distances and allow a little mutual understanding. Paradoxically enough, we bonded most often over a shared philosophy of communication. Privileging humanity over technology. Accepting the lack of communication, encouraging dialogue, removing the technical aspect of communication to rediscover humanist values. Accepting that communication is at least as much a matter of negotiation and compromise as it is an act of sharing. Communication as a political act of diplomacy.

The Big Subjects
Our conversations were conducted over twelve meetings between February 2016 and 2017, a considerable amount by Vatican standards. Particularly since nothing had been decided beforehand, in many cases, our discussions went beyond the strict framework of the book, and not everything appears directly in the text but to a large extent that explains the tone, the atmosphere and the freedom of our exchanges.

The Pope has obviously read the manuscript, and we easily reached agreement.

The themes addressed combine the political, cultural and religious questions that run through the world, and its violence: peace and war; the Church in globalization and its response to cultural diversity; religions and politics; fundamentalism of different kinds and secularism; the relationship between culture and communication; Europe as a territory of cultural cohabitation; the relationship between tradition and modernity; interreligious dialogue; the status of the individual, of the family, of morals and society; universalist perspectives; the role of Christians in a secular world marked by the return of religions; failure of communication and the uniqueness of religious discourse.

These themes are arranged in eight chapters. For each one, I complemented our discussions with extracts from sixteen big speeches delivered by Pope Francis since his election on March 13, 2013. These speeches, delivered all over the world, illustrate our dialogues. They are grouped so two appear in each chapter.

On the other hand, quite deliberately, there will be no references to political and institutional conflicts within the Church.

Apart from the fact that others are more competent than I am on this matter, and that the information is widely available, it had little to do with what I was interested in, namely the place of the Church in the world, and in politics, on the basis of the experience and analysis of the first Jesuit and non-European Pope of the Catholic Church.

One hypothesis concerning the Pope? Socially, he is a bit of a Franciscan; intellectually, a bit of a Dominican; politically, a bit of a Jesuit . . . In any case he is very human. We would probably have to factor in many other things to understand his personality.

Small Failures of Communication . . .

With the Holy Father, everything proceeds from religion and faith, including his approach to clearly political questions. Mercy plays an essential part, as does the depth of a history and an eschatology, or view of our final destiny, the roots of which go back more than four thousand years. My references are more anthropological, even if it is clearly impossible to eliminate spiritual dimensions from the deeds of humanity. Our visions of the world are often the same, even if we approach it from different angles.

22

Different kinds of rationality and logic do not always tally. The greatest aspect of communication lies in trying to understand one another and accept differences. There is, for example, the problem of the contemporary, visible and interactive world, in which performance and the speed of information create more misunderstandings and failures of communication than ever before. Here's a challenge: think of otherness in this open world, avoiding the monopoly of a single religious or political discourse, encouraging mutual understanding.

"Welcome, accompany, discern, integrate": the four key concepts of the Pope's *Amoris Laetitia (The Joy of Love,* March 2016) do, after all, have a certain general import. Particularly when it comes to rethinking questions that are essential in the modern world: work, education, the relationship between science, technology and society, globalization, otherness and cultural diversity, the media and public opinion, political communication, the urban environment. So many themes in which the work of the Church, and indeed its encyclicals, could help us to develop our ideas.

Conducting these discussions wasn't easy either. The Pope doesn't always answer the questions he is asked, or at least not in the

23

sense to which modern rationality has made us accustomed. We are very quickly diverted into references from several centuries ago, or metaphors, or the Gospels. Classical concatenations of ideas do not always apply. We inhabit different symbolic spaces. There were a lot of what I call "little failures of communication," which are the most interesting aspect of this encounter. Particularly since there is a third partner, the reader, and one never knows how he or she will receive these words. In short, it is a dialogue that does not have the "classic rationality" that goes hand in hand with habitual intellectual and political exchanges. All the better, even if it leads to the occasional surprise. This is a philosophy of communication that respects otherness.

The interesting thing about the Church is that it is hardly ever modern, it is not completely in the present, even if it is committed to the present in many of its struggles, and that attitude is clearly what is interesting about this vision of the world, even if it is sometimes alarming or puzzling. Being unconcerned about modernity means obeying values and timescales that do not coincide with our own times, which are dominated by speed, urgency and globalization. In the past, there was often an overlap between religion and politics, the spiritual and the temporal; the results were often dubious. Today, the spiritual no longer overlaps with the temporal, at least not in Christianity, and that distance from modernity in all its forms is in fact an opportunity, with the constant problem of knowing what distance to maintain between the two. Modernity, which vanquished tradition over a period of four centuries, has become an ideology. Placing a new value on tradition is probably a way of redressing the balance. The Catholic Church, along with all other resources — religious, artistic and scientific — can help with this. At any rate, all of these aspects necessarily encourage dialogue, tolerance and mutual understanding. In the present day, tradition, which modernity has rightly resisted for centuries, can be fueled by rationales other than its own. Anything but the continuing threat of one-dimensionality, and the reification of the world, as the Frankfurt School predicted in the 1920s.[1]

The work on this book took two and a half years overall. It provoked an emotional response within me, and led to a deep respect and real humility with regard to this man and all his huge responsibilities.

At the same time, this encounter, with its

25

atmosphere of genuine freedom, meant that many things could be said. A moment suspended in time. Always with the constant reality of globalization which collides with every area of life, with all values, and which we need to think about if we are to avoid new wars. Also, with the growing importance of communication and the lack of communication. In short, "to inform is not to communicate" and to "communicate is to negotiate, in the best instance to live together," concepts which lie at the heart of my attempts to bring about a reconciliation between visions of the world that are often different and often antagonistic to one another. Besides, a certain optimism is possible when we see some common points between secular and religious discourses around the challenges of globalization. We must do everything in our power to avoid the hatred of the Other. The concern of the Christian religion, in terms of its universalist vision, is to preserve dialogue, with the essential words of "respect," "dignity," "acknowledgment" and "trust," which are also at the heart of the democratic model.

— Dominique Wolton, Paris, July 2017

■ ■ ■ ■

1
PEACE AND WAR

■ ■ ■ ■

I

PEACE AND WAR

FIRST INTERVIEW —
FEBRUARY 2016

I have never met Pope Francis. With the translator, Father Louis de Romanet, a friend, I step inside the modest residence at Saint Martha's House,[1] just beside Saint Peter's Basilica. We are made to wait in a small, chilly room. Silence. A certain anxiety. All of a sudden, he comes in, warmly. Immediately, there is that deep and gentle gaze. We introduce ourselves. The discussions begin. Everything gradually becomes natural and direct. Something is happening. He replies seriously, the dialogue gets going, punctuated by laughter, which is very frequent throughout the twelve conversations. Humor, connivance, unfinished phrases and natural communication beyond words, in looks and gestures. No time limit. After an hour and a half he asks to stop because he has to go and see his confessor. I tell him he needs to. We laugh. We agree on a new date. He opens the door and leaves as simply as he came in. The intense emotion of

29

seeing that white-clad silhouette disappearing. Obvious frailty, and the huge power of symbols. We talked about serious matters, peace and war, the place of the Church in globalization and history.

POPE FRANCIS: You go first.

DOMINIQUE WOLTON: In January 2016 in Lesbos you said something strange and beautiful: "We are all migrants, and we are all refugees." At a time when the European and Western powers are closing their doors, what can we say, apart from this magnificent phrase? What can we do?

POPE FRANCIS: There is something I said — and migrant children wore it on their T-shirts: "I'm not a danger, I am in danger." Our theology is a theology of migrants. Because we all are, since the call to Abraham, with all the migrations of the people of Israel, and Jesus himself was a refugee, an immigrant, and existentially, by virtue of our faith, we are migrants. Human dignity necessarily implies "being on one's way." When a man or a woman is not on their way, they are a mummy, they are a museum piece. The individual is not alive.

It isn't just a matter of "being" on the way,

but of "making" one's way. You make your way. There is a Spanish poem that says: "you make your path by walking." And to walk is to communicate with others; when you walk, you meet people. Walking is perhaps at the root of the culture of meeting: people meet, they communicate, whether well, through friendship, or badly, through war, which is one extreme. Great friendship, and war too, are forms of communication, a communication of aggression of which mankind is capable. When I say man, I mean man and woman. When human individuals decide to stop walking, they fail. They fail in their human vocation. Walking, always being on the way, means always communicating. You may be on the wrong path, you may fall — as in the story of the thread of Ariadne, like Ariadne and Theseus, you may find yourself in a maze — but you walk, you walk, perhaps in the wrong direction, but you walk, you communicate. We have trouble communicating, but we communicate nonetheless. I say that because people who are "on their way" must not be rejected, because that would amount to a rejection of communication.

DOMINIQUE WOLTON: But migrants are being rejected and driven out of Europe?

POPE FRANCIS: If Europeans want to keep themselves to themselves, they'll have to have children! I think the French government launched actual plans, laws to give assistance to large families, but other countries didn't: they prefer the idea of not having children. For different reasons, using different methods.

DOMINIQUE WOLTON: In the spring of 2016,[2] Europe signed a crazy agreement to close the border between Europe and Turkey.

POPE FRANCIS: That's why I keep coming back to the walking man. Man is fundamentally a communicating creature. A person who is mute, in the sense that he doesn't know how to communicate, is a person who cannot "walk," who cannot "travel . . ."

DOMINIQUE WOLTON: A year and a half after those words that you said in Lesbos, the situation has got worse. A lot of people admired what you said, but afterward there was no follow-up. What would you say a year later?

POPE FRANCIS: The problem begins in the countries that the refugees come from. Why do they leave their home? Because of a lack of work, or because of war. Those are the two main reasons. Lack of work, because they have been exploited — I'm thinking of the Africans. Europe has exploited Africa . . . I don't know if one can say that! But some examples of European colonization . . . yes, they exploited Africa. I read that, with his first act of parliament, one African head of state proposed a law of reforestation for his country — and it was passed. The global economic powers had cut down all the trees. Reforestation. The land is dry from having been over-exploited, and there is no work. The first thing that needs to be done — and I said this when I spoke to the United Nations, to the Council of Europe, everywhere — is to find the sources of new jobs, and invest in them. It's also true that Europe needs to invest at home. Because there's an unemployment problem here too. The other reason for migration is war. If you invest, people will find jobs and won't need to leave, but if there is war, they will have to flee anyway. And who's making war? Who's giving them weapons? We are.

DOMINIQUE WOLTON: Not least the French . . .

33

POPE FRANCIS: Really? Other nations too; I know they're involved with arms dealing on a bigger or smaller scale, with all those things. We supply them with weapons so that they destroy themselves. People complain that migrants are coming to destroy us. But we're the ones who are sending them the weapons! Look at the Middle East. It's the same thing. Who's supplying the weapons? To Daesh, to those who support Assad in Syria, to the anti-Assad rebels? Who's supplying the weapons? When I say "we," I mean the West. I'm not accusing any country in particular. The West — and some non-Western countries also sell weapons. We're the ones who supply the weapons. We cause chaos, people flee, and what do we do? We say: "Come on, sort yourselves out!" I don't want to express myself too harshly, but we have no right not to help the people who arrive here. They are human beings. A politician said to me, "The one thing that overrules all agreements is human rights." And there you have a European leader with a clear vision of the problem.

DOMINIQUE WOLTON: This attitude of rejection can also encourage hatred, because today, with the globalization of the image, the internet, television, the whole world can see that Europeans are betraying human rights and rejecting immigrants, closing themselves selfishly away, while we have been indebted to migrants for fifty years, economically, obviously, but also socially and culturally. Europe is going to be struck by a boomerang effect. Europeans say they are the most democratic, but they are betraying their humanist and democratic values! The globalization of information will rebound on itself . . . and yet Europeans can't see that. Out of selfishness. Out of stupidity.

POPE FRANCIS: Europe is the cradle of humanism.

DOMINIQUE WOLTON: To come back to politics . . .

POPE FRANCIS: Every individual, every institution, throughout the whole world, already has a politics. On the subject of politics with a capital P, the great Pope Pius XI [1922–39], said that it is one of the highest forms of charity. Working toward a "good" politics means helping a country to advance, helping its culture to advance: that's politics. And it's a job. On my way

35

back from Mexico in mid-February 2016,[3] I learned from journalists that Donald Trump, before being elected president, said that I was a politician before declaring that, once he was elected, he would build thousands of kilometers of walls . . . I thanked him for calling me a politician, because Aristotle defines the human being as a *political animal,* and it's an honor for me. So at least I'm a person! As to walls . . .

The instrument of politics is closeness, it is about confronting problems, understanding them. There's another thing that we've forgotten how to do: persuasion. That may be the subtlest, the most refined political method. I listen to the other person's arguments, I analyze them and present him with mine . . . The other person tries to convince me, I try to persuade him, and, in that way, we walk together. Perhaps we don't arrive at a Hegelian-style or idealistic synthesis — thank God, because you can't do that, you mustn't do that, because it always destroys something.

DOMINIQUE WOLTON: The definition you give of politics — convincing people, arguing and above all negotiating — corresponds perfectly with the definition of communication that I defend, which stresses the impor-

36

tance of negotiation even in a situation of uncommunication![4] Communication is a concept inseparable from democracy, because it presupposes the freedom and equality of both partners. Communicating sometimes means sharing, but most often it means negotiating and living together . . .

POPE FRANCIS: Engaging in politics means accepting that there is a tension which we are unable to resolve. And yet to resolve something through synthesis is to destroy one party in favor of the other. There can only be a resolution upward, to a higher level, where both parties give the best of themselves, in a result which is not a synthesis but a common journey, a "walking together." Let's take globalization, for example. It's an abstract word. Let's compare the idea to something concrete: one might see globalization, which is a political phenomenon, in the form of a "bubble," each point of which is equidistant from the center. All the points are identical, and what prevails is uniformity: it is quite plain that this kind of globalization destroys diversity.

But we can also conceive of it as a polyhedron[5] in which all the points are united, but in which each point, whether it is a people or an individual, preserves its own identity.

37

Engaging in politics is seeking that tension between unity and people's own identities.

Let's move on to the field of religion. When I was a child, they used to say that all Protestants went to hell — all of them, absolutely all of them. (*laughter*) Ah, yes, it was a mortal sin. There was even a priest who used to burn the tents of the evangelical missionaries in Argentina. Here, I'm talking about the years 1940 to 1942. I was four or five, I was walking in the street with my grandmother and, on the other side of the pavement, there were two women from the Salvation Army, with their hats with the insignia. I asked, "Tell me, Grandma, who are those ladies? Are they nuns?" and she replied, "No, they're Protestants. But they're good people." So, the first time I heard an ecumenical speech, it came from an elderly person. My grandmother was opening up the doors of ecumenical diversity to me. We must transmit that experience to everyone. In the education of children, of young people . . . each one has their own identity . . . concerning interreligious dialogue; it must exist, but one cannot establish a sincere dialogue between religions if one does not take one's own identity as a starting point! I have my identity, and I speak with mine. We come closer to one another,

38

we find points in common, things we don't agree on, but on those points in common we forge ahead for the good of all, we do charitable works, we perform educational actions, together, lots of things. What my grandmother did with the child that I was at the age of five was a political act. She taught me to open the door.

In tense situations, then, we must not seek synthesis, because synthesis can destroy everything; we must tend toward the polyhedron, toward the unity that preserves all diversities, all identities. The master in this field — because I don't want to commit an act of plagiarism — is Roman Guardini.[6] In my view Guardini is the man who understood everything, and he explains it particularly well in his book *Der Gegensatz* — I don't know the English title, but in Italian it's *La Contrapposizione*. That first book that he wrote on metaphysics, in 1925, is his masterpiece in my view. In it, he explains what we might call the "philosophy of politics," but at the root of all politics lie persuasion and closeness. The Church must therefore open its doors. When the Church adopts an attitude that is not just, it proselytizes, and proselytism, I don't know if I can say this, isn't very Catholic! (*laughter*)

DOMINIQUE WOLTON: You acknowledge that for a long time the Church defended a more than inegalitarian concept of dialogue. What is the relationship between proselytism and interreligious dialogue?

POPE FRANCIS: Proselytism destroys unity. And that's why interreligious dialogue does not mean making everyone agree, it means walking together, each with his or her own identity. It's like when you set off on a mission, when nuns or priests go into the world to bear witness. The politics of the Church is its own witness. Going out of oneself. Bearing witness. Let me come back to Guardini for a moment. There is also a very short book on Europe by one of the thinkers who inspired him, Przywara, who also works on these very questions. But the master of oppositions, of bipolar tensions, as we might call them, is Guardini, who teaches us this path of unity in diversity. What's happening today with fundamentalists? Fundamentalists lock themselves up in their own identity and don't want to hear anything else. There is also a fundamentalism concealed within global politics. Because ideologies are not capable of engaging in politics. They help us think — besides, we need to know ideologies — but they are

40

not capable of engaging in politics. We saw a lot of those in the last century, ideologies that have given rise to political systems. And they don't work.

So, what must the Church do? Agree with one or with the other? That would be the temptation, it would send out the image of an imperialist Church, which is not the Church of Jesus Christ, which is not the Church of service.

Let me give you an example for which I can't claim any merit, which is down to two great men that I'm very fond of: Shimon Peres[7] and Mahmoud Abbas.[8] Those two men were friends, and they spoke to each other on the phone. When I went there, they wanted to make some kind of gesture, but they couldn't find the place to do it, because Abbas couldn't go to Jerusalem, to the nunciature. Peres said, "I'd happily go to the Palestinian territory, but the government won't let me go there without a significant escort, and that would look like an act of aggression." So both asked if they could meet here. I thought I couldn't organize the interview on my own with both of them, so I called Bartholomew I, the Orthodox Patriarch of Constantinople. So, four different religions came together, different, but all doing the same thing, because they all wanted peace and unity. Each one planted a seed of his own but a tree remained. We planted it together. The other thing that remained was the memory of a friendship, an accolade among brothers. The Church must serve politics by building bridges: that is its diplomatic role. "The work of Nuncios is to build bridges."

Here's something that is at the heart of our faith. God the Father sent His son, and He is the bridge. "Pontifex": the word sums up God's attitude toward humanity, and that must be the political attitude of the Church and of Christians. Let us build bridges. Let us work. Let us not find ourselves saying "But who are you?" Let us do everything together and then let's talk to each other. That's how things will get better. For example, I felt obliged to go to Caserta[9] and ask forgiveness from the charismatics, from the Pentecostalists. Then I felt the need, when I was in Turin, to go to the Waldensian Church — we did some terrible things to the Waldensians,[10] we even killed them — to ask forgiveness. Sometimes bridges are established when you ask forgiveness. Or when you go to other people's houses. You have to build bridges in the image of Jesus Christ, our model, who is sent by the Father to be the "pontifex," the one who establishes the bridges. In my view, that is the foundation of the political action of the Church. When the Church becomes involved in "low" politics, it is no longer engaging in politics.

DOMINIQUE WOLTON: Everyone says, "The Church doesn't get involved in politics." But the Church intervenes, with you, as it did with John Paul II, and Benedict XVI before that, about everything: migrants, wars, borders, climate, nuclear, terrorism, corruption, ecology . . . Isn't that politics? To what extent is the Church involved in politics and at what point does it turn into something else?

POPE FRANCIS: The French bishops wrote a pastoral letter in autumn 2016, following on from a letter that they wrote fifteen years ago, *Rediscovering the meaning of politics.* [11] There's big politics and there's little party politics. The Church mustn't get involved in party politics. Paul VI and Pius XI said that politics, big politics, is one of the highest forms of charity. Why? Because it is oriented toward the common good of all.

DOMINIQUE WOLTON: Yes, that's plainly where the greatness of politics lies.

POPE FRANCIS: But, given the diversity of political parties, the Church mustn't intervene. That's the freedom of the faithful.

DOMINIQUE WOLTON: Is that why you don't support the existence of Christian parties?

POPE FRANCIS: That's a difficult question, and one I'm worried about answering. I'm in favor of parties providing the great Christian values: they are values for the good of humanity. That I do support. But a party just for Christians or just for Catholics, no. That always ends in failure.

DOMINIQUE WOLTON: I think you're right. Because for 150 years there have been Christian parties, and the result . . .

POPE FRANCIS: It's a form of "caesaropapism,"[12] we agree on that, and it leads me to talk about something that's so dear to the French: *laïcité* — secularism.

DOMINIQUE WOLTON: The question of secularism has returned more powerfully today with the fundamentalism that seeks to unite political and religious power once again.

POPE FRANCIS: *"Laïcité,"* the separation of church and state,[13] is a healthy thing. There's a healthy way of separating the two. Jesus said, "Give unto Caesar the things that are Caesar's, and to God the things that are God's." We are all equal before God. But I think that in some countries — France for example — the separation of church and state is too much colored by the Enlightenment, constructing a collective imagination in which religions are seen as a subculture. I think that France — this is my opinion, not the official opinion of the Church — should "elevate" the level of secularism a little, in the sense of saying that religions are also part of culture, and how can that be explained in a *laïciste* way? By opening themselves up to transcendence, and everyone can find their own form of openness. In the French cultural legacy, the Enlightenment carries too much weight. I understand that legacy in historical terms, but broadening it out is a task that needs to be done. There are governments, whether Christian or not, which do not acknowledge the separation of church and state.

What does it mean for a secular state to be "open to transcendence"? That religions are part of culture, that they aren't subcultures. When they say that you mustn't wear crosses visibly around your neck, or that women mustn't wear this or that, it's a stupid mistake. Because both attitudes represent a culture. One person wears a cross, the other wears something else, the rabbi wears a kippah, and the Pope wears the skullcap! (*laughter*) There you have it, healthy secularism! The Second Vatican Council speaks about that very well, very clearly. I think that there are exaggerations about these subjects, particularly when the separation of church and state is placed above religions. Aren't religions part of culture? Are they subcultures?

DOMINIQUE WOLTON: With all the experience of the Church, its errors, its success stories, what can it contribute in terms of dialogue or living together? What can it do to unblock increasingly violent conflicts, wars and hatred?

POPE FRANCIS: I can only speak of my own experience, what I've said about Jews, the Orthodox and the Palestinians, and also about the experience that I had in the Central African Republic, in November 2015. I encountered so much resistance before I took that trip! But the people there, including the interim president, asked me to come. The interim president is a practicing Catholic, but he's very popular with the local Muslim community. Very well liked. I wanted to go there, even if that involved security problems, to tell them what the Church can do, for example. At Bangui, in the Muslim quarter, I went to the mosque, I prayed at the mosque, I took the imam for a ride in the popemobile . . . I'm not saying that I made peace, but I am saying that the Church needs to do things like that. There's a good archbishop there, there's a good imam and there's a good Protestant president. And all three are working together for peace. All three. They don't argue.

What can we do to ensure that people live in peace? It must be said that between the homeland, the nation and the people there is a higher interest than those individual parts. And for me it's a principle of geopolitics: the whole is greater than the parts.

DOMINIQUE WOLTON: But the journeys you take, are they tools of peace, communication or negotiation? Why do you travel so much, and talk constantly about violence, peace and negotiation?

POPE FRANCIS: I always say that I'm going as a pilgrim to learn — as a pilgrim of

47

peace. You've used a word that I haven't used before: negotiation. Negotiating. I said recently, at a meeting between businessmen and workers at Ciudad Juárez, "When we sit down at the negotiating table, we have an awareness, a certainty, that in a negotiation you always lose something, but everybody wins."[14] Negotiation is an instrument of peace, and one participates in it with the objective of losing as little as possible . . . One always loses something in negotiations, but everyone wins, and that's very good. To put it in Christian terms, a little bit of one's own life for the life of society, the life of all. Negotiation is important.

DOMINIQUE WOLTON: In this context, how do you see what you call "the new evangelization"? What's the connection between the two?

POPE FRANCIS: I'll repeat what I said before: evangelizing isn't the same as proselytism. And that's a phrase from Benedict XVI. Benedict XVI first said in Brazil, in Aparecida, and then many times again, that the Church grows through attraction, not through proselytizing.[15] Politics too. One person is Catholic, one Protestant, one Muslim, another Jewish, but it grows

48

through attraction, through friendship . . .
Bridges, bridges and more bridges . . . In
certain situations you have to reach a
negotiation because there is no other way of
doing things. But that is also a question of
political humility. Let us do what we can, as
far as we can . . .

In my view, at present, the most serious
political threats are uniformity and globalization. There's also a terrible thing that's
happening at the moment: *ideological colonization*. There are ideologies that infiltrate . . . The African bishops have told me
several times, "Our country obtained a loan,
but with imposed conditions that are contrary to our culture." Here we can see an
insidious ideology at work, and I explain it
both in *Evangelii Gaudium*[16] and in *Laudato
Si'*.[17] At the center of all this is the ideology
of worshipping "the money god" that runs
everything. On the contrary, we should put
man and woman back at the center, and
money must be at the service of their
development. Some ideologies want to
colonize Africa, a continent that has always
been exploited! As if it were Africa's fate to
be exploited!

DOMINIQUE WOLTON: When some priests,
or even bishops, revolt against the damage

49

done by globalization, their political action risks veering away from the Gospel and falling into socialist or Marxist political activity. For example, liberation theology, which has been criticized by Rome. How can one maintain a distance between political action and the spiritual dimension?

POPE FRANCIS: Liberation theology[18] is a way of thinking about theology which has often borrowed from non-Christian ideologies, whether they be Hegelian or Marxist. In the 1980s, there was a tendency toward a Marxist analysis of reality, which was then renamed the "theology of the people." I don't like that name very much, but that's the name I knew it by. Walking with the people of God and engaging in a theology of culture.

There is one thinker you should read: Rodolfo Kusch,[19] a German who lived in northwest Argentina, a very good anthropological philosopher. He helped me to understand one thing: the word "people" is not a logical word. It's a mythical word. You can't talk about a people logically, because it would just be a description. To understand a people, understand the values of that people, you must enter the spirit, the heart, the work, the history and the myth of its tradition. That point is really at the root of the so-called theology "of the people." It means going with the people, seeing how they express themselves. The distinction is an important one. And it would be a good idea for you, as an intellectual, to develop this idea of a mythical category! The people is not a logical category; it's a mythical category.

DOMINIQUE WOLTON: How does your experience of Latin America help you gain a better understanding of the contradictions of globalization? Is there a historical, political, cultural capital of Latin America in this regard? And if there is, what perspective does it grant you of internationalization, globalization, the pillage and destruction of cultural identities, etc.?

POPE FRANCIS: Latin America, since the "Aparecida Document,"[20] has become aware that the earth needs to be defended. Deforestation, for example. Amazonia, Pan-Amazonia — not only Brazilian Amazonia — is one of humanity's two lungs. The other is the Congo. They are in the process of reacting. The mines are in danger as well, with arsenic and cyanide. And all of that pollutes the water. There is something that I see as very serious . . . Every Wednesday I meet children here who are suffering from rare diseases. But where do these rare diseases come from? From atomic pollution, pollution from batteries . . . There is also talk of electromagnetic waves. There's a very serious problem that we have to attempt to denounce, which is what I meant in the encyclical *Laudato Si'*, which is the consequences of the money god. I studied chemistry. At that time, we were taught that if you grow maize you do it for four years, not more. Then you stop, you grow grass for the cows for two years, to raise the nitrogen levels of the soil. Then, again, three or four years of maize. That's how it is. Today, everything is planted with soya until the soil dies of it. And it's serious. Latin America is becoming aware of that, but it doesn't have the strength to react to the major farming exploitations. It doesn't even have the strength to resist the cultural exploitation of its own citizens.

I'm thinking of the country I come from. In Argentina, how many people have lost that sense of land, of homeland, of people? They have succumbed to ideology, in this globalized world.

Well, I'm aware that I've talked about a lot of things . . .

The Church has to enter into the people, it must be the people, make the people grow, and the culture of the people. The people must be able to do the liturgy in this way or that . . . That's the great contribution of Vatican II: inculturation.[21] We have to continue moving in that direction. The other day, I was in San Cristóbal de las Casas, in Chiapas: that indigenous liturgy, so dignified, so well conducted . . . they feel it . . . and it's beautiful . . . and Catholic.

DOMINIQUE WOLTON: Coming from Latin America, how do you see Europe? There are many connections between the two continents, cultural and political connections: How do you see the strengths and weaknesses of Europe, as a political and spiritual construction site?

POPE FRANCIS: Are you familiar with what I said in Strasbourg[22]?

DOMINIQUE WOLTON: Yes.

POPE FRANCIS: I think that Europe has become a "grandmother," while I'd like to see a Europe that's a mother. In terms of birthrates, France is at the head of the European countries, I think, with over 2 percent. But Italy, at around 0.5 percent is much lower. It's the same with Spain. Europe may be losing its sense of culture, of tradition. Just think, it's the only continent that has given us such cultural wealth, and I should stress that. Europe must find itself by returning to its roots. And not being afraid. Not being afraid of being Europe the mother. And I will say that in my speech for the Charlemagne Prize.[23]

DOMINIQUE WOLTON: So, what is your main worry for Europe, and your main hope?

POPE FRANCIS: I don't see a Schuman any more, I don't see an Adenauer[24] . . .

DOMINIQUE WOLTON: (*laughter*) Still, there's you. And there are others . . .

POPE FRANCIS: Europe, right now, is afraid. It's closing, closing, closing . . .

DOMINIQUE WOLTON: The subject of borders has always been very important for you. Why is there this constant desire to ask the Church to go beyond its borders, or to ask the Church to be at the borders?

POPE FRANCIS: Borders? I talk a lot about peripheries, which aren't the same as borders. The periphery may be geographical, existential, human. And our own internal peripheries are better at helping us see reality than the center. Because, to reach the center, you pass through filters, while, at the peripheries, you see reality.

DOMINIQUE WOLTON: You can see better from a distance.

POPE FRANCIS: But I don't talk much about borders.

DOMINIQUE WOLTON: Still, you say, "The Church has to get beyond borders."

POPE FRANCIS: Ah, no, there I'm talking about bridges. Building bridges.

DOMINIQUE WOLTON: Yes, you talk about bridges, but bridges between borders.

POPE FRANCIS: Building bridges and not walls, because walls come down. That's the idea.

DOMINIQUE WOLTON: "Periphery" — I don't think it's an idea that's been sufficiently developed. For thirty years, the return of borders has downgraded the problems involved with peripheries. If we upgraded peripheries again, it would allow us to relativize this obsession with borders, which is often accompanied by the hatred of others . . .

POPE FRANCIS: But borders and periphery aren't opposites. The periphery, on the other hand, is opposed to the center. Europe was better represented when Magellan reached the south. Suddenly, it wasn't represented only from Paris, Madrid or Lisbon, which were at the center of Europe. "Existential peripheries" also exist — for example, those of a society or those of a more personal order. The phrase that I like to quote is, "Reality is better understood from the peripheries than from the center." First of all, because the center is closed, while at the periphery you're with other people. There's also the fact that going to the peripheries is the commandment of the Gospel. The apostles went out from Jerusalem to the whole world. They didn't stay there, building a Church for intellectuals. So much so that the first heresy denounced by the Apostle John is Gnosticism, the elite that doesn't go toward the people.

DOMINIQUE WOLTON: That's what you said when you opened the doors for the Year of Mercy [2016]: "We must open them up because Jesus is inside and wants to come out."

POPE FRANCIS: Yes.

DOMINIQUE WOLTON: In a war, the chiefs of staff, the ones who make the decisions, are often far from the front. Because, at the front, you don't see anything. It's the same idea. And, these days, the same problem arises with the globalization of information: journalists can deal with everything "live," thinking that that means they are "closer" to reality and to truth. But they are so close that they have no distance from it. In a book I wrote about the first Gulf War, in 1990, *War Game,* I pointed a finger at the emergence of live global news and said, "Be careful, live global news can be dangerous too." Today, everything is "live." And it hasn't given us a better understanding of things. There is no more truth because there is no longer any filter . . .

POPE FRANCIS: This aspect of borders, as a clear limit, is no less real. And that's why I say again: yes, there are borders, but there must also be bridges. So that a border doesn't become a wall.

DOMINIQUE WOLTON: What are the bridges that the Church failed to build in the twentieth century, and which ones did it succeed in building?

POPE FRANCIS: I think the Church built lots of bridges, lots of them. But, in the first few centuries, it didn't always succeed . . . I'm thinking of the Reformation, five centuries ago. It didn't succeed in building a bridge with the Reformation thinkers because it was in a very, very complex political context. There was also a question of mentality, which wasn't mature. A mentality based on the principle *"Cuius region, ejus religio"* — "Whose realm, his religion"[25] — which is not a mature mentality. Let us go further back, to the time of the Crusades. Who was the first to understand how to behave with Muslims? Francis of Assisi, who went to talk to their leader. But making war was in the mentality of the age . . . Here, we're touching on a question which is very important in my view: an age must be interpreted with the hermeneutics of the same age. Not out of context.

DOMINIQUE WOLTON: Yes, definitely.

POPE FRANCIS: We shouldn't interpret the past with the hermeneutics of our time.

DOMINIQUE WOLTON: Epistemologically, that's the definition of history. Otherwise, you're guilty of anachronism. Sadly, we act anachronistically all the time . . . But let's talk about the interreligious meeting in Assisi.[26] What did it bring in the way of progress, in your opinion? At the meeting in September 2016 you produced three very strong phrases: you referred to "the Third World War in pieces": you said, "There is no such thing as a holy war," and, "There is no god of war." Can you give me an assessment of Assisi, thirty years on?

POPE FRANCIS: I think Assisi is a symbol of peace. And these meetings of religious leaders, of all religions, are testimony that all religions want peace and brotherhood. Making war in the name of God is not just; the only thing that is just is peace.

DOMINIQUE WOLTON: Do you think that, in thirty years, the Assisi meeting allowed the balance to tilt in the direction of peace?

59

POPE FRANCIS: Yes, yes. Maybe not concrete peace, because we're in a state of war. But yes, in terms of the idea that this war is unjust. Even today, we have to think in terms of the concept of "the just war." We have learned in political philosophy that, in order to defend yourself, you can make war and consider it just. But can you speak of a "just war"? Or even a "defensive war"? Because the only just thing is peace.

DOMINIQUE WOLTON: You mean you can't use the term "just war," is that it?

POPE FRANCIS: I don't like using it. You hear people saying, "I make war because I have no other possible way of defending myself." But no war is just. Only peace is just.

DOMINIQUE WOLTON: Yes, that's radical.

POPE FRANCIS: Because, with war, you lose everything. While, with peace, you win everything.

DOMINIQUE WOLTON: Well, in the end, peace doesn't always win, but . . . I understand the philosophy. From a hermeneutic point of view, it's important to separate the two.

Isn't there a gap between the wealth and diversity of the "sensors" that the Church has at its disposal, and what it does with them? The faithful, its priests, its congregations, its associations represent diversified and high-quality "sensors" for picking up the political stakes: it is not certain that the Church always uses that knowledge and that diversity of perceptions of the world . . .

POPE FRANCIS: Two words. Above all: closeness. When Church leaders, let's call them that, aren't close to the people, they don't understand the people and they don't do good. Second word: worldliness . . . Whether I'm a priest, a bishop, secular or Catholic, if I'm worldly, people are going to move away from me . . . The people of God have a sense of things!

DOMINIQUE WOLTON: Yes, but all peoples have intuition. I often write, "All peoples are intelligent, very intelligent, even if they are illiterate." Intelligence is never a matter of culture or diplomas.

POPE FRANCIS: The people have an understanding of reality.

61

DOMINIQUE WOLTON: Of course, perhaps those aren't necessarily the words one would use, but they see and feel.

POPE FRANCIS: Because the word "people," as I think I said before, is not a logical concept, it's a mythical concept. Not mystical, mythical.

DOMINIQUE WOLTON: Yes, they're not the same! Why do you specify "mythical and not mystical"?

POPE FRANCIS: Because, once, I said "mythical," and in *L'Osservatore Romano,* they accidentally got the translation wrong, talking about the "mystical people . . ."

DOMINIQUE WOLTON: *(laughter)* Oh, I didn't know that! They must have thought, "This Pope's crazy!"

POPE FRANCIS: And you know why? Because they didn't understand the meaning of the mythical people. They said to themselves, "No, it's the Pope who's made a mistake; let's put 'mystical!' "

DOMINIQUE WOLTON: What is the Church's main strength in globalization today? Its advantages, its strengths and its weaknesses?

POPE FRANCIS: In my view, its weakness lies in wanting to modernize without discernment. It's very general, but it sums up a lot of things. One other weakness, and that affects us, is rigid clericalism. Rigidity. You see rigid young priests. They're afraid of the Gospel and prefer canon law. But that's a caricature, just a manner of speaking . . . There is also rigidity in certain expressions, when the Lord has opened up such joy to us, such hope! Those are the two serious weaknesses that I'm familiar with: clericalism and rigidity. That's why I like to say — forgive me, I'm quoting myself — that priests must be "goatherds who retain a smell of goat." If you're a pastor, it's about serving people. Not looking at yourself in the mirror. The true wealth is the weak. The little people, the poor, the sick, the ones right at the bottom, the ones who are morally weakened . . . prostitutes, but those who are seeking Jesus, and who allow themselves to be touched by Jesus. When I went to Africa, there were sixteen prostitutes working with a group of nuns who were helping to take them out of human trafficking. That's where the wealth of the Church lies:

among the sinners. Why? Because when you feel you are a sinner, you ask for forgiveness, and by doing that you build a bridge. And the bridge becomes established! Little things, simple things: that's where the treasure lies. That's what does me good. I'm speaking from experience.

The two pillars of our faith, of our wealth: the Beatitudes[27] and Matthew;[28] the way in which we will be judged. That is where the treasure lies. That is where we must seek it. But you will say that I'm too simplistic a pope! (*laughter*) But thank God . . .

DOMINIQUE WOLTON: Off the top of your head, can you say what your greatest joy is?

POPE FRANCIS: I am at peace with the Lord. I have many joys. When priests come to me for help with their problems, I feel the joy of someone who is given a child; it's also a joy to celebrate Mass. I feel like a priest; I never, ever thought I would end up here, in this cage! (*laughter*).

DOMINIQUE WOLTON: (*laughter*) Keep your sense of humor. Because humor is a leveller of the intelligence. Everyone understands it, everyone.

POPE FRANCIS: I would even go further than that: the sense of humor is the thing, on the human level, that comes closest to divine grace.

ADDRESS OF THE HOLY FATHER
ON THE OCCASION OF HIS
MEETING WITH MEMBERS OF THE
GENERAL ASSEMBLY OF THE
UNITED NATIONS
ORGANIZATION, NEW YORK

(September 25, 2015)

[. . .] This is the fifth time that a Pope has visited the United Nations. [. . .] I can only reiterate the appreciation expressed by my predecessors, in reaffirming the importance which the Catholic Church attaches to this Institution and the hope which she places in its activities.

[. . .] The work of the United Nations, according to the principles set forth in the Preamble and the first Articles of its founding Charter, can be seen as the development and promotion of the rule of law, based on the realization that justice is an essential condition for achieving the ideal of universal fraternity. [. . .] To give to each his own, to cite the classic definition of justice, means that no human individual or group can consider itself absolute, permitted to bypass the dignity and the rights of other individuals or their social groupings. [. . .]

First, it must be stated that a true "right of the environment" does exist, for two reasons. First, because we human beings are part of the environment. [. . .] Second, because every creature [. . .] has an intrinsic value, in its existence, its life, its beauty and its interdependence with other creatures. [. . .] In all religions, the environment is a fundamental good.

The misuse and destruction of the environment are also accompanied by a relentless process of exclusion. In effect, a selfish and boundless thirst for power and material prosperity leads both to the misuse of available natural resources and to the exclusion of the weak and disadvantaged, either because they are differently abled, or because they lack adequate information and technical expertise, or are incapable of decisive political action. Economic and social exclusion is a complete denial of human fraternity and a grave offense against human rights and the environment. The poorest are those who suffer most from such offenses, for three serious reasons: they are cast off by society, forced to live off what is discarded and suffer unjustly from the abuse of the environment. They are part of today's widespread and quietly growing "culture of waste."

[. . .]

Our world demands of all government leaders a will which is effective, practical and constant, concrete steps and immediate measures for preserving and improving the natural environment and thus putting an end as quickly as possible to the phenomenon of social and economic exclusion, with its baneful consequences: human trafficking, the marketing of human organs and tissues, the sexual exploitation of boys and girls, slave labor, including prostitution, the drug and weapons trade, terrorism and international organized crime. Such is the magnitude of these situations and their toll in innocent lives, that we must avoid every temptation to fall into a declarationist nominalism which would assuage our consciences. We need to ensure that our institutions are truly effective in the struggle against all these scourges.

[. . .]

At the same time, government leaders must do everything possible to ensure that all can have the minimum spiritual and material means needed to live in dignity and to create and support a family, which is the primary cell of any social development. In practical terms, this absolute minimum has three names: lodging, labor, and land; and one spiritual name: spiritual freedom, which includes religious freedom, the right to education and all other civil rights.

[. . .]

The common home of all men and women must continue to rise on the foundations of a right understanding of universal fraternity and respect for the sacredness of every human life [. . .] This common home of all men and women must also be built on the understanding of a certain sacredness of created nature.

Such understanding and respect call for a higher degree of wisdom, one which accepts transcendence [. . .] and recognizes that the full meaning of individual and collective life is found in selfless service to others and in the sage and respectful use of creation for the common good. To repeat the words of

Paul VI, "the edifice of modern civilization has to be built on spiritual principles, for they are the only ones capable not only of supporting it, but of shedding light on it."

[. . .]

The praiseworthy international juridical framework of the United Nations Organization and of all its activities, like any other human endeavor, can be improved, yet it remains necessary; at the same time it can be the pledge of a secure and happy future for coming generations. And so it will, if the representatives of the States can set aside partisan and ideological interests, and sincerely strive to serve the common good. I pray to Almighty God that this will be the case, and I assure you of my support and my prayers.

Joint declaration made at the meeting between His Holiness Pope Francis and His Holiness Kirill, Patriarch of Moscow and All Russia, José Martí International Airport, Havana, Cuba

(February 12, 2016)

1. By God the Father's will, [. . .] we, Pope Francis and Kirill, Patriarch of Moscow and All Russia, have met today in Havana. We give thanks to God, glorified in the Trinity, for this meeting, the first in history. [. . .]
5. [. . .] Catholics and Orthodox have been deprived of communion in the Eucharist. We have been divided by wounds caused by old and recent conflicts, by differences inherited from our ancestors, [. . .] We are pained by the loss of unity, the

outcome of human weakness and of sin [. . .]

7. In our determination to undertake all that is necessary to overcome the historical divergences we have inherited, we wish to combine our efforts to give witness to the Gospel of Christ and to the shared heritage of the Church of the first millennium, responding together to the challenges of the contemporary world.
   [. . .]

8. Our gaze must firstly turn to those regions of the world where Christians are victims of persecution. In many countries [. . .] whole families, villages and cities of our brothers and sisters in Christ are being completely exterminated. [. . .] It is with pain that we call to mind the situation in Syria, Iraq and other countries of the Middle East, and the massive exodus of Christians from the land [. . .] in which they have lived since the time of the Apostles, together with other religious communities.

9. We call upon the international community to act urgently in order to

prevent the further expulsion of Christians from the Middle East. [. . .] we wish to express our compassion for the suffering experienced by the faithful of other religious traditions who have also become victims of civil war, chaos and terrorist violence. [. . .]

12. We bow before the martyrdom of those who, at the cost of their own lives, have given witness to the truth of the Gospel, preferring death to the denial of Christ. [. . .]

13. Interreligious dialogue is indispensable in our disturbing times. [. . .] In our current context, religious leaders have the particular responsibility to educate their faithful in a spirit which is respectful of the convictions of those belonging to other religious traditions. Attempts to justify criminal acts with religious slogans are altogether unacceptable. No crime may be committed in God's name [. . .]

15. [. . .] we are concerned about the situation in many countries in which Christians are increasingly con-

fronted by restrictions to religious freedom [. . .] It is a source of concern for us that there is a current curtailment of the rights of Christians, if not their outright discrimination, when certain political forces, guided by an often very aggressive secularist ideology, seek to relegate them to the margins of public life.

16. The process of European integration, which began after centuries of blood–soaked conflicts, was welcomed by many with hope, as a guarantee of peace and security. Nonetheless, we invite vigilance against an integration that is devoid of respect for religious identities. While remaining open to the contribution of other religions to our civilization, it is our conviction that Europe must remain faithful to its Christian roots. [. . .]

17. [. . .] We cannot remain indifferent to the destinies of millions of migrants and refugees knocking on the doors of wealthy nations.

[. . .]

19. The family is the natural center of human life and society. [. . .] Ortho-

dox and Catholics share the same conception of the family, and are called to witness that it is a path of holiness, [. . .].

21. We call on all to respect the inalienable right to life. Millions are denied the very right to be born into the world. [. . .] The emergence of so-called euthanasia leads elderly people and the disabled to begin to feel that they are a burden on their families and on society in general. [. . .]

24. Orthodox and Catholics are united [. . .] also by the mission to preach the Gospel of Christ in the world today. This mission [. . .] excludes any form of proselytism.

We are not competitors but brothers, and this concept must guide all our mutual actions as well as those directed to the outside world. [. . .].

28. [. . .] Much of the future of humanity will depend on our capacity to give shared witness to the Spirit of truth in these difficult times. [. . .]

30. With grace–filled gratitude for the gift of mutual understanding mani-

fested during our meeting, let us with hope turn to the Most Holy Mother of God, invoking her with the words of this ancient prayer: "We seek refuge under the protection of your mercy, Holy Mother of God." May the Blessed Virgin Mary, through her intercession, inspire fraternity in all those who venerate her, so that they may be reunited, in God's own time, in the peace and harmony of the one people of God, for the glory of the Most Holy and indivisible Trinity!

— Francis, Bishop of Rome,
Pope of the Catholic Church
— Kirill, Patriarch of Moscow
and all Russia

■ ■ ■ ■

2
RELIGIONS AND
POLITICS

■ ■ ■ ■

2
RELIGIONS AND POLITICS

INTERVIEW — JUNE 2016

The weather has improved. Spring has arrived in Rome, bright and mild. Same place, different atmosphere. Pope Francis arrives just as simply as he did on the first occasion. Without an escort. We immediately set to work. The central theme is the return of religions, secularism, fundamentalism. The same liveliness is in our exchanges, and the feeling of having time . . . Everything is calm. What a contrast when we go outside and find ourselves amid the bustle of Saint Peter's Square: full of noise and people. Only a few meters away from the crowd, I am working peacefully, trustingly, with the Holy Father. We are discussing serious matters. Strange paradoxes of experience and gaps in time. I'm walking silently, my head filled with our exchanges. Such freedom. No protocol.

DOMINIQUE WOLTON: How can the Church contribute to globalization today?

POPE FRANCIS: Through dialogue. I think that nothing today is possible without dialogue. But it must be a sincere dialogue, even if you have to say disagreeable things to each other's faces. Sincere. But not a dialogue along the lines of "yes, we agree," while secretly saying something completely different. I think the Church must contribute by building bridges. Dialogue is the "big bridge" between cultures. Yesterday, for example, I spent fifty minutes talking with Shimon Peres. He's ninety-three years old. He's a man with a vision, and our whole dialogue consisted of building bridges here and there. I felt I was truly in the presence of a great man, who shared the same feeling that the Church must build bridges, bridges . . .

DOMINIQUE WOLTON: What could the Church do that the UN isn't doing, to promote global peace?

POPE FRANCIS: I know that the UN does a lot of good things. I also hear criticisms, profound criticisms, which they direct at themselves. In this assembly, which will soon have to elect its new secretary general,[1] there is a current of healthy self-criticism, saying that they must "talk less and act more." Because the danger, whether for the Church or the UN, is that of nominalism[2]: merely saying "we must do this and that," and then having a clear conscience and not doing anything, or only small things.

But we must distinguish between the two, the UN and the Church. The UN should have more authority, global and physical. The Church is only a moral authority. The moral authority of the Church depends on the witness of its members, Christians. If Christians don't bear witness, if priests or even bishops become ambitious wheeler-dealers . . . or if Christians are constantly trying to exploit other people, if they contribute to the black economy, if they ignore social justice, they aren't acting as believers. Bearing witness is a necessary act in both institutions, but particularly in the Church. The UN must take decisions, develop a good plan and put it into effect. Not merely announce it. But, yes, they are both up against the danger of nominalism. Plato in the *Gorgias,* talking about information, about the sophists, says more or less this: "The words of the sophists are to politics what makeup is to health[3] . . ." Plato!

DOMINIQUE WOLTON: Where is God in globalization?

POPE FRANCIS: In globalization, as I understand it — as a polyhedron — He is everywhere, in everything. In each individual who gives him or herself and who brings his or her own contribution to the whole. In every country, in the whole world. But — and now I am talking as a Catholic — your question is addressed to Saint Basil of Caesarea[4] and goes beyond Saint Basil. What makes up the unity of the Church, and what its differences? The Holy Spirit. That same God who creates differences, meaning singularities, the great, beautiful variety of the world, is the same one who then establishes harmony. That's why Saint Basil says of the Holy Spirit that it is in harmony. God makes harmony in globalization.

DOMINIQUE WOLTON: How can we reconcile diplomacy and evangelization?

POPE FRANCIS: Evangelization is a mandate from Jesus Christ, and diplomacy is a behavior, a noble profession. The two things are on different levels.

DOMINIQUE WOLTON: Does diplomacy consist of relationships of strength, and evangelization of relationships of equality?

POPE FRANCIS: No, I don't think that's how it is. Because, in diplomacy, there are also fraternal relationships which are concerned with "seeking something together," there is a dialogue, there is a well-intended diplomacy. But very often the methods of evangelization are mistaken as well.

DOMINIQUE WOLTON: The Church is often chided for condemning violence more firmly than inequality. Of applying double standards.

POPE FRANCIS: That may be the case, but, as far as I'm concerned, I speak clearly and forcefully about both.

DOMINIQUE WOLTON: But throughout its history, the Church has been more responsive toward conservative governments, and more concerned about left-wing or progressive ones . . .

POPE FRANCIS: Both have done good things, and both have also committed errors. But in the Gospel it is very clear: we are children of God, and he who believed himself the less just, has become the more just. Jesus takes the greatest of sinners and leads them upward. He reestablishes equality from the outset.

And violence . . . Let us think of the great dictatorships of the last century. In Germany, there were Christians who didn't look on Hitler in an unfavorable light, but there were others who knew what he was really like. It was the same here in Italy. The violence of dictatorships . . . There are many forms of violence. But I am more afraid of violence in white gloves than in direct violence. Everyday violence, domestic violence, for example!

DOMINIQUE WOLTON: How can we ensure that globalization doesn't mean inequality, the increase of wealth only for the few?

POPE FRANCIS: In today's world, 62 people own as much wealth as 3.5 billion poor people. In today's world 871 million people are starving. There are 250 million migrants who have nowhere to go, who have nothing.

Today, the drug trade is worth about 300 billion dollars. And in tax havens, an estimated 2,400 billion dollars is "fluttering about," circulating from one place to another.

DOMINIQUE WOLTON: For a long time, the Church has condemned untrammeled capitalism. There are plenty of texts and declarations to say as much. Why hasn't the world heard more about it? Do people not know, or do they not want to know, to understand? What could be done to condemn this expansion of untrammeled capitalism, unleashed by globalization?

POPE FRANCIS: Think about the workers' movements today. There are popular movements all over the world. Those people are sometimes excluded even by trade unionists, because the trade unionists often come from the dominant classes, the upper middle classes at the very least. It is a strong movement claiming its rights. But there is also brutal repression in certain countries, and if you express yourself too freely you put your life in danger. One of the leaders of a popular movement, who took part in the first conference at the Vatican, was killed in Central America . . .

It's difficult, that's why the poor unite; they have great strength together. Religious strength as well.

DOMINIQUE WOLTON: Do you think that the reinforcement of inequalities within the context of globalization gives a boost to liberation theology?

POPE FRANCIS: I'd rather not talk about the liberation theology of the 1970s, because that's something specific to Latin America. But in very just and true theology there is a dimension of liberation because the memory of the people of Israel begins with the liberation from Egypt, doesn't it? The liberation from slavery? The whole history of the Church, and not only of the Church, but of the whole of humanity, is filled with such oppressors, a dominant minority.

DOMINIQUE WOLTON: Yes, but now, with globalization and the globalization of information, we see it more clearly. We see it every day. That has never happened in history before.

POPE FRANCIS: History is a history of sin . . . And here we must return to the source of the capacity for sin, or the root of sin which we all have, don't we? Without succumbing to pessimism, because of the redemption of Jesus Christ, which is the triumph over sin, the source is there, the wound is there, the possibility is there. If you are poor, and I am rich and I want to dominate everything, I corrupt you, and through your corruption I dominate you.

Corruption is really the method used by a

small number of people with the power and money to reach a large number of people.

DOMINIQUE WOLTON: On the subject of mercy, you had a lovely phrase: "Mercy is a journey that passes from our hearts to our hands."

POPE FRANCIS: That's very true. I think mercy[5] is at the heart of the Gospel. What advice does Jesus himself give us? "Be as merciful as the Father." But to complete its journey, the heart must be touched by compassion, by human misery, by any kind of misery. It's what ensures that the heart is moved, and that it begins its journey.

DOMINIQUE WOLTON: How can mercy open up a new path in the world, in this world of competition, of violence?

POPE FRANCIS: Let's speak at a simple level: what seems important to me are works. In this world of violence, for example, there are many men and women, priests, sisters, nuns who are devoted to hospitals, schools . . . So many good people. They are a slap in society's face. Because it is a form of witnessing: "I consume my life." When you go to cemeteries in Africa and you see those dead people, those missionaries — French ones, in particular — who died young, at forty, after contracting malaria . . . That wealth of mercy is moving. And people, when they receive that witness, understand and change. They want to be better people . . . Either that or they kill the one who bears witness! Because they are filled with hatred. Bearing witness involves that risk.

Did I tell you what I saw in Central Africa? A nun, aged about eighty-three or eighty-four, with a little girl of five. I greeted her: "Where are you from?" "I'm from over there, I came this morning by canoe." At eighty-three or eighty-four! "I come here every morning to do the shopping. I've been here since the age of twenty-three." (She came from Brescia.) "I'm a nurse, and I've brought 2,300 children into the world. And this poor little girl's mother died in childbirth, and she had no father, and I adopted her legally. She calls me mother."

That's pure tenderness. Devotion, a whole lifetime! The works of the merciful. For me, visiting the sick, going to prison, making a prisoner feel that he can have hope of becoming a member of society again — that's what the Church preaches. The

Church preaches more with its hands than with its words.

DOMINIQUE WOLTON: What's your evaluation of the 2016 Year of Mercy?

POPE FRANCIS: I can't give an evaluation of it, because when I say that word I think of the census of King David. And the Lord punished King David for that.[6] That's why I'm worried about doing that kind of thing. But I will only say objective things. It was excellent that the Jubilee wasn't held only in Rome. It stressed the synodality of the Church, of every diocesan church. The bishops in the diocesan churches could organize two, three, four Holy Doors. They organized them in prisons, in hospitals . . . That way, the whole of the people of God became involved in that dynamic. Because not many can come to Rome! Then, another very striking thing: the first Door of Mercy of the Jubilee which was opened was not the one at Saint Peter's, but the one in Bangui, in the Central African Republic, five days before. In the periphery . . . When I was preparing the trip to Africa — to Kenya, to Uganda and the Central African Republic — Monsignor Gallagher asked me, "Have you been to Africa before?" and

I said, "Never," and he answered, "You'll be in love by the time you come back . . ."

DOMINIQUE WOLTON: And it's true . . .

POPE FRANCIS: But I asked, "Please, in the liturgy, don't give me Masses lasting six hours." And they told me, "No, don't worry, no more than four hours!" For them, the Mass is a celebration that lasts all Sunday. They dance, but they dance religiously: the dance is there to carry the Word of God. We were all open-mouthed: a religious event. It was very, very beautiful. A real religious event. And then the Jubilee was helped a great deal by the Missionaries of Mercy. These were the priests put forward by the bishops, by the generals of the religious congregations, who went to all the dioceses to absolve all sins, even the ones reserved for the Holy See.[7] And then there was the fact of extending the power to absolve the sin of abortion to all priests. But be careful, that does not mean trivializing abortion. Abortion is a serious matter, it's a serious sin, the murder of an innocent. But, if there is a sin, pardon must be facilitated. Then, in the end, I decided that that measure would remain permanent. From now on, all priests would be able to absolve this sin.

DOMINIQUE WOLTON: Your open and humanist position prompts opposition from the Catholic Church.

POPE FRANCIS: One woman who has a physical memory of the child, because that is often the case, and who weeps, who has wept for years without having the courage to go and see the priest . . . When she heard what I had said . . . Can you imagine the number of people who are breathing at last?

DOMINIQUE WOLTON: Yes, because abortion is always a tragedy.

POPE FRANCIS: Let them at any rate find the forgiveness of the Lord and not sin again. Then there's the problem — and you French are very creative in this respect — of the Lefebvrists.[8] I have been thinking about the people who go to the Lefebvrist Masses, and I have given Lefebvrists the ability to absolve all sins. Not their own, because they still have some explaining to do. But the sins of the people who come to them. The Church is open to all. And that has done a great deal of good.

One other thing that has also done much good is the catechesis[9] on works of mercy,[10] because they had been forgotten. Let me give you an example: two years ago, I had a visit from some members of an apostolic organization, all lay people. It was around the time when I had announced the Year of Mercy. I asked them, "How many of you know by heart the list of works of mercy?" There were six of them. Six out of five thousand . . .

DOMINIQUE WOLTON: And you didn't ask those six people to recite them . . .

POPE FRANCIS: That's why I did a lot of work on the catechesis. I went to do them too. One Friday a month I went to a meeting place for people in difficult situations: people who were sick, whether terminally ill adults or children, priests who were in psychotherapy for serious reasons, refugees, migrants, prostitutes who had escaped from prostitution. I spoke to them. And I also went to see the priests who had left their ministry, because those defrocked priests are regarded with contempt. They are men who, at some point, for one reason or another, lacked the strength to go on and chose to ask for dispensation. Then they met a woman, or maybe they had met one before, we don't know. They started a family with the permission of the Church, they

go to church on Sunday . . . And I went to
see them. That was the idea: all of them.
What came to my mind was that passage in
the Gospel where the king organizes a wedding banquet that the guests don't want to
go to. What did he reply? "Go to the cross-
roads and invite everyone to the banquet,
good and bad, healthy and sick, blind, deaf,
all of them, all of them." That was the idea.
Everyone in the same pot. The pot being
God's mercy. I think that did a lot of good.
It's not something that I invented on a
pastoral level . . . It comes from Paul VI
after the Council . . . John Paul accom-
plished three powerful actions in this respect: the encyclical *Dives in Misericordia*,[11]
the canonization of Saint Faustina[12] and
the institution of the Feast of Mercy on the
first Sunday in Easter. I'm very happy about
it: a lot of people came to confession. I went
down to take confession in the square, and
I saw I don't know how many thousand
young people. There were two hundred
confessors on one side, and two hundred
on the other, and the young people were on
Via della Conciliazione. It was so beautiful!
That encounter with the Lord, the encounter with Jesus. That was an act of grace.

DOMINIQUE WOLTON: Yes, that is grace.

93

POPE FRANCIS: And that is balance. But don't talk about "evaluation." I would like to thank Monsignor Fisichella, who organized this Jubilee of Mercy.

DOMINIQUE WOLTON: What did you like best about World Youth Day in Poland, in the summer of 2016?

POPE FRANCIS: Krakow is a small town. And so many people! So many young people! And the enthusiasm of the young people! They want to hear the truth. The young people know they're being spoken to directly, that they're not being fed stories or lied to. And that's why it's very important to me that young people are in touch with older people. The elderly are the memory of a people, they are wisdom. Young people are strength, they are utopia. And we have to find this bridge, between young people and elderly people, because both of them today, in this world, are outcasts. The elderly are rejected, and rejecting them means throwing away the memory of a people, throwing away our roots. As for young people, only the most competitive can do well. The rest — with drugs, unemployment — are cast aside. And yet the wealth of the future, of the world, of a country really lies among those who have fallen by the wayside. Let them speak!

DOMINIQUE WOLTON: Yes, that's right, there isn't enough communication these days. Why are you holding a Synod on Youth in 2018?

POPE FRANCIS: The mechanism is the following: at the end of a synod, every synodal father hands in a piece of paper with three subjects written on it, and then we carry out a consultation among all the episcopal conferences. The three top themes were, first of all, young people, then the formation of priests, and, third, peace and inter-religious dialogue. I addressed the first and second of these. For me, the first theme doesn't only concern young people, it extends to the second: faith and vocational discernment. Why? Because young people, all young people, have a faith or a "non-faith." And yet we must grow in discernment. For that reason, I thought of merging the first and second subjects: young people and formation. But the term "formation" isn't good. So I chose "discernment and the vocational option." That's very important and we need to think about it: what exactly do young people believe in? As to vocational discernment, I think that, today, in the Church, it is one of the biggest problems: the lack of discernment.

DOMINIQUE WOLTON: There are more than seven billion people today . . . Is witnessing enough?

POPE FRANCIS: "The Church in the Kingdom of God is like a grain of mustard." To fail to understand that is to demonstrate triumphalism. So we need to undertake an examination of the Church.

DOMINIQUE WOLTON: By the way, do you like being called the "Pope for the Poor"?

POPE FRANCIS: I don't like it, because it's the imposition of an ideology. It's an ideological nickname. No, I'm everybody's Pope. The rich and the poor. The poor sinners, of whom I'm the first, yes, that's true.

DOMINIQUE WOLTON: In January 2016, you said: "Immigration is a natural historical phenomenon." A magnificent phrase, but Europe is rejecting all the refugees. What can we do?

POPE FRANCIS: Yes. Europe . . .

DOMINIQUE WOLTON: Europe is betraying its values.

POPE FRANCIS: Yes, that's true, while Europe was created by the Lombards[13] and other barbarians. Because they all mixed. The problem with immigration today is that it frightens people. But who's frightening whom?

DOMINIQUE WOLTON: Why is the Church no longer speaking out about accepting immigration and welcoming refugees?

POPE FRANCIS: I think that if it isn't, it's failing to do its duty. Let's remember what marks the beginning of the Church! Pentecost[14]!

DOMINIQUE WOLTON: The Church pays a lot of attention to ecology — we've read about that in your encyclical on the subject [*Laudato Si'*]. But war isn't ecology. War is human beings. It's a refusal of cultural diversity.

The Church's experience of the political issue of cultural diversity is much more essential than the question of ecology. Ecology is important, of course, but bearing witness to the greatness and wealth of cultural diversity is surely even more important . . . Why does the Church take a clear position about ecology, notably through your encyclical *Laudato Si'*, and much less about cultural diversity, when, in 2005, there was the UNESCO declaration, which is an exceptional text in favor of respect for cultural diversity?

POPE FRANCIS: As regards cultural diversity, the Church began on the day of Pentecost. That was when it opted for cultural diversity. If you read the Book of the Acts of the Apostles, the Apostle Philip is led to the treasurer of Queen Candace[15] of Ethiopia and baptizes him . . . Paul goes to Athens and talks about God . . . And centuries later, Matteo Ricci[16] "opens up" China . . . Often, Rome couldn't understand that attitude, because Rome was closed. That's true. The Church is always tempted into being defensive. It's fearful. It's a bad temptation, it's not good. Where in the Gospels does the Savior say that we must seek safety? On the contrary, he says, "Take risks, go on, forgive!" (*silence*) And evangelize. They wanted to halt Matteo Ricci in China, Roberto de Nobili[17] in India. And there were so many others . . .

DOMINIQUE WOLTON: You've written an encyclical about ecology. But why not an encyclical on the wealth of mankind and cultural diversity?

POPE FRANCIS: You know that liturgical celebrations are different across the world, in the East, in Africa: each one has its own liturgy.

DOMINIQUE WOLTON: The Church has a great deal of experience of cultural diversity. Why not talk about it more, even if only from the point of view of political anthropology?

POPE FRANCIS: The temptation is always toward a uniformity of rules . . . Take for example the apostolic exhortation *Amoris Laetitia.* When I talk about families in difficulty, I say, "We must welcome them, accompany them, discern with them and integrate them into the Church . . ." and then everyone will see the open doors. What happens, in fact, is that you hear people saying, "They can't take communion," "They can't do this or that." There you have the temptation of the Church. No, no, no! That type of prohibition is what you find in the clash between Jesus and the Pharisees.[18]

The same thing! The great people of the Church are the ones with a vision that goes further, the ones who understand: the missionaries.

DOMINIQUE WOLTON: What, in your view, is the greatest threat to peace in the world today?

POPE FRANCIS: Money.

DOMINIQUE WOLTON: You once called money "Satan's dung."

POPE FRANCIS: But that's in the Gospels. When Jesus talks about the division of the heart, he doesn't say, "Your wife or God," he says "Money or God."[19] It's clear, they're opposites.

DOMINIQUE WOLTON: You spoke in Assisi, in September 2016, about the "Third World War in pieces." Why?

POPE FRANCIS: Isn't it clear? The Middle East, the threat from North Korea in the Far East — we don't know how that will end — Africa, America, Central America and South America: there are wars, wars . . . and in Europe: Ukraine, the Danube Basin,

Russia . . . Europe is at war. There is no declaration of war, that seems to be something old and passé. You just make war, and that's what's happening! The problem is knowing who's behind it all. In my view it's a ghost: the arms traffickers. But is it legal to manufacture weapons? Yes, it's legal. It isn't illegal. Every country needs weapons for self-defense. But giving them to the traffickers, who infiltrate countries at war with themselves . . . And why? For money.

Right now, in Africa, and in Syria too — let's say in the Middle East so that we don't make a mistake . . . In the Middle East and in Africa, there are places to which the Red Cross doesn't have access for its aid missions, but weapons can get through. There are customs officials who let weapons through, but not humanitarian aid! In my view the arms trade is a terrible thing. And what can you say about a country that is as developed as the United States, and still has to fight so bitterly in Congress in the hope of obtaining a law that would forbid the free sale of weapons . . . ?

DOMINIQUE WOLTON: What urgent action might be carried out on behalf of the Christians in the Middle East? Can you give me an example of a failure, or indeed a success?

POPE FRANCIS: They're suffering terribly, and we're doing a lot of work for them, a lot of work. We don't talk about it, but we're doing a lot of work.

DOMINIQUE WOLTON: A positive sign, then? Some event that might take place? That might rehabilitate them? Or is it some sort of failure?

POPE FRANCIS: We're in constant contact, and we're doing everything to ensure that they keep their land.

DOMINIQUE WOLTON: Of course, but has anything positive happened in five, ten years?

POPE FRANCIS: A lot, a lot. The Church is working constantly.

DOMINIQUE WOLTON: So you're quite optimistic on their behalf?

POPE FRANCIS: Yes, that's the future. I don't know what will happen. They're suffering a lot, a lot. There's real persecution

102

in some places. But I'm confident.

DOMINIQUE WOLTON: But where is God in Auschwitz? And where is God in the crushing of the Eastern Christians?

POPE FRANCIS: I don't know where God is. But I know where man is, in that situation. Man manufactures arms and sells them. It's us, in our corrupt humanity. But people think it's easy to ask that question: "And why does God allow that?" But we're the ones who are doing all that! And why do we allow ourselves to do that? The arms trafficker selling weapons to one side fighting another, and then selling to the other side as well . . . Such corruption . . .

DOMINIQUE WOLTON: You come from Latin America, and you have European roots. How is South America unique in terms of globalization?

POPE FRANCIS: South America means new, young churches. The specific aspect is the youth of the church. They have a lot of faults, identical to those of the developed churches: for example, a certain freshness doesn't prevent clericalism.[20] The danger for the organized, older churches is rigidity.

In my view, it's one of the biggest dangers that the Church's clergy face right now.

DOMINIQUE WOLTON: What can the churches of Africa or Asia bring to the Catholic experience?

POPE FRANCIS: So many things! So many different things. Asia has a huge spiritual heritage, 2000 to 3000 years before Jesus Christ; Africa, less so. But Africa brings joy and freshness. A nuncio told me the other day that, in the cathedral in the capital of the country where he works, outside the Holy Door — because the Jubilee is being celebrated in every region of the world — there is a long line of people waiting to come in and celebrate the Jubilee. They come in, some of them approach the confessional, some pray; they are Catholic, Christian. And the great majority continue on to the altar of the Madonna: they are Muslims! Because even the Muslims want to celebrate the Jubilee, but they do it with the Madonna. And that is one of the sources of richness in Africa, that coexistence.

The richness of Africa! Africa is very big. Poor, but big. It knows how to celebrate!

DOMINIQUE WOLTON: Jean-Marie Lustiger

said to me[21] that the next pope would be Latin American, then African, then Asian. You come from Latin America. What does that experience and identity bring to your vision of the world? How do you differ from a European, an Asian, an African?

POPE FRANCIS: My case is a little bit complex, because in Argentina there have been a lot of waves of migration, and the phenomenon of mixing is very much apparent. I'm the son of an Italian; my father went to Argentina very young, at the age of twenty-two. I have Italian blood. It's a bit hard to say . . .

Let's say that what I feel is freedom. I feel I am free.

DOMINIQUE WOLTON: The Christians in the Middle East are having to endure massacres and terrible misfortunes. What things must be done as a matter of urgency? Is there something wrong with the Eastern Christians? It's still the first church! Just think about it, the Eastern Catholic churches, loyal to Rome; the Orthodox churches of the Byzantine Rite, the Armenian, Coptic, Western Syriac, Ge'ez churches . . .

POPE FRANCIS: It's a very difficult world. In Buenos Aires I was great friends with the Eastern Christians in the broadest sense. There are a lot of Ukrainians, but they aren't Eastern. Neither are the Armenians. But there aren't so many in Constantinople, in Antioch, the Melkites.[22] When they had a legal or economic problem, they went to see a Catholic lawyer, as if he was a normal priest. Sometimes they used our Curia. And, at Christmas, on January 6, I went to vespers with the Russians. I stayed with them for dinner, then to celebrate . . . We were very informal with each other.

DOMINIQUE WOLTON: Which is more urgent, interreligious dialogue with Islam or ecumenism?

POPE FRANCIS: The answer to that question depends on where you are in the world. In Syria, it has to be dialogue with Islam, but also within Islam, with the Alawites, the Sunnis — there's too much sectarianism. In other places, it's ecumenism, the most serious problem. In Armenia, for example, where I go, they are "apostolic" (Orthodox), and they suffered from a communication problem during the Council of Chalcedon.[23] The propositions set out there were

106

subjected to contradictory interpretations.

DOMINIQUE WOLTON: Why did you go to Armenia?

POPE FRANCIS: In 2015, they celebrated the centenary of the "word whose name must not be uttered," the one that gets on everyone's nerves: genocide. They came here, to Saint Peter's, Nerses Bedros XIX Tarmouni[24] and the two other patriarchs. I wasn't able to go there in 2015, and promised to go in 2016.[25]

DOMINIQUE WOLTON: And as regards dialogue with Islam, shouldn't we ask for a little reciprocity? There is no true freedom for Christians in Saudi Arabia and certain Muslim countries. Things are difficult for Christians. And Islamist fundamentalists are killing in the name of God . . .

POPE FRANCIS: They don't accept the principle of reciprocity. Some countries in the Gulf are also open, and they're helping us to build churches. Why are they open? Because they have workers who are Filipino, Catholic, Indian . . . The problem in Saudi Arabia is really a question of mentality. With Islam, however, dialogue is progressing well, because, I don't know if you know, the Grand Imam of al-Azhar[26] came to see us. And there will be a meeting there: I'm going.

I think it would do them good to engage in a critical study of the Qur'an, as we have done with our Scriptures. The historical and critical method of interpretation will help them to evolve.

DOMINIQUE WOLTON: What about traveling to a Muslim capital?

POPE FRANCIS: I've been to Turkey, to Istanbul. Ankara and Istanbul.

DOMINIQUE WOLTON: For Europe, you say, "We need to build bridges and break down walls." A beautiful phrase. But why wouldn't the Church set an example by organizing a meeting to promote interreligious and ecumenical dialogue in Europe? Since we have all the religions in Europe: Islam, Judaism and Christianity, not to mention the traditions of free thinking and socialism! It would be spectacular, to relaunch Europe, which is still the biggest democratic experiment in the world. And for the Europeans: an ecumenical and interreligious meeting would have real significance.

POPE FRANCIS: But bridges are going up. There are many bridges.

DOMINIQUE WOLTON: In another area: why has the Church, for over a hundred years, not been more critical about the destruction of the primary sector,[27] and the destruction of the world of the manual worker? More than eighty percent of the active population are found in the tertiary sector, in offices, at computers and so on. The Church doesn't talk much about this profound change affecting man and his relationship with work, nature, time, and which might almost be described as an anthropological catastrophe . . .

POPE FRANCIS: I talked about that a lot in *Laudato Si'*.

DOMINIQUE WOLTON: Yes, but from the point of view of ecology, not to conjure up a hundred years of industrialization, of rural exodus, the madness of the big cities around the world . . . Why hasn't the Church said much about this question? It seems as if it has espoused the modernist ideology, and that it has been afraid of being considered "conservative."

POPE FRANCIS: I do criticize the things you're talking about in my writings.

DOMINIQUE WOLTON: Yes, you do.

POPE FRANCIS: Others do too. Perhaps not everyone. But, yes, we are facing a phenomenon of self-destruction. I talked to you about an African politician whose first measure was in favor of reforestation, so that people would return to the countryside. Because the land is dead. The land is dead.

DOMINIQUE WOLTON: In the Catholic tradition, however, there is a condemnation of capitalism, but not much critical reflection on the disappearance, as a result of technology, of the balance between the three sectors of agriculture, industry and services, as well as the importance of maintaining a certain balance of relations between the city and the country.

POPE FRANCIS: I couldn't say . . . Let me come back to *Laudato Si'*. I've also taken some things from the theologians. Romano Guardini, for example. Guardini talked about the second form of "unculture." God gives mankind "unculture" so that it can be turned into culture. But then humanity takes that unculture and renders it so autonomous that it destroys itself and creates another unculture. The death of the land, for example, with monoculture.

DOMINIQUE WOLTON: We're familiar with that risk in Latin America.

POPE FRANCIS: Yes, monoculture . . . A politician told me what he said to Chávez: "Your shortcoming is monoculture," and he replied, "But there's oil." The man said, "Oil isn't enough. You need to grow tobacco, wheat . . . because you have a lot of land." He didn't do it. And the result is there. Then the multinationals arrive with new machines . . .

DW: Why does the Church not say more clearly that man can't be reduced to the economy and intensive urbanization?

POPE FRANCIS: Guardini talked about that. I mention him because I know him. There may be others too. There are a lot of quotations in *Laudato Si'* and *Evangelii Gaudium* . . . But perhaps you're right in saying that it hasn't been mentioned very much . . .

111

DOMINIQUE WOLTON: You say the state needs to exist and engage . . .

POPE FRANCIS: The liberal market economy is madness. The state needs to regulate a little bit. And that's what's missing: the role of the state as regulator. That's why, in my speech for the Charlemagne Prize [2016], I asked Europe to abandon economic liquidity to return to something concrete — the social market economy. I have retained the market, but the "social market."

DOMINIQUE WOLTON: Why does the Church, which is probably the global institution most committed to defending linguistic diversity, not say quite clearly that this diversity is an extraordinary heritage, particularly since Vatican II, which has officially recognized this cultural diversity and the importance of vernacular languages?

POPE FRANCIS: I can tell you what our liturgical discipline is. Each community, even the smallest, has the right to celebrate the rite in their own language. And there are many different missals. I would like to say, please trust the bishops who are in place.

DOMINIQUE WOLTON: Yes, but still, the Church could say something more officially, as it is able to do with other subjects. Couldn't it tell UNESCO that linguistic diversity is a treasure, a universal legacy?

POPE FRANCIS: Oh yes, of course, since the very foundation of the Church, with Pentecost, there has been linguistic diversity!

DOMINIQUE WOLTON: But the reference to "Pentecost," in 2016, isn't enough in the face of all the violence in the world. Why not write an encyclical on this major issue of linguistic and cultural diversity, in the age of globalization?

POPE FRANCIS: The Pope would die before it was finished! I would like to add something about the language of gestures. Because, in some countries, the culture prefers the greeting at Mass to be a handshake. In Argentina, for example, it is a hug.

DOMINIQUE WOLTON: In what respect is the Catholic Church modern?

POPE FRANCIS: The word "modernity" is a word with many meanings. You can talk of the spirit of modernity, you can talk of modernity as something that is needed today if we are to go forward: it's positive. You can talk of modernity as the negative spirit that the Lord warned us against. He asks the Father to defend the disciples against worldliness. I think I've spoken about all that in *Evangelii Gaudium*. The relationship with modernity. But there is another document which seems more and more wonderful to me each time I read it: the Epistle to Diognetus,[28] a letter from the second century. And that, precisely, is the spirit of the modernity of the Church. It explains that a Christian is open, modern. I've thought a lot about that word, "open:" I think what is specific to a Christian is being open. Open to the spirit. Closure is not Christian. Fidelity is Christian. If I close myself off, if I defend myself, that isn't Christian. Defending values through closure is not a Christian way. Values defend themselves by proclaiming themselves as they are, as Jesus gave them to us. They are Christian words. And they defend themselves through the teaching one makes of them, because we transmit them. The transmission of faith and the transmission of values. The role of parents and mothers, of grandmothers, fathers, grandfathers, etc.

Values defend themselves, but not through closure. The Christian spirit is open. Modernity is openness. Not being afraid.

When Paul arrived in Athens, poor man, he saw all those idolaters and still wasn't frightened. He knew from memory a poem by an idolater, and he recited it to them to get close to them, in an attitude of openness. But when they heard him talking about the Resurrection they were fearful and went away. And that's why I speak of the conversion of the Church in *Evangelii Gaudium*. I speak of a Church "that goes out."

DOMINIQUE WOLTON: Yes, going outside borders and from the periphery.

POPE FRANCIS: Going out of oneself. Not a closed Church. Speaking to the General Congregations before the conclave, I said this: "In the Book of Revelation, Jesus says, 'I stand at the door and knock, and if someone opens the door to me, I will come in.'" But very often Jesus is knocking at the door, but, because he is inside, we don't let him leave.

DOMINIQUE WOLTON: The Church defends tradition. Why does it not say something to relativize the exaggerated importance of speed in our societies? To place itself within time again? The Church could say something about temporal modernity. Modern time is instant. There is no longer any time for transmission. Is there a thought that might lend value to this Christian conception of time, a time of transmission and reflection, as opposed to instant time?

POPE FRANCIS: There is a swift transmission, that is true. There is always a transmission. That is a fact according to the new conception of time. In my view, that's not something to be condemned. But we have to find the right way of doing it.

DOMINIQUE WOLTON: Except, that swift transmission forgets time. And it makes the world horizontal. There is such a huge amount of contemporary information that there is no longer any view of history.

POPE FRANCIS: But I'm not in a position to give a fully formed opinion on that issue. I would need to think, to study the question . . . But it is true that man cannot live without memory. If this way of communicating does not leave room for transmission, it leaves no room for memory. And without memory there is no moving forward. You go into orbit. I would say that there is a danger of falling back into linear thinking. Linear thinking that doesn't take, doesn't develop and doesn't give. In my view, the three pillars of the historical reality of mankind, and also of communication, are the memory of the past — of my past, of the past of my culture; memory as a given that I receive — present reality, and promise, hope that is a promise. Note that hope is not the same thing as optimism. Hope, the future as hope. You have a great Christian who, I believe, died unbaptized, but a great Christian: Péguy.[29] Péguy was the one who most fully understood the role of hope in Christianity. He was more Christian than I am! Curiously, he never managed to join the Church, he died in the war, but he called hope the most humble of virtues. It is the one that carries you forward, but always with the past and with courage. Memory is the courage of the present and the hope of the future. Which is not the same thing as optimism.

On the contrary, the world of modernity, in inverted commas, is more optimistic than "hopeful."

DOMINIQUE WOLTON: Why are there no

ambitious Catholic architectural projects today? The way there are in Asia, with pagodas, or even in Islam . . . Why no grand architectural utopias? There were so many in the past. There is a legacy, but no utopia?

POPE FRANCIS: I would say one thing. Beauty is one of the three fundamentals: truth, goodness and beauty — and unity as well, a fourth one, but that's something that we, the Jesuits, say. We talk too much about truth, about defending truth: where is God to be found in truth? It's difficult . . . Finding God in goodness: ah, it's easier when we talk of goodness. Finding God in beauty: we don't talk about that very much, through the path of poetry, God's creative capacity. God is a poet, who makes things harmoniously. Of the three fundamentals, beauty is probably the least fully developed. In the Middle Ages, when there were no catechisms, catechesis was to be found in cathedrals. And cathedrals are monuments to the beauty of faith. Faith is beautiful.

There are two things today: the world of business, based on speed, and the world of makeup, where beauty does not exist "in itself," but is given artificially for a time and then goes away.

DOMINIQUE WOLTON: A great artistic utopia for the early twenty-first century?

POPE FRANCIS: It's true, that would be beautiful. But let me explain what I know. There are certain architects, painters, poets — great poets — but there is no Dante these days, that's true. I think it's a consequence of the world of business and the world of "makeup," which is the world of worldliness. Today, it's easier to make oneself up than to make oneself beautiful. I need to give more thought to that, because it's a beautiful question. But remember: truth, goodness and beauty. And then the rest: faith, hope, charity.

DOMINIQUE WOLTON: Do you experience things differently because of your Latin American origins and your Jesuit training?

POPE FRANCIS: One example comes to mind, but I don't know how to express it: I'm free. I feel free. That doesn't mean that I do what I want, it doesn't mean that. But I don't feel imprisoned, in a cage. In a cage, here, at the Vatican, yes, but not spiritually. I don't know if it's that . . . I'm not scared of anything. Perhaps it's a lack of awareness, or immaturity!

DOMINIQUE WOLTON: Both!

POPE FRANCIS: Yes, things happen like that, we do what we like, we take things as they come, we avoid doing things, some work out well, others don't . . . Perhaps it's superficiality, I don't know. I don't know what to call it. I feel like a fish in water.

Address of the Holy Father Pope Francis at the Expo Feria Exhibition Center, Santa Cruz de la Sierra, Bolivia

(Thursday, July 9, 2015)

Dear Brothers and Sisters [. . .]

The Bible tells us that God hears the cry of His people, and I wish to join my voice to yours in calling for the three "Ls" for all our brothers and sisters: land, lodging and labor. I have said it before and I say it again: these are sacred rights. [. . .]

1. Before all else, let us begin by acknowledging that change is needed.
   [. . .]
   You have mentioned the many forms of exclusion and injustice which you experience [. . .]
   If such is the case, I would insist, let us not be afraid to say it: we

121

want change, real change, structural change.

[. . .]

Today I wish to reflect with you on the change we want and need.

[. . .]

Once capital becomes an idol and guides people's decisions, once greed for money presides over the entire socioeconomic system, it ruins society, it condemns and enslaves men and women, it destroys human fraternity [. . .] and, as we clearly see, it even puts at risk our common home, sister and mother earth.

[. . .]

You, the lowly, [. . .] can do, and are doing, a lot. I would even say that the future of humanity is in great measure in your own hands, through your ability to organize and carry out creative alternatives, through your daily efforts to ensure the three "Ls" — do you agree? — (labor, lodging, land) and through your proactive participation in the great processes of change on the national, regional and global levels. Don't lose heart!

2. Secondly, *you are sowers of change.* [. . .] Change seen not as something which will one day result from any one political decision or change in social structure. We know from painful experience that changes of structure which are not accompanied by a sincere conversion of mind and heart sooner or later end up in bureaucratization, corruption and failure. There must be a change of heart. [. . .]

It is essential that [. . .] peoples and their social organizations be able to construct a humane alternative to a globalization which excludes. [. . .] Of the leadership I ask this: be creative and never stop being rooted in local realities [. . .] If you build on solid foundations, on real needs and on the lived experience of your brothers and sisters, [. . .] you will surely be on the right path.
[. . .]

3. Third and lastly [. . .] Neither the Pope nor the Church have a monopoly on the interpretation of social reality or the proposal of

solutions to contemporary issues. I daresay that no recipe exists. [. . .] I would like, all the same, to propose three great tasks which demand a decisive and shared contribution from popular movements:

3.1 The first task is to put the economy at the service of peoples. Human beings and nature must not be at the service of money. Let us say NO to an economy of exclusion and inequality, where money rules, rather than service. [. . .]

The economy should not be a mechanism for accumulating goods, but rather the proper administration of our common home. [. .]

Working for a just distribution of the fruits of the earth and human labor is not mere philanthropy. It is a moral obligation. [. . .] It is about giving to the poor and to peoples what is theirs by right.
[. . .]

3.2. The second task is to unite our peoples on the path of peace and justice. The world's peoples [. . .] want their culture, their language, their social processes and their religious traditions to be respected.

[. . .]

The new colonialism takes on different faces. At times it appears as the anonymous influence of mammon [. . .]: At other times, under the noble guise of battling corruption, the narcotics trade and terrorism [. . .] we see states being saddled with measures which have little to do with the resolution of these problems and which not infrequently worsen matters.

[. . .]

3.3. The third task, perhaps the most important facing us today, is to defend Mother Earth.

Our common home is being pillaged, laid waste and harmed with impunity. [. . .] There exists a clear, definite and pressing ethical imperative to implement what has not yet been done. [. . .] People and their movements are called to cry out, to mobilize and to demand — peacefully, but firmly — that appropriate and urgently needed measures be taken. I ask you, in the name of

God, to defend Mother Earth. [. . .]

4. In conclusion, I would like to repeat: the future of humanity does not lie solely in the hands of great leaders, the great powers and the elites. It is fundamentally in the hands of peoples and in their ability to organize. [. . .] I pray for you and with you, and I ask God our Father to accompany you and to bless you [. . .] I ask you, please, to pray for me. If some of you are unable to pray, with all respect, I ask you to send me your good thoughts and energy. Thank you.

Address of His Holiness Pope Francis to participants in the Third World Meeting of Popular Movements, Paul VI Audience Hall, The Vatican

(November 5, 2016)

Brothers and sisters!

[. . .]

At our last meeting, in Bolivia, [. . .] we listed three tasks essential for progressing toward a humane alternative to the globalization of indifference: (1) placing the economy at the service of peoples; (2) working for peace and justice; and (3) defending Mother Earth.

[. . .]

I would like to touch on some more specific issues, the ones I received from you. They have made me think, and now I hand them back to you.

First: terror and walls. [. . .]

Almost a hundred years ago, Pius XI foresaw the growth of a global economic dictatorship that he called "international imperialism of finance."[30] [. . .] It was Paul VI who [. . .] denounced the "new and abusive form of economic domination on the social, cultural and even political level."[31] [. . .] The entire social doctrine of the Church and the magisterium of my predecessors rejects the idolatry of money that reigns rather than serves, that tyrannizes and terrorizes humanity.

No tyranny can last without exploiting our fears. [. . .] Consequently, all tyranny is a form of terrorism. And when that terror, which has been sown in the outskirts, whether by massacres, plundering, oppression and injustice, explodes in the centers with different forms of violence, [. . .] citizens [. . .] are tempted by the false security of physical and social walls. [. . .] Some citizens behind walls, terrorized. Others excluded, dispossessed, and even more terrorized. [. . .]

Fear then is fed, manipulated . . . Because fear is not only good business for those who trade in weapons and death, it weakens us, throws us off balance, breaks down our psychological and spiritual defenses, anaesthetizes us to the sufferings of others, and in the end makes us cruel. [. . .]

Dear brothers and sisters: all walls collapse. All of them. Let us not be deceived. [. . .] Let us confront terror with love.

[. . .] Love and bridges.

[. . .]

The three Ls (land, lodging, labor), that cry of yours which I make my own, has a touch of that understanding which is humble, yet strong and healing. The bridge-project of peoples as opposed to the wall-project of money. The project that aims at integral human development. [. . .] We have to help heal the world of its moral atrophy. This atrophied system can offer a number of cosmetic implants that are not the true development: [. . .] a development that is not reduced to consumption [. . .]

Another point is: bankruptcy and salvaging.

Dear brothers and sisters, [. . .]

You devoted a whole day to the drama of migrants, refugees and displaced persons. [. . .] because here we have a shameful situation that can only be described by a word that came spontaneously to my lips in Lampedusa: a disgrace.

[. . .]

I echo the words of my brother, Archbishop Ieronymos of Greece: "Anyone who looks into the eyes of those small children we met in the refugee camps can immediately recognize, in its entirety, the 'bankruptcy' of humanity."[32] What is going on in the world today that, when a bank fails, scandalous sums of money suddenly appear to save it, but before this bankruptcy of humanity not even a thousandth part is allotted to save those brothers and sisters who suffer so greatly?

[. . .]

This brings me to the second major topic: [. . .] Popular movements [. . .] are not political parties [. . .] But do not be afraid to get involved in the great discussions, in politics with a capital P [. . .]: "Politics is one of the highest forms of charity, of love."

I would like to point to two risks involved in the relationship between popular movements and politics: the risk of being put in a straitjacket and the risk of being corrupted.

[. . .] As long as you are confined by

the straitjacket of "social policies," as long as you don't question economic policy or politics with a capital P, you are tolerated. [. . .] When you protest, when you lift your voice and presume to point out to the powerful a more integral approach, then you become intolerable. [. . .] Thus, democracy atrophies, turns into a slogan, a formality; it loses its representative character and becomes disembodied, since it leaves out the people.

[. . .]

The second risk [. . .] is that of being corrupted. [. . .] Corruption is not a vice limited to political life. [. . .] There is a "naturalized" corruption in some spheres of economic life [. . .] which gets less attention in the press than corruption directly linked to social and political life. [. . .] Those who have opted for a life of service have a further obligation. [. . .] One has to live his or her vocation to service with a strong sense of austerity and humility.

[. . .]

The example of an austere life of service to one's neighbor is the best way to promote the common good [. . .] I urge leaders not to tire of practicing

such moral and personal austerity [. . .]
Dear brothers and sisters,

I ask you, please, to pray for me, and those who cannot pray, they already know this, to think kindly of me and wish me well. Thank you.

■ ■ ■ ■

3
EUROPE AND
CULTURAL
DIVERSITY

■ ■ ■ ■

INTERVIEW — JULY 2016

There will be three meetings in three days! So much time and, for me, what a task: I have to do my best. It's very hot, Rome is filled with tourists — there are many more tourists than believers in Saint Peter's Square. A mixture of styles and attitudes . . . I'm getting to know the way. The Church and Europe, cultural diversity. Identities and men and women, the return of borders. The Church facing a different vision of globalization from its own. Churches old and new. How, in this very small territory, which seems to lie outside of time and space, and with so few people, there still exists, almost invisibly, the incessant motion back and forth toward the huge external reality. History and time are omnipresent. I'm feeling strangely dizzy. And at the same time, they are only a few, frail individuals, with an obligation to engage in dialogue and overcome the challenge of uncommunication . . .

DOMINIQUE WOLTON: What could be done in Europe, politically, culturally, on behalf of immigrants and refugees? What spectacular act could be, should be performed? On January 15, 2017, for example, in the Catholic Church, there will be the 103rd Day of Migrants and Refugees. To coincide with this event, might there not be an action by all religions, in Europe, on behalf of refugees and immigrants?

POPE FRANCIS: Europeans do not agree on this subject. In the three speeches that I have delivered on the subject of Europe, two in Strasbourg and one for the Charlemagne Prize, I talked about all that. It's all there.

DOMINIQUE WOLTON: Yes, but nothing's happening.

POPE FRANCIS: I think some efforts have been made.

DOMINIQUE WOLTON: The Germans have done something. Merkel. Not the French. The two most courageous peoples are the Italians and the Greeks, because they are giving concrete help to refugees, they have shown solidarity and generosity. On October

136

13, 2016, you said that "Christians who close their doors to refugees or to those who need aid are hypocrites." That's all well and good, but then what happens? Of course, surely it doesn't depend on you, but on a symbolic act by all the religions in Europe for refugees? On the part of Christians, Muslims, Jews?

POPE FRANCIS: Yes, you can talk about it, all religions talk about refugees. But there are political problems, and some countries don't have enough room, others don't have the necessary courage, and others are frightened. Others didn't know how to integrate immigrants and ghettoized them. It's very complex. Let's consider the problem of Africa, for example. They're fleeing war and hunger, and when there is war and hunger over there, the problem eventually reaches us, and we also have to wonder why there's a war down there. Who's supplying the weapons?

DOMINIQUE WOLTON: Of course, the historical and economic explanation is crucial, but we still need to know why the hatred of the Other has reemerged so powerfully in Europe. We didn't expect Europe to have such a hostile reaction to immigrants.

Particularly since Europeans are often themselves second- or third-generation refugees ...

POPE FRANCIS: It's also because it's mixed up with terrorism.

DOMINIQUE WOLTON: Yes, but not just that.

POPE FRANCIS: Not just that, perhaps, but it's very important.

DOMINIQUE WOLTON: Let's say that the economic crisis makes it possible to combine the two, but sadly I think that suspicion of the Other carries more weight than terrorism alone.

POPE FRANCIS: That's how life is. *C'est la vie.*

DOMINIQUE WOLTON: It's true, that's life! What contribution can Catholics — who played a very important historical part in the creation of Europe, between 1945 and 1960 — make to relaunch this project? While political Europe was still under construction, the commitment of the churches disappeared. The origin of Europe lies with socialists and Christian democrats. As we move toward a political Europe, why can't the five spiritual families of Europe — Christianity, Judaism, Islam, socialism and free thinking — take a common initiative?

You talked about celebrating the soul of Europe at the Charlemagne Prize: how, today, could we mobilize in favor of what is the greatest democratic utopia in the history of mankind? Never before have twenty-seven countries, or 500 million inhabitants with more than twenty-five languages, tried to live together in peace.

POPE FRANCIS: Pope Benedict XVI invited agnostics to the last meeting of his pontificate in Assisi. That's important. You can't ignore the fact. I clearly expressed my thoughts on Europe in my two speeches in Strasbourg, and in the third speech that I made when I received the Charlemagne Prize. I didn't want to receive that prize, because I've never accepted distinctions, I don't like it. It isn't humility — perhaps it's pusillanimity, I don't know. But it's clear that it isn't humility.

I don't like distinctions. I don't like high decorations.

DOMINIQUE WOLTON: . . . Austere.

POPE FRANCIS: I don't know if it's austere. I didn't like it, but I accepted it after much discussion. I accepted it for the good of Europe. Because I think that Europe is in crisis at the moment. The unity of Europe is in crisis. One of the things I said, and which I have stressed a great deal, is dialogue. Our children, from primary school onward, need to learn to engage in dialogue.

In our schools, they teach maths, reading, physics, chemistry, but dialogue? That's also part of the phenomenological structure of school, of teaching. It's "I talk and you listen. If you don't understand something, you ask me and I reply." You could say that it might be the start of a process that would go further, and which would teach children to engage in dialogue.

I remember once, in my first year as bishop, in 1992, I went to a school where a girl asked me, "Why can't I have an abortion?" and I immediately thought that, if I answered starting with "Because . . ." nobody would accept the answer. I said, "That's a good question. Let's all think about it together." And everyone started looking for the "why." In schools, you have to teach people to find their way while looking for things. Learning by looking. And not just "question, answer; question, answer."

You have to start at school, but keep going after that. We've lost — think of the parliaments — we've lost, and to such an extent, the culture of listening!

DOMINIQUE WOLTON: So, why wouldn't the big spiritual families try to say, on this question of the construction of Europe, to say, "Let's get involved a bit." There might be an initiative by religions.

POPE FRANCIS: But there are meetings, dialogues . . .

DOMINIQUE WOLTON: From the point of view of public democratic space, it's not visible . . . In Havana, in February 2016, with the Patriarch of Russia, you said these words: "At last we see each other." Why not do the same thing with all the religions and the spiritual families for political Europe? Meaning that, even if you're an atheist, even if you're a Freemason, even if you're a socialist, even if you're Jewish, even if you're a Muslim . . . Because Europe is still the biggest workshop for peace and democracy.

POPE FRANCIS: I think it's part of the art of politics, but politics in the noble sense of the term. The churches have to enter into dialogue, and think about what's happening in Europe today. Because Europe isn't in a good way.

DOMINIQUE WOLTON: So why not a formal meeting of everyone? You see, we're very different, from the point of view of religions, of our relationship with the world, but we have a common love of what Europe represents: the biggest peaceful democratic workplace in the history of the world, and we support it. You could perform a political act with a capital P, with all the religions and all the intellectual currents. Because if we Europeans succeed, it will be a lesson of hope. If we fail it will be disastrous. Not just for us, but for the rest of the world. So why don't the churches organize a formal event to say, "It's fundamental"? You see, it would be symbolic.

POPE FRANCIS: I share your concerns. You say "We must," and I take that "We must" and I will try to spread that idea, and hold a meeting about Europe. I would like to have a meeting about Europe with European intellectuals. I would like to do that. But you can also do it with the churches. There's a lovely phrase that says Europe extends from the Atlantic to the Urals . . .

DOMINIQUE WOLTON: Yes, that's the same phrase that General de Gaulle used — "from the Atlantic to the Urals" — and he even included Russia, hoping to take Russia away from communism.

POPE FRANCIS: There are common values, but in our interreligious dialogues there are also more specific theological questions. These are two different types of discourse. But you can engage in dialogue by bringing the religions into a more general dialogue about Europe. I was very touched when President Hollande, who telephoned me and then sent me a lovely letter, sent the Minister of Education to the award ceremony for the Charlemagne Prize.

DOMINIQUE WOLTON: Europe is cultural coexistence, and the Catholic experience is also, in the end, an experiment in coexistence on the global scale. Christian universality and cultural coexistence, as a condition for peace in the twenty-first century, are points in common. In the political utopia, there is a point in common between the rather secular utopia of the European coexistence and the universal dream of the Catholic Church. Could the Catholic

Church represent the initiative of a kind of symbolic meeting of everyone?

POPE FRANCIS: Yes, it could.

DOMINIQUE WOLTON: (*laughter*) I'm too utopian . . . Because even multiculturalism is an essential part of the history of the Catholic Church and also of the history of Europe. The Catholic Church has a considerable historical and philosophical legacy on the question of relations with the Other, with coexistence, with dialogue. Of course, in the past there were massacres and colonial rule, but that has changed today, and everything's still too closed. You should open up more. Without necessarily engaging in evangelization!

POPE FRANCIS: Yes, we can do that.

DOMINIQUE WOLTON: Yes, why not? (*laughter*) An example, in your view?

POPE FRANCIS: It would be a good service to perform. But I must say that there is a dialogue between us about political and social problems — not to mention talking about religious dialogue, which works — but also about a lot of sociopolitical problems. For example about the death penalty.

144

DOMINIQUE WOLTON: Yes, but in Europe we all agree about the death penalty. There is no longer a death penalty in Europe.

POPE FRANCIS: Yes, but what I'm saying is that this dialogue is taking place. And we also talk about welcoming refugees, about integrating families . . . and then Europe, which has a very strong history of cultural integration, multiculturalism, as you say. Forever. The Longobardi, the Lombards today, are barbarians who arrived here a long time ago . . . and then everything got all mixed up and our culture came into being. But what is European culture? How would I define European culture today? Yes, Europe has important Christian roots, that's true. But that's not enough to give a definition of Europe.

There are our abilities. Our abilities to integrate, to receive other people. There is also language in culture. In our Spanish language, 40 percent of words are Arabic. Why? Because they were there for seven centuries, and they left their trace.

DOMINIQUE WOLTON: Yes, people don't know enough about that. And the Europeans have forgotten their Arabic and Jewish roots, and all the others . . .

POPE FRANCIS: At the time, politics consisted in hounding out the Jews. The politics of the sixteenth century was "too" Catholic. That "too" hurts. It's normal to say, "We think like that," but if I think "too much like that," then something's gone wrong, and that leads to fundamentalism, to isolation, to closure of dialogue and to other people's words.

DOMINIQUE WOLTON: Europe today is confronted with the same temptation to turn in on itself, to seek a hypothetical identity that is under threat from globalization.

POPE FRANCIS: A society mustn't be homogenized . . . Homogenization is never fruitful, it always leads to sterility.

DOMINIQUE WOLTON: Given this twofold risk of conflict and homogenization, why do spiritual forces not mention the importance of this political project? Europe is a fragile political project.

POPE FRANCIS: There was a voice. I said it, but there were other voices as well. Bartholomew I, as well as other religious leaders. But how can we remake that unity in

Europe? How can it be found again? I think you mustn't forget the role of women in Europe. Women have this maternal capacity to unite; children argue among themselves, but the mother imposes unity. I think Europe needs more courageous women. There are some. But we need more courageous women who can, as women, carry out this work of unification and reconciliation among peoples, of dialogue between peoples. I'm reading an article that was published in *L'Osservatore Romano* about motherhood as unity. Did you read that?

DOMINIQUE WOLTON: No.

POPE FRANCIS: I'll bring it next time, it's very relevant. There's a real dynamism in women and women's qualities. Some women say to me, "Why can't we become deaconesses?"[1] And that's an office. We can think about that. But I like that more than the function and role of women in a developed society, which some people confuse with the demands of women, as if it were "machismo in a skirt." But no, it's something else; machismo is brutality, a negative thing. "Machismo in a skirt" is the same thing. It doesn't represent what women must represent in society. And yet they have a big part to play in European unity. In the wars. In both World Wars, the true heroines were women.

DOMINIQUE WOLTON: Yes, the role of women is largely undervalued. Let me come back to the separation of church and state. The strength of Europe and the Church lies in the acknowledgment of that separation. And yet, with the return of fundamentalism, once again there is a risk of the merging of religion and politics. The Catholic Church should clearly be able to say, "No, do not go down this path." The Catholic Church and even Christianity could denounce this illusion of the merging of politics and religion because we've seen the consequences over three or four centuries . . .

POPE FRANCIS: It's curious, these European fundamentalist movements that always carry the flag of Christianity, of the Church. It's a fundamentalism that needs to use the Church, but against the Church, because it misrepresents the Church.

DOMINIQUE WOLTON: And why don't you say anything?

POPE FRANCIS: Without naming any countries in particular, we can talk in general about this principle: the Church is sometimes used to justify a fundamentalist attitude.

DOMINIQUE WOLTON: The idea of withdrawing is a temptation, like fundamentalism. It would be something new if the Catholic Church were the first to say, "No, this is a dead end." You would play a leading role in terms of the European challenge and European utopia: *coexisting in spite of all our differences.*

POPE FRANCIS: I often preach on this subject at morning Mass, here at Saint Martha's.

There's nothing new under the sun. It's the same problem as it was in Jesus' time, when Jesus Christ began preaching. The people understood him perfectly, and they were filled with enthusiasm because he spoke with authority. On the other hand, in those days, the Doctors of the Church were closed. They were fundamentalist. "You can go so far but no further." That's the battle that I'm fighting today with my exhortation *Amoris Laetitia*. Because some people are still saying: "You can do that, you can't do that." But there is another logic. Jesus Christ did not respect habits that had become commandments, because he touched lepers, which you weren't supposed to do. He refused to stone the adulteress, when other people did. He talked to the Samaritan woman, when people weren't supposed to do that because it made one impure. He allowed himself to be touched by a woman who had a discharge of blood, and that was impure. Did Jesus Christ not respect the law, or was the law of the others wrong? It was degenerate, yes. As a result of fundamentalism. And Jesus Christ responded by going in the opposite direction.

I think that applies to all aspects of culture. When I destroy harmony intentionally — because the destruction of harmony is always intentional — when I take one element and render it absolute, I destroy harmony: that's what fundamentalists do.

DOMINIQUE WOLTON: One last question on Europe: do you have one thing to say about Europe? A dream, a utopia, a wish?

POPE FRANCIS: There is a problem in Europe. Europe is not free. The economy of Europe is not a productive economy of the land, a concrete economy. It has lost its "concreteness." It is a liquid economy. Finance. That's why young people are out of work.

DOMINIQUE WOLTON: Finance is too inegalitarian a model of liberalism. Finance has devoured the economy, which has devoured politics . . . . Europe is the only part of the world today that is completely economically liberal. Regulation has returned everywhere, except in Europe where the liberal economic values of the 1980s have survived!

POPE FRANCIS: It is the virtual state as against the real. The virtual detached from reality, whose sole mode of activity is a factor of destruction.

DOMINIQUE WOLTON: You said "Europe isn't free because finance . . ." Would you like to go on?

POPE FRANCIS: . . . This is what an ambassador said to me when he came to drop off some letters of credence: "We have fallen into the idolatry of money." And Europe has succumbed to that. And, besides, I would like to talk about people, about European leaders. Talking to the politicians who come here, I have noticed that the young ones express themselves in a different tone. They're obliged to negotiate, but they have a different ideal. I have a lot of confidence in the younger European politicians. I think we need to help them. There are great European leaders at the moment . . . Merkel is indisputably a great European leader. Have you talked to Tsipras?

DOMINIQUE WOLTON: No, I have never talked to him.

POPE FRANCIS: Talk to him. The day I went to Lesbos, he was very discreet. He went away and he didn't show his face. But, in the end, when we decided to bring back the twelve Syrian refugees, all Muslim, he made a comment. And he said something very brave: "Human rights go beyond all treaties." A politician who can think like that is a politician of the future, who is reflecting on the meaning of Europe. There are a lot of young people who think like that. Let's think about popular movements. I'll talk about that afterward.

DOMINIQUE WOLTON: I'd like to come back to Europe and Latin America: what strikes you about the comparison between the two?

POPE FRANCIS: Popular piety in Latin America is very strong. The same phenomenon exists in certain parts of Europe. The people of Europe have been protagonists in history and in catechesis. It's the same in Latin America. We are "underdeveloped," but we are also under domination, subject to the power of ideological and economic forms of colonization. We are not free. Of course, we have our way of being, but multinationals have done their work! Take Brazil . . . But that's a different subject.

DOMINIQUE WOLTON: Two questions about Latin America. Why have the bishops been on the side of conservative rather than progressive regimes?

POPE FRANCIS: Most of them . . . Because some of the bishops are progressive in the good sense of the term. Pastors of the people. There is an ideological progressivism connected with your May '68.[2] That ideological progressiveness has disappeared. But there is a theology that is said to be "of the people." The people bring the faith forward. That's very highly developed in

153

Latin America. But in some countries there is also the problem of priest patrons, priest princes, lord bishops . . .

DOMINIQUE WOLTON: Will you gain ground with the subject of the "theology of the people"? With the inequalities of globalization, won't Marxism get going again, and with it the subject of "liberation theology"? What could become of the theology of the people?

POPE FRANCIS: Yes, that will happen. Yes, because the people never accepted those little groups.

The people have their piety, their theology. They are healthy and concrete. They are based on the values of the family, of work. Even the sins of the people are concrete sins. On the other hand the sins of these ideological theologies are too "angelical." The most serious sins are those that are very angelical. The others have very little angelicality, but a lot of humanity. Do you understand me? I like to use the word "angelicality" because the worst sin is pride. The pride of the angels.

DOMINIQUE WOLTON: Yes. Just one point. You talk a lot about "the people," and in

Europe that's a word that is treated with suspicion. Europeans will talk instead about societies, communities, individuals, but not use the word "people," which is a beautiful word but which brings us back to populism, which is linked historically to the excesses of the extreme right and the extreme left.

POPE FRANCIS: "The people" also exists in Europe.

DOMINIQUE WOLTON: Of course.

POPE FRANCIS: But "the people" is not a logical category. It is a mythical category. It's a "mythos." To understand the people, you need to go to a village in France, Italy or America. They are the same. And, there, you live the life of the people. But you can't explain it. You can explain the difference that exists between a nation, a country and a people. A country is what lies within borders. A nation is the legal and judicial constitution of that country. But a people is something else. The first two are logical categories. The people is a mythical category. To understand the people, you have to live with the people. And only those who have lived with the people understand . . . I'm thinking of Dostoyevsky. He understood the people: "He who doesn't believe in God doesn't believe in the people." That's Dosto-yevsky.

DOMINIQUE WOLTON: That needs to be said over and over again. Because the word "people" isn't a word that is used often enough in political categories, except pejoratively in terms of populism, and demagogical and authoritarian excesses. It's true that it would be useful to reappraise the word "people" in the anthropological sense in which you use it.

POPE FRANCIS: Because the word "people" is used too much as a logical category. Populism, for example — "that's a populist party" — has some of the same logic. Even in France there's a writer, Joseph Malègue, who wrote a novel called *Augustin.* He has a lovely expression: "the middle classes of holiness."[3] He has an intuition, on the level of holiness, of what the people is. Péguy — there is another one who understood the people. He understood very well.

DOMINIQUE WOLTON: Yes, but, in France, Péguy is almost "anathematized," because he's "reactionary." He's a great poet, of course.

POPE FRANCIS: He understood the people, and very well. On the other hand, Léon Bloy didn't really understand them. His attitude can be understood as an ideology of the people. And there is another remarkable Frenchman: Bernanos. He understood the people, he understood that mythical category. *A contrario,* Action Française,[4] Cardinal Billot[5] . . . You know what happened to Billot in the end?

DOMINIQUE WOLTON: No.

POPE FRANCIS: Cardinal Billot had very strong connections with Action Française. Pius XI is supposed to have sent him a very, very severe letter. When there was a meeting of the cardinals, Billot came with the others. The Pope greeted them and, when he came to Billot, Billot said, "Holy Father, I'm sorry for what I've done, but forgive me, I'll renounce my vows as a cardinal." And do you know what Pius XI did? He took his biretta and said "I accept!" That's a historical fact.

DOMINIQUE WOLTON: (*laughter*) What year was that?

POPE FRANCIS: 1927, I think.

DOMINIQUE WOLTON: What should you do to escape the ideology of modernity, which says, "The Church is ahead," "The Church is lagging behind"?

POPE FRANCIS: For me, modernity has a double meaning. There are modern worlds, you just have to watch that Charlie Chaplin film, *Modern Times* [1936] . . . There's the modernity that we see now. And the Church has to accept today's ways of life. But there is another meaning, which assimilates worldliness. That's a negative word for Christians. Christians cannot be worldly. They must live in the world, and experience the modernity of the world, but without being worldly. They have a different message for the world. They have to take the good part of the world, and engage in dialogue with the world.

DOMINIQUE WOLTON: Two more questions. Civil society, democracy and societies have changed a lot in 150 years, with health education, democracy, politics, freedom, equality. What has secular political progress brought to the Church? The Church never says, "Thank you, the modern world is great." More often, it says, "Be careful!"

POPE FRANCIS: I think Vatican II opened the doors in that direction.

DOMINIQUE WOLTON: There are two parallel histories: there's the history of the Church and there's the history of progress and democracy. Obviously, there are connections, but the Church seldom mentions what modernity has brought . . .

POPE FRANCIS: I think what you're saying is a little exaggerated.

DOMINIQUE WOLTON: In what respect?

POPE FRANCIS: I think that, in its documents, its speeches, the Church has a great deal of praise for the modern world. You just have to look at Paul VI, but also Pius XI. Pius XI launched Radio Vatican and a lot of modern things. Let's analyze it on three levels: in the texts you find that respect and that openness to the modern world, with some "be carefuls," with a number of warnings, but you do find it. Secondly, in the ruling class of the Church, some are opposed to it, but others are courageous. Last of all, the people of God, in principle, are the ones who suffer most. Laypeople are more easily enslaved by the bad sides of modernity. More easily — I'm not saying "always." When you see obesity in children, because they're eating modern food with chips, hot dogs and Coca-Cola . . .

DOMINIQUE WOLTON: Where fast food is concerned, of course. But the Church can both say that there is progress in modernity, which is true, and at the same time condemn a modernity which has no meaning, which has no generosity, which is very selfish. You can say both. What I mean by that is that the Catholic Church, with all its history, is well placed, without dogmatism, to say, "That's what's good about modernity and progress, and that's what leaves man all alone." In your view, where does politics start and finish for the Church?

POPE FRANCIS: The Church must be charitable, and my predecessors, Pius XI and Paul VI, said that one of the highest forms of charity is politics. The Church must enter "high" politics. Because the Church engages in "high" politics. The politics that carries people forward on the basis of an evangelical proposition. But it must not get involved in the "low" politics of parties and all that sort of thing. On the other hand, the Church is used by "low" politics to such an extent . . . Used so much. By the fundamentalists, we've talked about that before. Think about your history.

Think of the history of France. The famous *Monsieur l'Abbé.* And who were those abbots? They were priests who served the court and engaged in low politics. They weren't pastors. True pastors are the Curé d'Ars,[6] they're Saint Pierre Fourier,[7] who was confessor to the court, but who always kept himself apart. He waited for people to come and talk to him about what was on their minds. But he didn't engage in low politics. I don't think it's good at all, having pastors and priests at receptions, at airports . . .

DOMINIQUE WOLTON: You said to the Christian Life Community, in May 2015, in Bogotá, I think, "A Catholic can't just watch from the balcony." Does that mean you have to get involved in politics?

POPE FRANCIS: Yes! But not in "big" politics.

DOMINIQUE WOLTON: Of course.

POPE FRANCIS: I think I said that in Rio

de Janeiro. "Watch from the balcony." Watch history passing.

DOMINIQUE WOLTON: Why is the Church more severe with left-wing Catholics, worker priests, liberation theology, than it is with right-wing Catholics, the Society of Saint Pius X,[8] or often with dictatorships. Why?

POPE FRANCIS: I don't really see what you're getting at. Why is the Church more severe with left-wing Catholics than right-wing ones?

DOMINIQUE WOLTON: Historically, in the twentieth century . . .

POPE FRANCIS: Perhaps in the sense that the left is always trying out new paths. On the other hand, when you maintain the status quo, when you rigidify, that isn't a threat, that lets you live peacefully . . . but at the same time the Church doesn't grow. I don't see that as a threat. But let's call that the left, it's not the left, but the left of Jesus Christ was very dangerous for them. Often the left . . . But I don't like that word.

DOMINIQUE WOLTON: Perhaps, but that's the political vocabulary in democracy, where there are generally two camps.

POPE FRANCIS: The Gospel . . . The Church is often identified with the Pharisees. And not with sinners. The Church of the poor, the Church of sinners . . .

DOMINIQUE WOLTON: You've said, "A poor Church for the poor." Yes, but that's the Gospel and it's you. But, after that, there's the institution of the Church.

POPE FRANCIS: There are the sins of the rulers of the Church, who lack intelligence or allow themselves to be manipulated. But the Church is not bishops, popes and priests. The Church is the people. As Vatican II put it: "The People of God, as a whole, is not mistaken." If you want to know the Church, go to a village where the life of the Church is lived. Go to a hospital where there are so many Christians who want to help — laypeople, nuns . . . Go to Africa, where you will find so many missionaries. They are burning up their lives down there. And they are making real revolutions. Not to convert, talk of conversion is from another era, but to serve.

DOMINIQUE WOLTON: The Church's most

radical message has always, from the Gospel onward, been to condemn the madness of money. Why is that message not being heard?

POPE FRANCIS: Perhaps the message isn't getting across? But why do some people prefer to speak of morality, in homilies or theology departments? There's a big danger for preachers, which is that of falling into mediocrity. Of only condemning morality — forgive me — "below the waist." But the other sins, the more serious ones, hatred, envy, pride, vanity, killing other people, taking life away . . . Those priests don't talk so much about that. Joining the mafia, making secret agreements . . . "Are you a good Catholic? Then hand over the money."

DOMINIQUE WOLTON: I agree. What do you have to say to people who are always stressing the crimes and abuses of the Church over the centuries?

POPE FRANCIS: When the Church ceased to be a servant and became a mistress?

DOMINIQUE WOLTON: Yes, that lasted for a long time.

POPE FRANCIS: Yes, but it was also a culture of the time. The Church has lost that culture.

DOMINIQUE WOLTON: It's the historical context . . . Do you think that's a good enough explanation?

POPE FRANCIS: There's a historical context that was determining, and the Church made choices. I don't know if I've talked about medieval catechesis, the one learned in the cathedrals. The people learned the true faith in cathedrals. In 1974, when there was a conflict between the Society[9] and the Vatican Curia, I was in the general congregation. The traditionalists took their flowers to the Church of the Twelve Apostles, which holds the tomb of Clement XIV, hoping that the Society would be dissolved, as had happened in his day. The Society, and it's a proud Jesuit talking to you, had the glory of imitating the death of Jesus Christ, because it was abolished by the Pope, and abided by that decision before being reborn under a different Pope. The Society was saved by a German Protestant, who then became Orthodox — a great woman, Catherine II. She was the one who saved the Society. The great Maria Theresa held out until the end, but she had to give in because all her children had married Bourbons.

DOMINIQUE WOLTON: Yes, it's a long story. What's the simplest message you could give advising people to get involved in politics?

POPE FRANCIS: Do it to serve. Do it out of love. Don't do it out of personal interest, out of greed or a desire for power. Do it as the great European politicians did. Think of the three founders, Schuman, Adenauer and De Gasperi.[10] They are three models, and there are many others.

DOMINIQUE WOLTON: In May 2016, you said of the Charlemagne Prize: "We must build bridges and knock down walls." Can you give me an idea about that? An example?

POPE FRANCIS: Shake hands. When I shake somebody's hand, I'm building a bridge. When I see the other person over there and I'm interested in him, I begin to build a bridge.

In my view, that is the most human bridge, the universal bridge: shaking hands. If someone isn't capable of shaking hands by doing this with the other person (the gesture

166

accompanies the words), they aren't capable of building bridges.

DOMINIQUE WOLTON: And a bridge today in Europe? An example, a symbol?

POPE FRANCIS: Welcoming refugees. When they are welcomed . . . And also go to them, to their countries, and help them survive by making peace and creating sources of work so that they aren't forced to flee. Invest.

DOMINIQUE WOLTON: Yes, because Europe is very rich.

POPE FRANCIS: But you can't take money with you! I've never seen a removal van behind a hearse . . .

ADDRESS OF HIS HOLINESS POPE FRANCIS AT THE CONFERRAL OF THE CHARLEMAGNE PRIZE, SALA REGIA, THE VATICAN

(May 6, 2016)

[. . .] Creativity, genius and a capacity for rebirth and renewal are part of the soul of Europe. In the last century, Europe bore witness to humanity that a new beginning was indeed possible. After years of tragic conflicts, culminating in the most horrific war ever known, there emerged, by God's grace, something completely new in human history. The ashes of the ruins could not extinguish the ardent hope and the quest of solidarity that inspired the founders of the European project. They laid the foundations for a bastion of peace, an edifice made up of states united not by force but by free commitment to the *common good* and a definitive end to confrontation. Europe, so long divided, finally found its true self and began to

168

build its house.

This "family of peoples,"[11] which has commendably expanded in the meantime, seems of late to feel less at home within the walls of the common home. At times, those walls themselves have been built in a way varying from the insightful plans left by the original builders. Their new and exciting desire to create unity seems to be fading; we, the heirs of their dream, are tempted to yield to our own selfish interests and to consider putting up fences here and there. Nonetheless, I am convinced that resignation and weariness do not belong to the soul of Europe, and that even "our problems can become powerful forces for unity."[12]

In addressing the European Parliament, I used the image of Europe as a grandmother. I noted that there is a growing impression that Europe is weary, aging, no longer fertile and vital, that the great ideals that inspired Europe seem to have lost their appeal. There is an impression that Europe is declining, that it has lost its ability to be innovative and creative, and that it is more concerned with preserving and dominating spaces than with generating processes of inclusion and change. There is an impression that Europe is tending to become increasingly "entrenched," rather than open to initiating new social processes capable of engaging all individuals and groups in the search for new and productive solutions to current problems. Europe, rather than protecting spaces, is called to be a mother who generates processes.[13]

[. . .] Robert Schuman, at the very birth of the first European community, stated that "Europe will not be made all at once, or according to a single plan. It will be built through concrete achievements which first create a *de facto* solidarity."[14] Today, in our own world, marked by so much conflict and suffering, there is a need to return to the same *de facto solidarity* and *concrete generosity* that followed the Second World War, because, as Schuman noted, "World peace cannot be safeguarded without making creative efforts proportionate to the dangers threatening it."[15] The founding fathers were heralds of peace and prophets of the future. Today more than ever, their vision inspires us to build bridges and tear down walls.

[. . .]

The community of European peoples will thus be able to overcome the temptation of falling back on unilateral paradigms and opting for forms of "ideological colonization." Instead, it will rediscover the breadth of the European soul, born of the encounter of civilizations and peoples. The soul of Europe is in fact greater than the present borders of the Union and is called to become a model of new syntheses and of dialogue. The true face of Europe is seen not in confrontation, but in the richness of its various cultures and the beauty of its commitment to openness. [. . .]

If there is one word that we should never tire of repeating, it is this: dialogue. We are called to promote a culture of dialogue by every possible means and thus to rebuild the fabric of society. The culture of dialogue entails a true apprenticeship and a discipline that enables us to view others as valid dialogue partners, to respect the foreigner, the immigrant and people from different cultures as worthy of being listened to. Today we urgently need to engage all the members of society in building "a culture which privileges dialogue as a form of encounter" and in creating "a means for building consensus and agreement while seeking the goal of a just, responsive and inclusive society."[16] [. . .]

This culture of dialogue should be an integral part of the education imparted in our schools, cutting across disciplinary lines and helping to give young people the tools needed to settle conflicts differently than we are accustomed to do.

[. . .]

Lately I have given much thought to this. I ask myself: How can we involve our young people in this building project if we fail to offer them employment, dignified labor that lets them grow and develop through their handiwork, their intelligence and their abilities? How can we tell them that they are protagonists, when the levels of employment and underemployment of millions of young Europeans are continually rising? How can we avoid losing our young people, who end up going elsewhere in search of their dreams and a sense of belonging, because here, in their own countries, we don't know how to offer them opportunities and values?

[. . .]

I dream of a Europe that is young, still

capable of being a mother: a mother who has life because she respects life and offers hope for life. I dream of a Europe that cares for children, that offers fraternal help to the poor and those newcomers seeking acceptance because they have lost everything and need shelter. I dream of a Europe that is attentive to and concerned for the infirm and the elderly, lest they be simply set aside as useless. I dream of a Europe where being a migrant is not a crime but a summons to greater commitment on behalf of the dignity of every human being. I dream of a Europe where young people breathe the pure air of honesty, where they love the beauty of a culture and a simple life undefiled by the insatiable needs of consumerism, where getting married and having children is a responsibility and a great joy, not a problem due to the lack of stable employment. I dream of a Europe of families, with truly effective policies concentrated on faces rather than numbers, on birth rates more than rates of consumption. I dream of a Europe that promotes and protects the rights of everyone, without neglecting its duties toward all. I dream of a Europe of which it will not be said that its commitment to human rights was its last utopia. Thank you.

ADDRESS OF HIS HOLINESS POPE FRANCIS TO THE HEADS OF STATE AND GOVERNMENT OF THE EUROPEAN UNION FOR THE CELEBRATION OF THE SIXTIETH ANNIVERSARY OF THE TREATY OF ROME, SALA REGIA, THE VATICAN

(Friday, March 24, 2017)

Distinguished Guests,

I thank you for your presence here tonight, on the eve of the sixtieth anniversary of the signing of the Treaties instituting the European Economic Community and the European Atomic Energy Community. I convey to each of you the affection of the Holy See for your respective countries and for Europe itself, to whose future it is, in God's providence, inseparably linked.

[. . .]

March 25, 1957, was a day full of hope

and expectation, enthusiasm and apprehension. Only an event of exceptional significance and historical consequences could make it unique in history. [. . .]

This was very clear to the founding fathers and the leaders who, by signing the two Treaties, gave life to that political, economic, cultural and primarily human reality which today we call the European Union.

It was clear, then, from the outset, that the heart of the European political project could only be man himself. It was also clear that the Treaties could remain a dead letter; they needed to take on spirit and life. The first element of European vitality must be solidarity. [. . .]

Solidarity gives rise to openness toward others. "Our plans are not inspired by self-interest," said the German Chancellor, K. Adenauer.[17] The French Minister of Foreign Affairs, C. Pineau, echoed this sentiment: "Surely the countries about to unite . . . do not have the intention of isolating themselves from the rest of the world and surrounding themselves with insurmountable barriers." In a world that was all too familiar with the tragedy of walls and divisions, it was clearly important to work for a united and open Europe, and for the removal of the unnatural barrier that divided the continent from the Baltic Sea to the Adriatic. What efforts were made to tear down that wall! [. . .]

In today's lapse of memory, we often forget another great achievement of the solidarity ratified on March 25, 1957: the longest period of peace experienced in recent centuries.

[. . .]

The world has changed greatly in the last sixty years. If the founding fathers, after surviving a devastating conflict, were inspired by the hope of a better future and were determined to pursue it by avoiding the rise of new conflicts, our time is dominated more by the concept of crisis. There is the economic crisis that has marked the past decade; there is the crisis of the family and of established social models; there is a widespread "crisis of institutions" and the migration crisis. So many crises that engender fear and profound confusion in our contemporaries, who look for a new way of envisioning the future. Yet the term "crisis" is not necessarily negative. It does not simply indicate a painful moment to be endured. The word "crisis" has its origin in the Greek verb *kríno,* which means to discern, to weigh, to assess. [. . .]

So what is the interpretative key for reading the difficulties of the present and finding answers for the future? Returning to the thinking of the founding Fathers would be fruitless unless it could help to point out a path and provide an incentive for facing the future and a source of hope. [. . .]

Their answers are to be found precisely in the pillars on which they determined to build the European economic community. I have already mentioned these: the centrality of man, effective solidarity, openness to the world, the pursuit of peace and development, openness to the future. [. . .]

Europe finds new hope when man is the center and the heart of her institutions. I am convinced that this entails an attentive and trust-filled readiness to hear the expectations voiced by individuals, society and the peoples who make up the Union. Sadly, one frequently has the sense that there is a growing "split" between the citizenry and the European institutions, which are often perceived as distant and inattentive to the different sensibilities present in the Union. [. . .] The European Union was born as a *unity of differences* and a *unity in differences*. What is distinctive should not be a reason for fear, nor should it be thought that *unity is preserved by uniformity*. Unity is instead *harmony* within a community. The founding fathers chose that very term as the hallmark of the agencies born of the Treaties and they stressed that the resources and talents of each were now being *pooled*. [. . .]

[. . .] Forms of populism are instead the fruit of an egotism that hems people in and prevents them from overcoming and "looking beyond" their own narrow vision. There is a need to start thinking once again as Europeans, so as to avert the opposite dangers of a dreary uniformity or *the triumph of particularisms*. [. . .]

Europe finds new hope when she refuses to yield to fear or close herself off in false forms of security. Quite the contrary, her history has been greatly determined by encounters with other peoples and cultures; hers "is, and always has been, a dynamic and multicultural identity."[18] [. . .] It is not enough to handle the grave crisis of immigration of recent years as if it were a mere numerical or economic problem, or a question of security. The immigration issue poses a deeper question, one that is primarily cultural. What kind of culture does Europe propose today? The fearfulness that is becoming more and more evident has its root cause in the loss of ideals. Without an approach inspired by those ideals, we end up dominated by the fear that others will wrench us from our usual habits, deprive us of familiar comforts, and somehow call into question a lifestyle that all too often consists of material prosperity alone. Yet the richness of Europe has always been her spiritual openness and her capacity to raise basic questions about the meaning of life. [. . .] Europe has a patrimony of ideals and spiritual values unique in the world, one that deserves to be proposed once more with passion and renewed vigor, for it is the best antidote against the *vacuum of values* of our time, which provides a fertile terrain for every form of extremism.

[. . .]

Europe finds new hope when she is open to the future. When she is open to young people, offering them serious prospects for education and real possibilities for entering the work force. When she invests in the family, which is the first and fundamental cell of society. [. . .]

Distinguished Guests, Nowadays, with the general increase in people's lifespan, sixty is considered the age of full maturity, a critical time when we are once again called to self-examination. The European Union, too, is called today to examine itself, to care for the ailments that inevitably come with age, and to find new ways to steer its course. Yet, unlike human beings, the European Union does not face an inevitable old age, but the possibility of a new youthfulness. [. . .]

For my part, I readily assure you of the closeness of the Holy See and the Church to Europe as a whole, to whose growth she has, and always will, continue to contribute. Invoking upon Europe the Lord's blessings, I ask Him to protect her and grant her peace and progress. I make my own the words that Joseph Bech proclaimed on Rome's Capitoline Hill: *"Ceterum censeo Europam esse aedificandam"* — "Furthermore, I believe

that Europe ought to be built."
Thank you.

■ ■ ■ ■

4

CULTURE AND
COMMUNICATION

■ ■ ■ ■

INTERVIEW — JULY 2016

The atmosphere is always more relaxed in the morning. The security team and the Swiss Guards are getting to know us, and they speak French as well. There's always that same sense of trust. The Holy Father is always just as direct, just as forthcoming . . . He's at home, he goes in and out unhindered. We work, but we also laugh and chat, quite naturally, while the themes we approach are boundless, inexhaustible, sometimes tragic. I'm constantly struck by the simplicity with which he speaks. So alert, so comprehensible, so unstuffy. How does he do it? I have to pinch myself sometimes to accept that I'm really having a conversation with the Pope. He likes the French "style" (because there is one). Such freedom, such serenity, almost. Both trust and empathy are present at our meeting. We're talking about history, again, still. About the evangelization of the Church in an open world, about pastoral work, about the experiences of the past, dictatorships and democracies, about the action of the Church. Translation isn't to the fore, but it's still necessary. The Holy Father speaks better French than he says he does; or at any rate he understands it. Exchanges are complemented by the priceless language of the eyes, of gestures and behavior. There is something miraculous about the whole atmosphere . . .

DOMINIQUE WOLTON: You know, I'm thinking about the relative solitude in which you live here. Do you know what I mean?

POPE FRANCIS: Yes.

DOMINIQUE WOLTON: All on your own.

POPE FRANCIS: No.

DOMINIQUE WOLTON: No, of course not. But you can't leave, you can't go for a walk, for a stroll.

POPE FRANCIS: Yes, but I'm happy.

DOMINIQUE WOLTON: The theory of communication that I've been defending for years is a humanistic and political theory, it's not a technical and economic one. Just like you! But that humanist theory is very much in the minority because everyone prefers technology and the economy.

But the most important thing is humanity, dialogue, not technology. And besides, looking at it closely, beyond the breathtaking performance of technology, what we're in search of is always human relationships . . . That comes back to your quest for bridges. And the first of those, the handshake!

POPE FRANCIS: I'm very fond of talking about the language of gestures. It's a fine form of communication. Because of the five senses, touch is the most important . . .

DOMINIQUE WOLTON: The March 2016 issue of my journal, *Hermès,* was called "The Way of the Senses."[1] With a view to placing a new value on touch, sense, smell, in relation to vision and hearing, which are overvalued these days. We find ourselves on common ground again. I'll send you a copy!

POPE FRANCIS: I was at death's door at the age of twenty-one because of a serious pulmonary infection. Part of my lung was removed. And everyone came to see me, my friends, my family, and everyone said "Good luck!" And I just wanted to send them all back to the village, all of them! And then a nun came to see me, an elderly lady who had prepared me for my first Communion. She took my hand. She gave me the sign of peace . . . As she left, she said, "You're imitating Jesus." She left like that! And think about what you hear when you go to funerals. People saying, "Oh, Mama!" Rather than hugging one another, embracing each other! You can't say anything in the face of the mystery of another person. And I have to communicate the very depths of my mystery, my experience, as silently as possible. And in extreme situations, just through touch. If you think about it, it's the language of children. When I look at a child, when I find myself faced with a child, I don't ask, "How are things at school?" I do this, and that (*gestures*). It's about expressing proximity through gestures.

DOMINIQUE WOLTON: The first time I saw you, I needed to touch you. To have contact. In fact, I don't know if you're allowed to touch a pope, but I felt the need to do so . . .

POPE FRANCIS: When I was studying philosophy at the age of 28, I don't know if I've said this, I read an article by a German writer who said that touch is the most human of the senses.

DOMINIQUE WOLTON: While we're on the subject, I have some questions about silence, about silence and communication.

POPE FRANCIS: From my own experience, I can say that I can't communicate without silence. In the most authentic experience of friendship, and also of love, of love of one's father, one's mother, one's brothers and sisters, the most beautiful moments are the ones when words, gestures and silence mingle. A friend came to see me last week: "How are you?" "I'm well, thank you." There we were, the two of us . . . We talked about a number of things. He talked to me about his wife, his children and grandchildren. It was fine. And then, eventually, we sat in silence. In peace. It was beautiful. And then he asked me a question, and I asked another one. We spent an hour together, but during that hour I don't think we spoke for more than half the time. There was a communication of peace, of friendship. It was beautiful. I was happy and he was too. And that silence mustn't be like starch that you put on shirts to make them stiff; then it becomes rigidity, a formal silence, and that's not silence any more.

DOMINIQUE WOLTON: That's protocol . . .

POPE FRANCIS: It's no longer silence. Silence is tender, affectionate, warm. And it's equally painful at difficult moments. You can't have a communication of any quality without the capacity for silence. It's in silence that the capacity for listening is born, the capacity for understanding, trying to understand, suffering when you can't understand. I don't understand and I suffer. But true communication is human.

Let's move on to God. Communication is a trinity, a mystery in the way it is transmitted. But the Bible tells us that God made man and woman in his own image. The same is true of the way in which they communicate with each other. With words, with caresses, with sexuality, with silence . . . And all of that is sacred. You can't buy communication. You can't sell it. It is given. One can communicate authentically, as we are doing now. On the other hand, pretending to communicate involves manipulation, trickery. I have seen programs on television — I stopped watching television in the 1990s, it's a vow I made to the Virgin — with important people, an artist, a doctor, a scientist, a student, talking among themselves.

But I've very seldom witnessed real communication.

DOMINIQUE WOLTON: Were they only acting out roles? But you know, communication is always something more complicated. Sometimes something happens that the protagonists are unaware of . . .

POPE FRANCIS: I think again of what I wrote for young people before meeting them in Krakow, in 2016. I had taken the image of building bridges, not walls. And I don't know if I said this to you, I already had it in mind: Which is the fundamental bridge? What bond can a human being have with another human? The most human bridge? Taking their hand. When I shake hands with someone, I make a bridge.

DOMINIQUE WOLTON: Yes, of course . . . That's the first bridge. Will you invite everyone to make bridges in front of you?

POPE FRANCIS: Yes. The first time that idea came to me spontaneously, it was in Kenya. In the big stadium in Nairobi, all the young people were there. And the president of the

Republic was there too, his government, all the ministers. I'd been told that one of the "hottest" topics was tribalism, which is very powerful in Africa. But Kenya is a country with a large majority of Christians — Catholic and Anglican — and the president is Catholic. But they were all there — Christians, Muslims, everybody. There were also Africans from opposite tribes. And I don't speak English well because I have a phonetic problem — I don't even speak Spanish well. I have trouble with the pronunciation, I have to make a big effort to ensure that my pronunciation is correct. But I had to deliver that speech. Thank God, I had an excellent translator, a priest from here, who comes from Gibraltar, and who has two mother tongues, Spanish and English. He understands what I want to do, and he can convey what I am saying because he knows me very well. At one point I said to him, "I can't talk like that in front of a stadium full of young people." So I started improvising in Spanish. And he followed me straight away. If he didn't understand something, he made it up. Along the same lines. Eventually, when I got to the crucial subject of tribalism, I said, "Stop tribalism! Repeat after me: 'Stop tribalism!' But say it with your hands, let's make bridges!" And the whole stadium shook hands, even the president of the Republic. They made bridges, and they started thinking about the fact that the first human bridge is a handshake.

DOMINIQUE WOLTON: And that's also what's done at Mass. Yes, communication is human first and foremost, and it's physical.

POPE FRANCIS: We aren't angels!

DOMINIQUE WOLTON: Of course. And what I like in Latin America, and in Africa, is that everyone touches each other. On the other hand, in the United States, those beautiful smiles people give one another are often a way of keeping each other at a distance. It's icy. Everyone is afraid of harassment . . .

POPE FRANCIS: And why? I think I've already touched on this elsewhere, talking about the film *Babette's Feast.* I'm speaking as a Catholic, but it's a bit risky to say so, because it might be perceived as non-ecumenical. And yet it's hard to imagine, among Christians, a celebration based on words alone. You need to break bread, to drink from the chalice, to hug, to greet one another . . . And what you see clearly in that film is the transformation of people who have been "locked up" in words and who, after a period of failure in their lives, have the good fortune, thanks to the cook, to learn to be happy in a different way. And there's one more thing I'd like to say about communication.

Personally, I barely drink. Not every day. But, in a human sense, it's impossible to imagine communication of any quality taking place without drinking, or eating, or doing anything together. *Touching, eating, drinking.* Wine is the symbol of that. Wine, as the Bible says, cheers the heart of man. Nehemiah, in the Book of Ezra, seeing people weeping in the temple after hearing the words of the law, says to them, "Do not weep, but go home, eat, drink, give food to those who have prepared nothing." And that's how the feast of God ends . . . Communication always ends, and I'm not saying that religiously or in a sacred way, but humanly . . . There is true communion in eating and drinking.

In Argentina there's a lovely expression: when you want to talk to someone you say to each other, "let's meet up and have a coffee." Have a coffee. Not to talk, but to "have a coffee." It's understood that it's to talk business, to communicate . . . But it's still a "coffee." Here in Italy, I think the archetype is wine. An anecdote to make you laugh. In Armenia, they gave me a Noah's ark. I'm sure you've seen it on television: a big bronze ark that weighs a ton, I think. And here we have a little olive tree, a real one, which we planted in the ground with the Patriarch. But the ark hasn't arrived yet, because it's too heavy, it's supposed to be coming on a special boat. I asked the Patriarch, "Is Noah in it?" And he said, "No, no!" And I added, "But I wonder if he's still drunk," because he invented wine. And the Armenians say they have the best cognac in the world. They sell it under the Ararat brand. The Patriarch said no, he wasn't drunk on wine, but on Ararat cognac . . . There's a lovely Biblical scene, even with the excess of wine: the drunkenness of Noah — because it's a very tender scene. There's the son looking at his father (Noah), who is naked, drunk, laughing. And the two other sons talk to him and cover him up. The excess of wine also provokes tenderness. All to say that you can't establish genuine communication without making a bridge, and without eating. Words on their own aren't enough. There is another free way of communicating: dance.

DOMINIQUE WOLTON: Yes, it's magnificent, and it's physical.

POPE FRANCIS: The people communicate through dance. That is to say that they communicate with their bodies, with their whole bodies. There's also another way of communicating: weeping . . . Weeping together. When a wife and her husband sit by the bedside of a sick child, they weep together, hoping that the child will be cured. Dancing, shaking hands, kissing, eating and drinking together, weeping . . . If you don't do those things, communication is impossible. It's happened to me several times, and I'm telling you this sincerely, that I've been preaching and I've had to stop because I wanted to weep. When I was truly immersed in a sermon, I was communicating with the people. I'm going to finish on ways of communication with an essential term, without which there is no communication: play. Children communicate through play. Play has the property of developing the capacity for invention. Children are creative!

DOMINIQUE WOLTON: Yes. They invent things all the time.

POPE FRANCIS: Our football these days is

a fallen thing, it has lost the human sense of communication that amateur football used to have. These examples are intended to illustrate the dimension that I don't want us to forget: there is no true communication without selflessness. Selflessness means being capable of wasting time. I don't know if I've talked to you about that couple who were celebrating their sixtieth wedding anniversary? Here, at the Wednesday audiences, we have a lot of young married people. Some of them have been married for six months, and sometimes, when they come for blessing, the wife already has a big belly and they ask me to bless the belly. But it's beautiful. And then, among them, there are old people, who have been married for fifty or sixty years. And I always ask them questions to make them laugh: "Which of you has more patience?" And the answer is always the same: "Both of us!" I saw one couple, still young, because the wife had married at the age of fifteen and the husband at seventeen. So, after sixty years of marriage they were seventy-five and seventy-seven. But they were beautiful, their eyes were glorious. I asked them: "Have you ever argued?" And they said, "Constantly." "But now you're happy about this journey?" They stayed silent, but then they looked each other in the eyes and they said to me, "We're in love." But how did they communicate about their love? First of all, they looked, then they answered. The gesture spoke for itself.

Elderly people have a greater capacity for good communication — not all of them: some get annoyed and declare war on others. They have that capacity because they have wisdom. The wisdom that comes with the passing years.

Elderly people talk to me a lot, I have great tenderness for old people. When I see elderly people, particularly old ladies, with that beautiful gleam in their eyes, I stop the popemobile. The things they say are so wise. I think today is the time of the elderly, of grandparents.

This world claims to be the world of efficiency and work, but it leaves out young people because it doesn't give them any work, and it leaves out old people because it puts them in retirement homes. It's on the way to suicide. There's this prophetic passage from Joel 3, 1: "The old will dream, the young will prophecy." The time has come for the elderly to dream and tell us their dreams. For young people to accomplish their prophecies and change the world. It isn't a time of adults, of mature people. No, the protagonists who will save the world will be those two groups. As long as old people dream and tell their dreams, and young people pick up those dreams and carry them forward.

There's a scene in the Gospel that I find very moving: the story of the presentation in the temple. Four times, that passage from the Gospel[2] says that it was young people who were going to enforce the law, and three times they say that it was two old people, Simeon and Anne, who were moved by the Spirit. They were granted by the ability to dream by the Spirit. Young people must receive those dreams and fulfill the prophesies. It sounds as if I'm preaching!

DOMINIQUE WOLTON: When you receive heads of state or other people, in your personal meetings is there time for silence?

POPE FRANCIS: Generally speaking, no. No, because there is protocol. With some young people, not heads of state, but with two heads of government and some young MPs, I've managed to remain silent.

DOMINIQUE WOLTON: Why don't you systematically request a moment of silence with the heads of state? Perhaps it would be good, in international meetings, to suggest a moment of silence. Then something might happen, an authentic communication. Because the world today is so mad about speed, interactivity and noise, if on an official trip you were to say, "If you like, we could have a few moments of silence," that might be possible, and it might have real power.

POPE FRANCIS: But I can do that in Saint Peter's Square with the crowd. At the Angelus, or at other times, I ask for silence, and the square responds well to that request for silence.

DOMINIQUE WOLTON: On the evening of your election, when you came out on the balcony, you asked the crowd to give a moment's silence.

POPE FRANCIS: A moment of silence, of prayer. And they responded well.

DOMINIQUE WOLTON: This theme of silence, if you can bring it to a wider audience, it's essential in a world that is always noisy and fast. Finding a little silence would be an astonishing human contribution. How can you express goodness, love of others, mercy, in a world saturated with noise, words and interactions?

POPE FRANCIS: According to my experience of the media and the world of communication, they keep what suits them. The media faces four pitfalls. I'm not talking about communication, but about the media. The first is disinformation. Saying only a part of things, the part that suits them. I'm thinking about newspapers: they lead the reader to form an incorrect judgment about reality, because they only give half the facts. The second danger is slander. Sullying other people's reputations.

Slander, as *The Barber of Seville* has it, is not a gentle breeze, it is a hurricane. The third is defamation. A person may have made mistakes in a past life. Then they may have changed, they may perhaps have asked for forgiveness. You can tell that their behavior is different. The danger is that the media, in order to sap their authority, bring up that past. That's defamation. The fourth is a very ugly illness in the media: coprophilia — I'm expressing it nastily — which is sad, unpleasant and disagreeable. Wallowing in the most scabrous, brutal and voyeuristic stories and references.

Those pitfalls are everywhere in social

communication, in the media.

DOMINIQUE WOLTON: It's the same with the internet.

POPE FRANCIS: And we're used to that. We're used to it. It's very hard to find someone in the media who discusses a situation without sullying it, without only saying a part of things, without attacking other people's dignity.

DOMINIQUE WOLTON: Yes, the dignity of the person.

POPE FRANCIS: In my view the media must protect the dignity of the person.

DOMINIQUE WOLTON: Everything you're saying, I've been writing it for twenty, thirty years. But no one hears me. I hope that people will listen to you more. On the other hand, why does the Church talk not of "communication" but of "social communication"? Particularly since Vatican II.

POPE FRANCIS: But you don't find much about the anthropology of communication in the texts. You know where there might be something? In *The Theology of the Body* by

John Paul II. He spoke about marriage, and he developed this theology of the body that shocked a lot of people. But he said how a woman and a man communicate, without fear but quite naturally. I think that was the first time a pope, or the Church officially, talked about personal, not social, communication. But communication is always a social matter, even when it's personal.

DOMINIQUE WOLTON: Yes, always. Because communication is a relationship, it is about the other.

POPE FRANCIS: And to communicate is to put oneself in the hands of the other.

DOMINIQUE WOLTON: And, please, read the five pages of the summary that I have given you about my theory of communication, because that's exactly what I've been writing for thirty years . . .

POPE FRANCIS: But, in that case, why are we doing yet another book on the subject?

DOMINIQUE WOLTON: This book will interest people beyond Christians and Catholics. It will be of great interest to laypeople, because you are often better liked among laypeople and atheists than you are among Catholics, as you know. (*laughter*).

Yes, but it's true! You're the last "communist" in Europe . . .

POPE FRANCIS: I received some French politicians the other day, with Cardinal Barbarin. And before that, on the Sunday[3] before the Feast of Christ the King, I had received the pilgrimage of the poor of Europe, also with Cardinal Barbarin.[4]

DOMINIQUE WOLTON: Yes, I know him.

POPE FRANCIS: He's a good man

DOMINIQUE WOLTON: He's very intelligent.

POPE FRANCIS: He came to the conclave by bike!

DOMINIQUE WOLTON: The idea of bringing the poor together here is a very good one. So what will your successor do? He'll have to keep it going! (*laughter*)

POPE FRANCIS: But the Holy Spirit will provide . . .

DOMINIQUE WOLTON: Yes, perhaps. But

the difference between the two of us is that, for you, the Holy Spirit is always there, and, for me, it's far from certain. You see? (*laughter*)

POPE FRANCIS: You'll go to hell! (*laughter*)

DOMINIQUE WOLTON: (*laughter*) Yes. You have more authority than I do. But we agree on lots of things. You know, these days, things are all about the madness of technology, the media, the internet, social networks, the insanity of speed, of interactivity. When I maintain that technical communication is always easier than human communication, which explains its success, I encounter real resistance. Technology is so seductive, human relationships are so difficult, and yet the only thing that matters is other people, love and otherness.

POPE FRANCIS: But . . . something happened to me one Sunday when I was about to leave for the palace, for the Angelus. A bishop comes to see me and he tells me he's brought in a little group of a hundred people who have come for a blessing, but I don't need to go to them, they're just there for a blessing. At first, I thought, "If I do that blessing from a distance, I should do it like that" (*gesture*). But then I went outside, and I saw the people waiting for me. That isn't theory, it isn't politics: it's a human need. And, all of a sudden, they all came to touch me, the young people, their parents . . . They tried to take a photograph, a selfie. And I didn't say a single word. In fact, I did say something to one of them, a twelve-year-old boy who had a lovely T-shirt with the words: *My mother always performs miracles, but with me she outdid herself.* And I asked him, "Where's your mother?" And he said, "That's her." All of a sudden, we walked toward one another. In the end, I had to establish a bit of order and say, "Let's do something, let's stand together, we'll take a photograph and then we'll say goodbye." I really had to leave for the Angelus; I didn't have much time. I explained the situation, and they understood. We prayed to the Madonna, a Hail Mary, a blessing, we said goodbye and I left. You might ask, "But what catechesis did you give them?" I have no idea, but I think that catechesis must be given by a priest who is close to his people, who laughs with his people, who allows himself to be disturbed by his people. And that's communication. I don't like it when I encounter a priest who has listed his times of availability in his parish church: "From this time to this, from this time to this . . ." And when the member of the congregations says, "All right, then," and they go at the time shown and, instead of finding a priest, they find a secretary, sometimes a rather surly one, who tells them the priest is too busy! That's anti-communication and anti-Gospel . . .

DOMINIQUE WOLTON: Yes, that's true. Often, priests are so busy that they aren't available. You don't dare to speak to them. You have the impression that they're doing very important things when they're talking to God, obviously more important than we are . . .

POPE FRANCIS: Jesus himself was very busy. And yet, when a man told him that his son or a servant, I can't remember which, was dead, and he asked him to heal him, Jesus said, "I'll come." The man told him he didn't want to trouble him, but Jesus said, "No, I'll come!" When Jesus saw, by the gates of Naim, that a widow's only son was being buried, he went over, touched her and began to weep. Then, he touched the child's coffin and performed a miracle. He approached. And that's the conclusion I want to come to: there cannot be a Church of Jesus Christ that is far from the people. The Church of Jesus Christ must be attached to the people, connected to people. The opposite would be to do as some politicians do — not all of them, let's not condemn them en masse — who are only interested in people during election campaigns and then forget about them after that. And, for me, closeness, even in pastoral life, is the key to evangelization. You can't evangelize without closeness.

I once heard a story, told to me by a layman who witnessed it: "A rich man had parted ways with his family, and lost all connection with them. Eventually, he was put in hospital with a terminal illness. In the bed next to him, there was another man, with the same illness. The chaplain came and talked to the other patient, but he couldn't get a word out of our man. Completely closed up, he didn't say a word to anybody. One day, the man in the next bed asked him to bring him the spittoon, and, for the first time, he got up and went to get it. Then the other man asked him to wash the spittoon. He went to the bathroom and washed it and brought it back. At that point, the man started feeling a sense of anxiety, a great anxiety . . . and he started talking to the nurses, to the others, as if this act of service, of closeness, of communication through the suffering flesh had opened a door for him. And, three days later, when the chaplain came back, our man called to him and started telling him about his life . . . I don't know what he said to the chaplain, but he asked him for Communion, and he died the same evening." That story made me think about the parable of the eleventh hour, the parable of the workers in the vineyard. How an act of closeness, a dirty and humble service performed for someone else, opened his heart. It liberated him.

Here, I'm going to mention a historical thing that happened, involving communication. In the Piazza del Risorgimento, there was a homeless Polish man who was often drunk, and he said he had been a fellow seminarian and fellow priest of John Paul II, and then he had left the priesthood. No one believed him. Someone mentioned this to John Paul II. "There's someone saying this and that." And John Paul II said, "Well, ask him what his name is." And it was true! "Bring him in." They made him take a shower and presented him to the Pope. And the Pope received him: "So, how are you?!" And he hugged him. He had basically abandoned the priesthood and run off with a woman. "So, how are you?" And then eventually John Paul II looked at him. "My confessor was supposed to be coming today, but he's not here. Take my confession." "What are you talking about?" "Yes, yes, I give you permission." And he knelt down and confessed. And then he did the same thing for his visitor, and the man ended up as chaplain at the hospital, helping the sick. An act of closeness and humility.

Another word comes to mind. I said selflessness, but it's humility. You can't communicate with pride. The only key that opens the door of communication is humility. Or at least a partial attitude of humility. You communicate as equals. You communicate upwards. But, if you only communicate downwards, you will fail.

DOMINIQUE WOLTON: That's hierarchy.

POPE FRANCIS: Talking of hell — it's a subject I don't want to talk about — but . . . Have I talked to you about the portal at Vézelay?

DOMINIQUE WOLTON: No.

POPE FRANCIS: The Way of Saint James

begins at the Cathedral of Mary Magdalene in Vézelay. It has a magnificent portal. On one side, there is Judas, who has hanged himself and died, and on the other side, there is the good shepherd, who has taken him and is carrying him on his shoulders. And, when you see that, you wonder if Judas has been saved. But, if you look at the face of the good shepherd, who is Jesus, one half of his face is sad, the other half smiling. That's the mystery of hell. Selflessness, humility: those are words to assist communication. Sharing a meal. Drinking, dancing, celebrating.

DOMINIQUE WOLTON: But then, since you maintain a real distance from technology, why are you the champion of Twitter?[5] Why do you tweet? Why you? Why, since you say that human communication is much more important than technical communication?

POPE FRANCIS: I have to use every means available to get close to people. It's a way of getting close.

DOMINIQUE WOLTON: Yes, but then there's no difference, if you're doing the same as everyone else. Don't you issue warnings about omnipresent technical communication, saying yourself that it is very limited?

POPE FRANCIS: I don't stop there. I just do it to open doors. But I want to go beyond that. In 2016, I received eleven or twelve YouTubers from all over the world and talked to them live on the web. One girl, I can't remember what country she came from, said to me, "How can I communicate with a person who . . ." I said to her, "To communicate, you must be personally a part of the group; if you are not, you have no identity, and if you have no identity, you can't communicate." She said, "But how can I communicate with someone who has no identity?" I gave this answer: "You, yourself, just have to give them a virtual identity. And from that virtuality you reach the concrete, you reach the reality." I tweet to open doors, I'm sure those tweets touch people's hearts . . .

DOMINIQUE WOLTON: But insofar as there is a globalization of communication technologies and less and less human communication, why not at least deliver a neutral address about the strengths and limits of technical communication? There is individual freedom, but behind that there is the incredible power of GAFA (Google, Apple,

Facebook, Amazon). And others . . . They are the biggest networks in the world, with a lot of power, money, influence and control! That has nothing to do with human communication, even if each individual feels they are free. Free in terms of use. Terribly compromised and controlled in terms of organization. Why isn't the Church saying, "Be careful, be careful"? You could say, yes to technical communication, but in moderation, while stressing the value of human communication and its specificity. In fact, if technical communication happens very quickly, human communication goes very slowly. And that's the most difficult thing, the most important, and the one that needs to be saved. You could say things like that. Why does the Church not say anything?

Why has there been no encyclical on the challenges of human and technical communication? It would be useful, given the current silence on the matter. Particularly given that the Church very quickly adopted a position on radio and television. On computers, then on the internet, nothing. You could say yes to technical progress, but don't forget human communication.

POPE FRANCIS: Perhaps. And there are some very serious problems. For example the people who lock themselves away in an exclusively technical communication. People who have meals each with their own computer, dad, mum, the children . . . They aren't talking to each other, they're writing. In the past, they used to watch television; now, only the father and mother do. At least that was something you could comment on together. That needs talking about, I agree.

DOMINIQUE WOLTON: Yes, the Church can say "be careful" because, in the world, the technical, financial and economic matters at stake are considerable. The American communication-technology industry makes more money than the arms trade. But, since everyone is fascinated by these performances, they let it go. The internet is still identified with "freedom," and all regulation is considered retrograde . . . Some public figures talk about the "knowledge society," about "digital civilizations." But the point isn't so much that technology has to be humanized: human beings must themselves be made human and protected . . .

POPE FRANCIS'S ADDRESS TO THE ITALIAN COUNCIL OF THE ORDER OF JOURNALISTS, 400 JOURNALISTS, CLEMENTINE HALL, THE VATICAN

(September 22, 2016)

[. . .] Few professions have such a great influence on society as journalism. The journalist has a role of great importance and, at the same time, a great responsibility. In a certain sense you write the "first draft of history," by setting the agenda of the news and leading how people interpret events. That is very important. Times are changing, and journalism is changing too. Both print journalism and television are losing relevance compared to the new media of the digital world — particularly among young people — but journalists, if they do their job professionally, remain a pillar, a fundamental element in the vitality of a free and pluralist society. [. . .]

Today, I would like to share with you a reflection on some aspects of your profession of journalism, and how this may serve to improve the society in which we live in. For all of us, it is essential to stop, to think about what we are doing and how we are doing it. In the spiritual life, this often takes the form of a day's retreat, of inner contemplation. I think that, in our professional lives too, we also need some time to stop and think. Certainly, it isn't easy in a field such as journalism, a profession constantly based around "deadlines" and "expiry dates." But, at least for a moment, let us try to gain a better understanding of the reality of journalism.

I shall focus on three elements: the love of truth, a fundamental thing for everyone, but especially for journalists; living professionally, something that goes far beyond rules and regulations; and a respect for human dignity, which is much more difficult than it might seem at first glance. [. . .]

Loving the truth means not only affirming it, but living it and bearing witness to it through one's work. This means living and working with coherence in relation to the words you use for a newspaper article or a television report. Here, it is not a question of "being or not being a believer." It is a question of "being or not being honest with yourself and with others." This relationship lies at the heart of all communication. Especially for those who do this as a profession. And no relationship based on dishonesty can survive and endure over time. I realize that, in contemporary journalism — an uninterrupted flow of facts and events related twenty-four hours a day, seven days a week — it is not always easy to reach the truth, or at least to get close to it. Not everything in life is black and white. In journalism too, you must be able to discern between the shades of gray of the events you are called upon to narrate. Political debates, and indeed many conflicts, are seldom the result of clear and distinct dynamics in which it is possible to recognize unequivocally who is wrong and who is right. Comparison and sometimes conflict are indeed born precisely out of this difficulty in establishing a synthesis between these different positions. That is the difficult and necessary work — we might even call it a mission — of a journalist: to get as close as possible to the truth of events and never say or write anything which we know in the depths of our conscience to be untrue.

Second element: living professionally means, above all — beyond what we find written in deontological codes — understanding and internalizing the deeper meaning of one's own work. Hence the need not to submit your profession to the logic of partisan interests, whether they be economic or political. The task of journalism, I would even say its vocation, is thus — through attention and a concern to seek the truth — to enhance the social dimension with a true sense of citizenship. In this perspective of opening horizons, acting professionally therefore means not only responding to the preoccupations, however legitimate, of one particular part of society, but to have at heart one of the pillars of the structure of a democratic society. Dictatorships — of any orientation and "color" — which have always sought to seize the means of communication and impose new rules on journalism, should always give us food for thought.

And thirdly: respect for human dignity is important in every profession, but particularly in journalism, because behind the simple account of an event there lie feelings, emotions and, most importantly, people's lives. I have often spoken of gossip as a form of "terrorism," capable of killing a person through language. If that applies to individuals, whether in their family life or at work, it applies even more so to journalists, because their voices can touch everyone, and this is a very powerful weapon. Journalism must always respect the dignity of the person. An article is published today, and tomorrow it will be replaced by another, but the life of a person slandered unjustly may be destroyed forever. Certainly, criticism is legitimate, and I would go so far as to say that it is necessary, like "denouncing" evil, but it must always be done with respect for others, for their lives and their emotions. Journalism must not become a "weapon of destruction" of people or indeed of peoples. Nor must it fuel fear in the face of changes or phenomena such as forced migrations due to war and famine.

My wish is that journalism, more and more, and everywhere, should become a constructive instrument, a factor for the common good, an accelerator of the process of reconciliation; that it should be able to reject the temptation to foment confrontation with a language that stirs the fire of divisions, but instead encourage the culture of encounter. You journalists remind all of us each day that there is no conflict that cannot be resolved by women and men of goodwill.

Thank you for this meeting; I wish you good luck in your work. May the Lord bless you. I hold you in my prayers and in my heart, and ask you please to pray for me. Thank you.

ADDRESS OF HIS HOLINESS POPE FRANCIS TO THE NEWLY APPOINTED BISHOPS PARTICIPATING IN THE FORMATIVE COURSES ORGANIZED BY THE CONGREGATIONS FOR BISHOPS, CLEMENTINE HALL, THE VATICAN

(September 16, 2016)

[. . .] You have almost reached the end of these fruitful days spent in Rome to deepen your reflection on the richness of the mystery to which God has called you as bishops of the Church. [. . .] I am happy to receive you and to be able to share with you some thoughts which get to the heart of the Successor of Peter when I see those who have been "caught" by God's heart to guide His holy people.

1. **THE THRILL OF HAVING BEEN LOVED FIRST**

Yes! God precedes you in His loving knowledge! He has "caught" you with the hook of His surprising mercy. His nets were mysteriously tightened and you could not help but let yourselves be captured. [. . .]

2. **ADMIRABLE KINDNESS!**

It is good to allow oneself to be pierced by the loving knowledge of God. It is consoling to know that He truly knows who we are and is not alarmed by our smallness. [. . .]

3. **CROSS THE THRESHOLD OF THE HEART OF CHRIST, THE TRUE DOOR OF MERCY**

These are the reasons why I invite you, next Sunday, when crossing the Holy Door of the Jubilee of Mercy, which has drawn millions of pilgrims to Christ, both from the city and the world, to live an intense personal experience of gratitude, of reconciliation, of total abandonment, delivering your life unreservedly to the Pastor of Pastors. [. . .]

4. THE TASK OF MAKING MERCY PASTORAL

It is a difficult task. Ask God, who is rich in mercy, the secret of making mercy pastoral in your dioceses. [. . .]

Do not be afraid to propose mercy as the summary of all that God gives to the world, because man's heart can aspire to nothing greater. [. . .]

5. THREE RECOMMENDATIONS FOR MAKING MERCY PASTORAL

[. . .]

5.1. *Be bishops capable of enchanting and attracting:*

Make your ministry an icon of mercy, the only force capable of seducing and permanently attracting the heart of man. [. . .]

5.2 *Be bishops capable of initiating those entrusted to your care:*

All that is great needs a way to enter. This is even more true of the divine mercy, which is inexhaustible! Once one is seized by mercy, it requires a way in, a path, a road, an initiation. [. . .]

Be bishops capable of initiating your churches into this abyss of love. Today, too much fruit is asked of trees that have not been sufficiently well cultivated. We have lost the sense of initiation, and yet the truly essential things in life can be reached only through initiation.. [. . .]

Please attend to the initiation structures of your churches with special care, particularly the seminaries. Do not allow yourselves to be tempted by the numbers and quantity of vocations, but rather seek the quality of initiation. Neither numbers nor quantity: only quality. [. . .]

5.3. *Be bishops capable of accompanying:*

[. . .] Dear brothers, let us now pray together and I will bless you with all my heart as pastor, father and brother. Blessing is always the invocation of the face of God upon us. The face of God that never darkens is Christ. By blessing you, I will ask Him to walk with you and give you the courage to walk with Him. It is His face that attracts us, that imprints itself within us and accompanies us. So be it![6]

■ ■ ■ ■ ■

5
OTHERNESS,
TIME AND JOY

■ ■ ■ ■

■ ■ ■ ■

5

OTHERNESS,
TIME AND JOY

■ ■ ■ ■

INTERVIEW — JULY 2016

We're almost getting used to these interviews, after seeing each other for three days in a row. Everything is simple and familiar in this dialogue, which exists both outside of time and at all times at once within this vast history. Everything here makes one modest. A tiny territory, but one with such a long history. An obvious intermingling between the culture of our societies, gnawed away by events and immediacy, and this apparently serene, still and eternal space. We continue our discussions very seriously, following the planned order of the book. The Holy Father is scrupulous, our dialogue is always just as natural and humorous as ever. Humor, that huge and eternal short-circuiting of the intelligence. . . .

The Church in modern society. Mutual support and confrontation. The Church, communication, human beings and technology, the gaps between experience and the vision of the world. Where does modernity lie? How can this man shoulder the weight of the vast symbol that he embodies? How can he live with the responsibilities he has assumed? There is modesty here, in this building, but right next door the solemnity of Saint Peter's is a constant presence, its bells regularly reminding us of the openness to the world, the relationships between civilizations and the huge problem of the coexistence of different cultures. Time, the time that defines all of us.

What a thought. And in his company, in his words, there is always the essential, vital, ontological reminder of the role of prayer. An object lesson, as people used to say. In any case silences, dreams and deep reflection . . . Besides, our exchanges are a perfect illustration of this difficult and indispensable dialogue between the religious and the layman. Between someone who is steeped in values and references different from those of the intellectual, whose codes are closer to anthropology.

DOMINIQUE WOLTON: How do you engage in dialogue with atheists and non-believers who acknowledge neither original sin nor error? How do you engage with them, since we are often in a secular and not a religious world?

POPE FRANCIS: They are a part of reality. Part of different powers. And when we speak of reality, we immediately collide with different viewpoints. But reality builds bridges between different viewpoints. Reality is truth. The bridges exist in our conversation. But we must take reality, not theory, as our starting point. We can talk about squaring the circle until the end of time, it would be pointless. What is reality? Everyone sees reality in his or her own way. And I see it as I think it is. I understand it as it is. So we must seek together. It's a quest, a search.

DOMINIQUE WOLTON: Still, what must we do, what must we say, to people who are atheists? How do you respect people who are atheist? What is the dialogue? Atheists have done a great deal, a very great deal, for social and political liberation, for democracy since the eighteenth century. What does the Church say? The Church often says, "We will wait for them." But if they are atheists they aren't waiting for anything. And they don't need you to wait. So how do you engage in dialogue? Particularly since they are often people of peace! What is to be done with atheists? Because, of course, the Church has killed lots of them.

POPE FRANCIS: In another time, some people said, "Leave them alone, they'll go to hell anyway!"

DOMINIQUE WOLTON: (*laughter*) Of course!

POPE FRANCIS: But we must never talk in adjectives. True communication is made with nouns. With a person, that is. The person may be agnostic, atheist, Catholic, Jewish . . . but those are adjectives. I talk to a person. You have to talk to a person. It's a woman, it's a man, like me. In Krakow, a young man asked me the same question at a lunch with a group of young Catholics of twelve or fourteen. Girls and boys, two for each continent and two extra ones for Poland. A young man asked me, "What do you say to an atheist?"

DOMINIQUE WOLTON: But that's not my question. Mine is: how do you engage in dialogue with them?

POPE FRANCIS: "What do you say to an atheist?" I told him this: "The last thing you should do is address yourself [preach] to an atheist. You have to live your life; you listen to them, but you mustn't deliver an apologia.[1] No apologias. If the atheist asks you something, you answer according to your human experience." Dialogue must be carried out on the basis of human experience. I'm a believer, but faith is a gift, a gift from God. No one can have faith from themselves alone. No one. Even if you study a whole library. It's a gift. And if you don't have that gift, God will save you in a different way. And you can talk about lots of things that we have in common: ethical problems, mythical matters, human matters . . . Lots of things. About what you think, human problems, how to behave. You can talk about the development of humanity . . . Talk about things you have in common. The atheist will have a different point of view, and I will have a different point of view as well. But you can speak, and when you reach the problem of God, each one of you will express your choice. But while listening to the other person with respect.

I once had the following experience: a lady told me she had heard a sermon, or a lecture, I can't remember which. She told me she was an atheist, but at that moment she began to doubt the nonexistence of God. That was what had touched her. Agnostics too. They are different.

DOMINIQUE WOLTON: There's a phrase from the Church which I think is devastating: "By forgetting God, we forget mankind."

POPE FRANCIS: Yes.

DOMINIQUE WOLTON: Yes, but for an atheist?

POPE FRANCIS: There's another idea involved there. You're right. Let's take a concrete example, an atheist like Hitler, with the precept that I quoted to you . . .

DOMINIQUE WOLTON: Hitler was hardly an ordinary atheist.

POPE FRANCIS: But by forgetting God, we forget mankind.

DOMINIQUE WOLTON: That's what Monsignor Jean-Marie Lustiger said to me when we talked together. But the question remains: by forgetting God, do we forget mankind? First of all, there are priests and believers who have killed lots of people throughout history. And then, today, there are lots of atheists who are as humanistic as believers . . . Because, if you say, "By forgetting God, we forget mankind," that means that there is no solution other than God. And yet an atheist will say, "I'm an atheist and sometimes I do good, just as much as believers do." And that's a strange thing: there is interreligious dialogue, there is ecumenism, but what do we do with atheists? For example, the Year of Mercy. How do you get across that message of the Year of Mercy? How do you express that to atheists? They don't get it.

POPE FRANCIS: Do something good for somebody. Do it. And, if you aren't interested in the subject, think of those in need. Think of the children in Syria. Think a merciful thought. An internal emotion.

DOMINIQUE WOLTON: You often say, "How do we make people understand that humanity is both wounded and saved?"

POPE FRANCIS: The experience of each individual. Each man, each woman, falls and gets up again. How do you get back up after falling many times, and find a new path? You can speak without being afraid, since you are an atheist and I'm not . . . but let's talk to each other! We will both end up in the same place. We will both be eaten by worms!

DOMINIQUE WOLTON: What do you think about that phrase of Pius XII, when he said, "The tragedy of our age is that we have lost the sense of sin"? Would you say the same thing?

POPE FRANCIS: Yes, that's true. I think that's true, the age has lost the sense of sin. Today, when you see fifty people being blown up and killed by a suicide bomber . . . When you see traffickers drowning people in the Strait of Sicily . . . If an honest person wonders, "Why are they doing that?" the answer is that those people have no moral compass. That at the very least. And the moral compass is one that is accepted by everyone. From there to talking about sin, there's a journey, because to talk about sin is also to talk about our relationship with God; sin presupposes faith. But having no moral compass is an idea that touches everyone. Even atheists. And even a convinced and honest atheist will say to him or herself, "Yes, the world lacks a moral compass." If an ultraliberal economist reads certain passages in *Laudato Si'*, he will end up saying to himself that the economy lacks

234

a moral compass. Morality is a requirement of our social behavior. But it does not have the strictness or rigidity of the commandments. Morality means paying your workers honestly, paying your housekeeper honestly . . . And sometimes there are terrible contradictions.

There was a rich woman, very Catholic, who was part of a very active charity group, with three children, three adolescent boys, of sixteen, seventeen and twenty, and she said to me, "I recruit my housekeeper very carefully," because, listen to this, "I don't want my children to go looking elsewhere; I want them to have the complete service at home." That's immorality.

There's a social problem today, one for which I blame the media. Today, the whole world is shocked, thank God, by child abuse. But, in this world, there are businessmen who produce films — not for television, but for the internet — videos in which young boys and young girls, men and women, can watch "filth," sexual relations with minors, homosexual, heterosexual, every possible way.

DOMINIQUE WOLTON: Yes, that's hypocrisy.

POPE FRANCIS: Who allows that? The same

government that condemns child abuse. And sometimes they put out films showing how to abuse children . . .

DOMINIQUE WOLTON: Pornography is one of the biggest industries in the world . . .

POPE FRANCIS: That's it, that's the contradiction I'm underlining. We all have a moral compass within us. We can all sense if a thing is good or bad.

DOMINIQUE WOLTON: After thirty years of economic liberalization, the question of morality will return. For thirty years, money has ruled! Money alone, in the name of economic liberalism. Perhaps morality will return as an investigation of meaning, not as a sequence of prohibitions.

POPE FRANCIS: May the Lord hear you! But how do we Catholics teach morality? It can't be taught with precepts like, "You can't do that, you have to do that, you must, you mustn't, you can, you can't." Morality is a consequence of the encounter with Jesus Christ. It is a consequence of faith, for us Catholics. And for others, morality is a consequence of the encounter with an ideal, or with God, or with oneself, but with the best part of oneself. Morality is always a consequence.

DOMINIQUE WOLTON: But it has often been said that there is no morality in the economy. It is false, of course, to say there is morality in the economy. For thirty years, liberal capitalism has been like that, without morality. Particularly since globalization and the fall of communism.

POPE FRANCIS: It will come to an end eventually.

DOMINIQUE WOLTON: Yes, of course.

POPE FRANCIS: I don't think I'll live to see that . . .

DOMINIQUE WOLTON: One has a sense that the Church is progressive on the subject of the love of the Other, of immigrants, but that, in the areas of the family, of the couple, of morals, of homosexuality, it is much more "rigid." You yourself have even mentioned the "whip" that should "hang in the sacristy."[2] Where morals, the family and sexuality are concerned, one still has the impression that the Church is the "whip."

237

POPE FRANCIS: But great progress has been made in explaining the position of the Church, from Pius XI to the present day. For example, the whole anthropology of the family carried out by John Paul II is very important. And then there is what I did after the two synods, *Amoris Laetitia* . . . It's something clear and positive, which some people with excessively traditionalist inclinations resist, saying that it is not the true doctrine. On the subject of wounded families I say in the eighth chapter that *there are four criteria: welcoming, accompanying, discerning situations and integrating.* And that isn't a fixed norm. It opens up a way, a path of communication. I was immediately asked, "But can you give Communion to divorcees?" I reply, "Talk to the divorced man, talk to the divorced woman, welcome, accompany, integrate, discern!" Sadly we priests are used to fixed norms. Unshakeable norms. And that's difficult for us: "accompanying along the way, integrating, discerning, saying good things." But that is my proposition. John Paul II as well, with his theology of the body, which is very important, traveled a long way in terms of sexuality and the family. I quote him in my exhortation *Amoris Laetitia,* which I was just talking about, because it contains everything. One sentence in it shocked a few people: "Sex is a good and beautiful thing."

DOMINIQUE WOLTON: You must admit that it is complicated for laypeople to hear priests, who have renounced physical love, saying that physical love is beautiful.

POPE FRANCIS: To renounce sexuality and choose the way of chastity or virginity is a life consecrated to God. And what is the condition without which this path dies? It is that the path must bring you to spiritual fatherhood or motherhood. One of the evils of the Church is the "old bachelor" priests and "old spinster" nuns. Because they are filled with bitterness. On the other hand, those who have attained spiritual father-hood, either through the parish, or through the church or the hospital, are fine . . . And the same applies to nuns, because they are "mothers."

DOMINIQUE WOLTON: Philippe Barbarin[3] encountered a lot of difficulties on these subjects. André Vingt-Trois, the Archbishop of Paris, and a few others supported him . . .

POPE FRANCIS: Were the others like Pontius Pilate?

DOMINIQUE WOLTON: A lot of them are like Pontius Pilate and wash their hands of him.

POPE FRANCIS: I know Monsignor Philippe Barbarin very well. He came here, he's a brave man. It's a problem that dates back to forty years ago, and he thought there was prescriptiveness. He's free. He's a free man, and he's also very generous. He was a missionary in Madagascar . . .

DOMINIQUE WOLTON: He needed the Pope's authority, because the pressure of the media and public opinion was very strong in terms of saying, "Resign! Resign!"

POPE FRANCIS: Catholic priests represent more or less 2 percent of pedophiles. That doesn't sound like much, but it's too many. Even one Catholic priest doing that is horrible. Zero tolerance! Because the priest must bring children to God, not destroy their lives. And then there's the chain of consequences: of four abused children, two will become abusers.

DOMINIQUE WOLTON: On the subject of pedophilia, I have found the Church to be very much on the defensive. Of course, it closed its eyes too often, it covered up unacceptable things, but still, the time of the Church is not the same as the time of society. It isn't the time of the media, either. And yet today the media has become the court of morals.

Why can't the Church say, "Yes, I respect the law, but I am in charge of problems of conscience, of peace, of morality, which do not adopt the logic and rhythm of the media or public opinion"? I think that, for fifty years, the Catholic Church has often been on the defensive, without explaining the difference in temporality or logic. It is too keen to adapt to modern times. The Church is not outside the law, but it is something other than the law.

POPE FRANCIS: And there is also the issue of doctors, *mutatis mutandis,* professional secrecy, and other things going in the same direction as the problem you raise. Most child abuse is committed by family members or neighbors.

DOMINIQUE WOLTON: And nothing is said about the absolute power of the family.

POPE FRANCIS: In the past, the priest would have been moved, but the problem

241

would have moved with him. The current policy is the one that Benedict XVI and I put in place through the Commission for the Protection of Minors, which was founded two years ago, here in the Vatican. The protection of all minors. It was intended to raise awareness of the problem. The Mother Church teaches how to warn, how to encourage a child to speak and behave in such a way that it can tell its parents the truth, tell them what happens, and so on. It's a constructive path.

The Church must not move toward a defensive position. If a priest is an abuser, it means he's a sick person. Out of every four abusers, two were abused when they were children. Those are psychiatric statistics. But, in this way, the Church is trying to protect children.

DOMINIQUE WOLTON: That's the question I asked you just now: how can the Church get across the idea that of course it must respect the law, but that it also has to deal with the age and its different values?

POPE FRANCIS: It must get that across. The time. It takes time to grow, to die, to repent, to weep. Each thing in its time. That's the mystery of time.

DOMINIQUE WOLTON: Yes, but today everything's happening very quickly. And the Church is going faster and faster as well. It can't impose a different temporality, a different vision of things; it is running toward modernity, it's conforming with the law of the age, while, as you say, everything is becoming much more complicated. And yet, like you, psychiatrists and psychoanalysts say that everything is very slow, that everything is very complicated. Besides, we don't hear much from psychiatrists or psychoanalysts on this matter, the complexity of time . . .

POPE FRANCIS: We must begin by experiencing it. Doing it over time. Taking people's hands, walking with them. The four criteria in the exhortation *Amoris Laetitia:* welcome, accompany, discern, integrate. It takes a very short time to welcome somebody. But accompanying is a long road. Discerning, the wisdom of discernment, is the wisdom of fatherhood, of motherhood, the wisdom of the elderly. It takes a whole life to learn it.

DOMINIQUE WOLTON: In globalization, the Christian churches, particularly the Catholic Church, should be able to say something that removes us from the tyranny of the event, the moment, public opinion. Because of its theoretical and historical legacy, the Church should say, without a hint of arrogance, that there is more than the time of modernity, that there is more than just speed, that there is more than individual freedom. The Church's experience, in spite of its mistakes, lies in saying something quite different. And, after a while, that "something else" might be heard. And, in fact, I have a question about joy. Yesterday, you told me that joy is one of your favorite words. But why isn't there more joy in the Church?

POPE FRANCIS: But you do find joy in the Church . . .

DOMINIQUE WOLTON: Yes, but, by and large, the Church isn't always much fun. Except for the World Youth Days, which have the joy of youth. You're more joyful at twenty than you are at sixty. But what about the Church's message of love and joy? The difference between Christians and fundamentalists should be joy. And there's no sign of that everyday cultural, psychological joy. The joy of the Church would be most valuable for peace, as a political issue. In the same spirit, there should be some discussion about joy. We need joy, happiness, to combat the hatred that arises out of different forms of selfishness and fundamentalism.

POPE FRANCIS: Essentially, when the rulers of the Church, the ones who are called pastors, bishops, priests, become detached from the people — and here I'm talking about the people of God — and when they become *too serious,* too restrictive, they start looking "starched."

DOMINIQUE WOLTON: Yes, a starched Church, that's exactly it.

POPE FRANCIS: That happens when they become detached from the people and also, one might say, from God.

DOMINIQUE WOLTON: But you know that from this point of view it's the same utopia as communism. Communism had the same utopia of the people, at the beginning. Just like utopian socialisms, between 1850 and 1900, which also talk about the "People," communism has failed, but the values of communism are extraordinary. Freedom, equality, love. Those are Christian too!

POPE FRANCIS: Someone once said to me: "But you're a communist!" No. The true communists are Christians. It's the other lot who stole our banner.

DOMINIQUE WOLTON: *(laughter)* It's true, but it didn't really work. The Church isn't always terrific, but over ten or fifteen centuries, it's still better than communism . . .

POPE FRANCIS: Pope Paul VI wrote an encyclical about joy. A beautiful encyclical, in 1975: *Gaudete in Domino.*[4]

DOMINIQUE WOLTON: Yes, I'd forgotten that one . . . But that could be picked up again, because joy in globalization wasn't the context of Paul VI. And it's quite alarming how much has changed in forty years. This kind of "transparent," interactive world in which you don't understand anything is a worrying one. You see, but you don't understand. You have something to say about this important subject of "understanding."

In the time of Paul VI, there were still some structures, there was still East–West, there was capitalism, socialism. Now there's nothing else. Now, there's only capitalism. No values, no identity. What is the Church waiting for? It's not just joy, it's humility. Everyone is in search of meaning. And religious meaning doesn't have a monopoly, but it still constitutes a witnessing. An encyclical.

POPE FRANCIS: I've written three. One encyclical and two exhortations. The three are called "joy." *Evangelii Gaudium, Amoris Laetitia* and *Laudato Si'.*

DOMINIQUE WOLTON: That's true, but joy is primarily human. And yet you use tweets a lot, technical communication, the internet. You have 32 million online followers — a record — and that's great. You use technology to spread your message. But, at the same time, those communication technologies, particularly with the internet, have become an economic, financial and political empire: GAFA[5] controls all the social media. That critical reflection on the limits of the internet, an experience which is not human, which is too technological, should let the Church say something else. And, in the world at present, no one is saying anything very much. Not the states, not individuals to any great extent, because everyone feels "free" to communicate. The Church could relativize those aspects of technical communication which risk devaluing human communication. It says nothing.

If the Church doesn't say it, no one is going to say it. One day states will do it. There is bound to be a democratic awakening. But when? What price?

Priests are often sad people. One day, I was giving a lecture to the bishops of France, in Lourdes. I went into the hall, there were eighty bishops, all quite sad. I said to them, "Come on, smile! God is with you!"

POPE FRANCIS: I think Teresa of Ávila said that a sad saint is a sorry saint. No, really, joy is at the heart of the Gospel! Take the first pages of the Gospel. They are pages of joy. Look at what people hear when they listen to Jesus speaking. It's full of joy. Because he speaks as someone who has authority, not like the others, who are so sad.

DOMINIQUE WOLTON: Yes, but, from your experience as a priest, why are there so many who are so sad?

POPE FRANCIS: Go and see the nuns of Mother Teresa, you'll see that they aren't sad. Joy! There's so much joy!

DOMINIQUE WOLTON: Yes, but they aren't necessarily the majority.

POPE FRANCIS: When you talk about them, you call them "the Church," but they're Christians without Jesus.

DOMINIQUE WOLTON: Nicely put.

POPE FRANCIS: They're ideological Christians. They have a Christian ideology. If you prefer, a Christian doctrine. They all know the catechism. They even know Denzinger.[6] Jesus is the opposite.

DOMINIQUE WOLTON: I'm an intellectual and I don't like the coldness of intellectuals. Intellectuals are like priests, it's always . . .

POPE FRANCIS: But in the Gospel, the Lord puts us on guard against that. If you aren't like children, you won't be allowed back into the Kingdom. The child's joy, the child's hope . . . without closing oneself off. Sad people have closed-off horizons. A church without resources. But, in the Book of Revelation, there is that beautiful passage about Jesus, who says, outside the church, "I am the door and I am knocking, let me

249

in." Jesus is the door, and he is knocking. But he is inside and we don't let him out. And that's why some people can feel un-happy.

DOMINIQUE WOLTON: In the churches in Africa, in Vietnam, in Latin America, they dance and sing. Even in Eastern Europe, it's joyful. Why don't you try to say, joyfully, "We know man's weaknesses and betrayals, we know everything about man, but there is always something else? . . ." What I mean is that the Church has "expert knowledge" of the human soul, which no institution has as much as yours. Because it has lived through all kinds of betrayals. And all kinds of redemptions. And, last of all, the Church has greater expert knowledge of human communication than anyone!

POPE FRANCIS: The Church says those things. But it only says them, and that's not enough. I would make a distinction. What you are looking for is for the Church to bear witness more, it's a matter of witnessing. Christianity isn't a science. It's not an ideology, it's not an NGO: Christianity is an encounter with a person. It's the experience of amazement, of wonder at having encountered God, Jesus Christ, the word of God

— that's what amazes me. And the Church is the guardian, the mother of that wonder, of that encounter. When the Church forgets that, and goes beyond it, it turns itself into an NGO. And that isn't bearing witness. It's when there is wonder that there is witnessing.

DOMINIQUE WOLTON: Can't the Church invent something else to be heard better? In your writing on mercy, you talk of the "apostolate of listening." How can you enlarge the conditions of listening for others?

POPE FRANCIS: That's the change that the Church has to make. In *Amoris Laetitia,* when I give the four criteria — welcome, accompany, discern, integrate — that's what you're talking about.

DOMINIQUE WOLTON: It's a huge political program, in fact . . .

POPE FRANCIS: When the Church becomes moralistic . . . The Church isn't a morality, Christianity isn't a morality. Morality is a consequence of the encounter with Jesus Christ. But if there is no encounter with

Jesus Christ, that "Christian" morality is worthless.

DOMINIQUE WOLTON: What you say is very surprising . . . I'd like to return to languages. A billion people in the world speak Romance languages.[7] The languages that have come out of Latin. Latin is the womb of those billion speakers. It's an extraordinary and innovative power, and not at all a dead language that has emerged from the past . . . Why doesn't the Church develop that treasure? And also, why not say solemnly that linguistic diversity is an issue of peace and war for tomorrow? That identities, particularly linguistic identities, must be safeguarded in order to preserve cultural diversities? Besides, Vatican II was a pioneer in that sense. It legitimized all the vernacular languages! Today, everyone prays in their own language. That's considerable progress, unthinkable a hundred years ago. What an extraordinary strength for the Catholic and, more broadly, the Christian world!

It opens up another space in relation to English, Russian, Chinese. It awakens a communion of a billion Italians, French, Spanish, Romanian . . . and 500 million Latin Americans. And it's not only the West. In global communication, the Catholic

Church, without pretention, without a monopoly, might say that Romance languages represent a considerable patrimony of humanity, wealth, diversity. In a word, you have a treasure trove in the Latin language.

POPE FRANCIS: The womb? It's the great grandmother!

DOMINIQUE WOLTON: (*laughter*) Yes. That's right — Europe is the grandmother.

POPE FRANCIS: Living languages come from the same mother. But they are living. And they go forward.

DOMINIQUE WOLTON: Yes, but knowing that a high proportion of those living languages have Latin roots constitutes a patrimony.

POPE FRANCIS: Yes, a patrimony. A family patrimony. But the universality of the Church today imagines that it is talking to everyone. That's in the nature of a mother. Adding. Never stopping. The Church must take the good in everything. Not hold it back. And that was the intuition of Vatican II. But what happened afterward? The weight of sins, habits, interests, ideology stopped all that.

DOMINIQUE WOLTON: Conversely, what has the world brought to the Church in the last fifty years?

POPE FRANCIS: So much. So much. In communication, so many good things. There are communicators today who have learned not only the techniques but also the profundity of communication. And the Church has learned that from them. Just think, when I was a child, on Easter Saturday, there was a ceremony when twelve readings were held in Latin. It was interminable. It was as tiresome as a day without bread. Then the bells rang. And what did the grandmothers and the mothers do to the children who stayed at home? They turned on the tap and washed our eyes. So that the water of Christ would wash us. That gesture was more communicative than the three-hour ceremony. There is another experience in communication that I have never forgotten. At my home, there was a wall, not very high, between the garden of my house and the garden of the house next door. The women, my mother and the others, talked and chatted on either side, and we played. I will never forget that moment. It was in 1945. The neighbor leaned over from the other side of the wall: "Where is your mother?" "She's inside." "Call her!" "Mum! Mum, you're wanted!" And my mother said, "What's happened?" "The war's over!"

I'll never forget that gesture of communication. The joy of the women who were not concerned — they had no family in Europe — but who nonetheless had the joy of passing on a piece of good news, communicating the joy of some good news. I will never forget that gesture. They hugged each other, they wept with joy. I remember it as if it were yesterday. I was nine years old. Eight or nine. It was magnificent!

For communication, we must return to primal gestures. The primal gestures and words of communication. And from that starting point, undertake the reconstruction of that aseptic, pharmaceutical, laboratory, entirely technical, lifeless communication.

DOMINIQUE WOLTON: Today, with new technologies, computers, social media, radio, television, technical communication is everywhere. And yet there has never been so much incomprehension, or perhaps I should say, the globalization of communication doesn't bring more peace.

POPE FRANCIS: True, because the other person isn't there . . .

DOMINIQUE WOLTON: I say the same thing again . . . Why isn't the Church more active, not in condemning, but in smiling on those technical performances which are seductive but limited . . . ? Smiling with a hint of irony at technical ideology?

POPE FRANCIS: Because I think there is a certain shame. A certain complex about lagging behind. That's what's regrettable about novelties: everything that's new is supposed to be good. But no, it isn't . . .

DOMINIQUE WOLTON: I agree. The Church has this complex, sadly, of not being modern when there's no point in being modern. Particularly in terms of communication. And if the Church said that joyfully, that would be useful, because the whole world is on its knees before technical ideology, it has been for thirty years, and that will last. Apart from the encyclical on communication, there might be three others about the political issues of cultural diversity and about the place of knowledge in globalization. Three areas in which political, cultural and anthropological challenges are considerable and in which the experience of the Church would enable it to say offbeat and useful things . . .

Many people believe that there is a "backwardness" in the Church, at the moment, concerning the three great problems of cultural diversity, knowledge and human communication . . . But thinking about these subjects, the Church isn't lagging behind; it may even be ahead!

POPE FRANCIS: Yes, but I don't know how to reply. We'll have to work on that.

DOMINIQUE WOLTON: The Church has a huge amount of experience in human communication, accumulated over centuries. Today, there is a conflict between modern communication, with technology, speed and the Church's communication, marked by silence, slowness, words . . .

POPE FRANCIS: The Dutch made up a word, about forty years ago, "rapidation," which is geometrical motion in terms of rapidity. I'm not saying that we need to stop, but that at least we should turn it into something less inconsistent. At the dinner table, when the family and the children are there, the father is watching television, the mother doing something else, they're not talking to each other. Everything is inconsistent. Everyone is communicating . . . but they don't know with whom. We need to communicate more concretely. With "concreteness." That occurs through human relations.

All right, let's talk about a mode of communication that makes me smile — and yet it doesn't need new machines, computers. At orations, at funerals, at the cemetery, they deliver a speech. They say, "He did this, and that. . . ." "Words, words, words . . ." as Mina[8] sang. Here's an example of inconsistent communication, without concreteness. Approaching those who suffer as a result of that person's death means hugging them, shaking hands with them, touching, without words. Concrete communication. Rediscovering the sense of touch. Perfect communication is done through touch. Touch is the best form of communication.

DOMINIQUE WOLTON: As I told you, we published an issue of my journal at the CNRS[9] in May 2016, about the five senses of communication.[10] I say exactly the same thing as you. The importance of touch, of smell . . . as opposed to sight and hearing.

258

When you were in Sweden to bring the Catholics and Protestants closer together, the Catholic journal *La Croix* had a very good headline: "So near, so far." Isn't that an image of ecumenism?

POPE FRANCIS: Yes. Don't worry about tensions. Here we're talking about tension. How do you resolve a tension? At a higher level.

DOMINIQUE WOLTON: That's the German philosopher, Hegel . . .

POPE FRANCIS: Hegel does synthesis. I'm saying something else; I'm saying that synthesis occurs on a level higher than both sides of the argument. And what you find on the higher level preserves in its roots the two initial points of view. Because life is always in tension, it is not in synthesis. Synthesis is not truly vital. Tension, though, is vital. Physically, when the body loses its tension between the balance of fluids and the electricity of the heart, the air in the lungs, everything falls out of balance.

DOMINIQUE WOLTON: In a century or 150 years, there has been a lot of progress in human communication — independently of technology: liberty, equality, equality between men and women, children . . . Why has the Church, which has this experience in communication, even down to its etymology [*communicare,* "share"], stopped joining in with the fight for this freer and more authentic communication?

POPE FRANCIS: Perhaps what you say is true. But there is still a lot of communication in the Church. When the Church communicates best, it's when it communicates with the poor, with the sick . . . It is on the path of the Beatitudes. If you read them carefully, they too are rules for communicating better.

I had an experience in Buenos Aires, where we had a hospital that was tended by German nuns. Unfortunately for the poor nuns, their congregation had become much smaller and they had to leave the hospital. A Korean priest told me he knew some nuns from Korea who wanted to come. And some nuns actually arrived from Korea. They spoke Spanish the way I speak Chinese: not a word! They arrived on Monday, on Tuesday they installed their belongings and on Wednesday they came down to the hospital, without speaking a word of Spanish. But the patients were all happy. And why? Because they knew how to communicate with their eyes, with their smiles. And, on that level, the Church is a mistress of communication. Before learning the language, you're already communicating. It's a concrete experience. Where there are works of mercy, where the Beatitudes exist as a criterion, I think the Church has already reached an exceptional level of communication. It's truly, truly remarkable.

And we mustn't forget the two pillars of Christianity, of the Church: the Beatitudes and Matthew 25, the protocol on which we will be judged. The works of mercy.

These two pillars — whether the Beatitudes or Matthew 25 — make the Church a champion of communication. When you tell me that the Church doesn't communicate, you're talking about a Church of the elite, closed and intellectualist. I don't use the word intellectual, but intellectualist.

DOMINIQUE WOLTON: To stay with the long story of the liberation of communication, the Church could have relied on Matthew 25. Why hasn't the Church been saying, for a century, "We are happy that people are trying to communicate better, it's our own philosophy, so we'll find one another again"? Of course, you aren't accountable for Church history!

POPE FRANCIS: Yes, when you read certain ecclesiastical texts, they tell the truth, but it's terribly tiresome. They don't have the joy, the lightness of beautiful communication.

DOMINIQUE WOLTON: It's a very long time since the Church last said anything much about the omnipotence of technology in communication. Perhaps because it doesn't want to be seen as "reactionary"?

POPE FRANCIS: That fear of being seen as "reactionary" may be real. And not only where this matter is concerned. It's a temptation of today's Church. You have to be "modern." If being modern means that the children bring themselves up, that a sixteen-year-old child takes the car keys . . . That's the temptation today, that's true. The temptation to be afraid that one isn't modern. That can lead to terrible things.

DOMINIQUE WOLTON: Let's take the example of education. The biggest market in the world on the internet is in education. That is to say that there will be computers everywhere, electronic schoolbags, personalized interactive systems. They say that if a three-year-old child knows how to use a computer, that child will be more intelligent and will therefore be at an advantage for them . . . The Church doesn't have a monopoly on education, but it does have experience of it. It says nothing about the economic, financial and cultural power of these technologies. For fear of finding itself on the wrong side of the ideology of modernity? That's a considerable disproportion compared to everything it says about morals . . .

POPE FRANCIS: I think the Church is carrying out some interesting experiments in the field of education. When I was in Buenos Aires, I founded the School of Neighbors, to create a form of mutual education. Now, that school exists globally, as a meeting place for young people from all over the world. In Buenos Aires, with this system of the "school of neighbors," we had twenty-four laws drawn up on the basis of young people's discussions, and approved in the city parliament. But these are small things. I agree with you: the educational pact has been broken. And the Church needs to be active in rebuilding all that.

DOMINIQUE WOLTON: Yes, because, for now, given technical absolutism, in education and elsewhere, everyone is silent. That's what interests me. That silence. Why is the Church involved in that silence? On bioethnics, on morals, its voice is heard! So why is there nothing about education, in which the Church has genuine expertise?

POPE FRANCIS: Some people say so. Officially, I don't know what to reply. But I think we need to talk about it.

DOMINIQUE WOLTON: That touches on education, on knowledge, on personal relationships? Absolutism is "Mammon"; it's like money. Today's global ideology lies in communication technologies. Because it's both a humanist utopia, but particularly it's a considerable technical, financial and political enterprise. And no one is in any hurry to regulate it. And, in the past, the Church had things to say about education, science, even work . . . Today, much less. As if there was no particular reflection about work, education, science, technologies and culture in general.

POPE FRANCIS: Catholic universities are doing good work.

DOMINIQUE WOLTON: Yes, perhaps. But there's a gap. About bioethics, the Church says what it thinks, but, for example, on culture, science, technology, but also about chemistry, nuclear power, relationships between science, technology and society, you don't have a sense that it is currently truly interested.

POPE FRANCIS: In the universities, yes.

DOMINIQUE WOLTON: What has changed in relations with the Other, over the last fifty years?

POPE FRANCIS: A word comes to me, but I'm worried about getting it wrong. Everything has changed, but the foundations remain. The modalities of the relationships have changed. But the foundation, the essence, the elements that are really part of the human person have not changed. The need to communicate has not changed, even if a lot of things have changed.

DOMINIQUE WOLTON: I'll take an example. Societies are increasingly multicultural, and for a very long time the Church has used the *concept of brotherhood*. How could that patrimony be useful in contributing to

thought about peace in multicultural societies?

POPE FRANCIS: That is done often, and it
works well. Just think about something
that's been working for twenty years: Daniel
Barenboim's Israeli-Palestinian orchestra —
and he's Argentinian! (*laughter*) The WYDs,
too, the World Youth Days that John Paul II
set up in 1986, which have been an intuition
of encounters. There, young people encounter one another, they see a different culture,
a different way of thinking. They build
bridges. The experience of a bridge, however
ephemeral, will remain. Today is a time of
encounters, to talk about social laws, laws
of labor, of our relationship with medicine . . . There is a need for encounters, for
experiences, and not only in order to have
scientific conferences. "How do you do
that?" "I do it this way. . . ." Giving. It's
very, very important. Through encounters
you can travel much further along the path
of communication, because there is freedom, a lot of freedom, in those encounters.
There is a different atmosphere. Study how
an encounter develops. On the first day,
everyone's very solemn. Everyone has that
form of solemnity.

Then there is the speech, and, by the end,

they're saying, "Ciao, see you next time, ciao." They may never see each other again, but, in their consciousness, there is an experience that will never be erased.

DOMINIQUE WOLTON: In the society of speed, of noise, the strength of the Church remains in silence, slowness, pilgrimages and monasteries. Why not say so more clearly?

POPE FRANCIS: Yes. Today people talk a lot about Charles de Foucauld,[11] the saints of the Church, the cloistered nuns.

DOMINIQUE WOLTON: A classic question about the relationship with the world. Catholicism is a religion of love and sharing, and yet priests have to renounce physical, sexual, carnal pleasure.

POPE FRANCIS: It's a voluntary renunciation. Virginity, whether it be masculine or feminine, is a monastic tradition that preexists Catholicism. It is a human quest: renunciation in order to seek God at the origin, to encourage contemplation. But a renunciation must be a fruitful renunciation, which preserves a kind of fruitfulness that is different from sexual fruitfulness.

Even in the Church, there are married priests. All the Eastern priests are married, so there's that. But renouncing marriage for the realm of God is of value in itself. It means renouncing in order to serve, to improve one's contemplation.

DOMINIQUE WOLTON: The paradox is that the Catholic Church condemns capitalism, money, inequalities, but those criticisms go rather unheard. On the other hand, on morals, it knows how to make its critiques and condemnations heard . . .

POPE FRANCIS: The least serious sins are the sins of the flesh.

DOMINIQUE WOLTON: All right, but that needs to be said more forcefully, because the message isn't getting across.

POPE FRANCIS: The sins of the flesh are not necessarily (always) the gravest. Because the flesh is weak. The most dangerous sins are those of the mind. I have talked about angelism[12]: pride and vanity are sins of angelism. I understood your question. The Church is the Church. Priests have been tempted — not all of them, but many of them — to focus on the sins of sexuality.

That's what I've already talked to you about: what I call "below-the-waist" morality. The more serious sins are elsewhere.

DOMINIQUE WOLTON: What you say is not being heard.

POPE FRANCIS: No, but there are good priests . . . I know a cardinal here who is a good example. He admitted to me, talking about these subjects, that when people come to see him to talk to him about these below-the-belt sins, he says, straight away, "I've got it; let's talk about something else." He stops them, as if to say, "I've understood, but let's see if you have something more important." "I don't know." "But do you pray? Do you seek the Lord? Do you read the Gospel?"

He makes them understand that there are more important failings. Yes, it is a sin, but . . . he lets them know, "I've understood," then moves on to something else.

Conversely, some priests, when they receive confession of a sin of this kind, ask, "How did you do it, and when did you do it, and for how long? . . ." And they have a "film" playing in their head. But those priests need a psychiatrist.

DOMINIQUE WOLTON: That's true, there are much more serious "sins" than the sins of the flesh, but what you say is not in the cultural tradition . . .

Final question: humanism. There is no monopoly on humanism. There is a crisis in humanism today, because technology, the economy, money . . . eat everything up. Why does the Church, which has no monopoly on humanism, but which has real experience of it, not say anything? It is one of the resources that would enable us to re-enchant the world.

POPE FRANCIS: The times in which the Church has best understood its mission are the moments when it has respected humanism. It respected the dignity of the human person. It did not reduce it. We have two very serious threats to humanism, and we can call them "heresies": Gnosticism, which consists, more or less, of saying that everything is ideas, and which appeared in the time of the Apostles, and Pelagianism,[13] of which you French are the champions. Think of Port-Royal and Pascal. But the great Pascal almost fell into Pelagianism, and he was a master of the mind and of humanism. Today we are in a Pelagian and Gnostic world, which rejects the flesh. The flesh. I challenge you to find in the work of Dosto-yevsky a single manifestation of Pelagianism or Gnosticism. I advise you to read Romano Guardini's book about the religious universe of Dostoyevsky[14] — a very fine book.

DOMINIQUE WOLTON: The strength of the Church, since Vatican II, has lain in assuming a tension between linguistic identity and universalism. And yet globalization is standardization and rationalization. And hence the disappearance of linguistic diversity.

POPE FRANCIS: That's globalization, in the form of a sphere. It's bad. On the other hand, the Church talks about globalization in a polyhedron and it's better . . .

DOMINIQUE WOLTON: In global cultural contradictions, what the Church has at its disposal, in terms of expert knowledge about the relationship between language and universality, is a "universal" patrimony. Conflicts are going to be more and more cultural, violent and linguistic against the crimes of globalization, which is reduced to liquid economy.

POPE FRANCIS: Perhaps . . .

DOMINIQUE WOLTON: Thank you! (*laughter*). So, I'm not going to burn in hell straightaway?

Address of Pope Francis
to the participants in
the World Meeting of
Popular Movements,
Old Synod Hall,
The Vatican

(October 28, 2014)

[. . .] The poor not only suffer injustice, they also struggle against it!

You are not satisfied with empty promises, with alibis or excuses. Nor do you wait with arms crossed for NGOs to help, for welfare schemes or paternalistic solutions that never arrive; or if they do, then it is with a tendency to anaesthetize or to domesticate . . . and this is rather perilous. One senses that the poor are no longer waiting. You want to be protagonists. You get organized, study, work, issue demands and, above all, practice that very special solidarity that exists among those who suffer, among the poor, and that our civilization seems to have forgotten or would strongly prefer to forget.

[. . .]

This meeting of ours responds to a very concrete desire, something that any father and mother would want for their children — a desire for what should be within everyone's reach, namely *land, housing and work.* However, nowadays, it is sad to see that land, housing and work are ever more distant for the majority. It is strange but, if I talk about this, some say that the Pope is communist. They do not understand that love for the poor is at the center of the Gospel. Land, housing and work, what you struggle for, are sacred rights. [. . .]

Land. At the beginning of creation, God created man and woman, stewards of his work, mandating them *to till and to keep* it. I notice dozens of farmworkers here, and I want to congratulate you for caring for the land, for cultivating it and for doing so in community. The elimination of so many brother and sister *campesinos* [farmers] worries me, and it is not because of wars or natural disasters that they are uprooted. Land and water grabbing, deforestation, unsuitable pesticides are some of the evils

274

which uproot people from their native land.

[. . .]

Second: housing. I said it and I repeat it: a home for every family. We must never forget that, because there was no room in the inn, Jesus was born in a stable; and that his family, persecuted by Herod, had to leave their home and flee into Egypt.

[. . .]

Third: work. There is no worse material poverty — I really must stress this — there is no worse material poverty than the poverty which does not allow people to earn their bread, which deprives them of the dignity of work. But youth unemployment, casual or underground work, and the lack of labor rights are not inevitable. These are the result of an underlying social choice in favor of an economic system that puts profit above man. [. . .]

Today, a new dimension is being added to the phenomena of exploitation and oppression, a very harsh and graphic manifestation of social injustice: those who cannot be integrated, the excluded, are discarded, the "leftovers." This is the throwaway culture, and I would like to add something on this that I just remember now, I do not have it written down. This happens when the deity of money is at the center of an economic system rather than man, the human person. Yes, at the center of every social or economic system must be the person, image of God, created to "have dominion over" the universe. The inversion of values happens when the person is displaced and money becomes the deity.

[. . .]

Recently I said and now I repeat, we are going through World War Three, but in installments. There are economic systems that must make war in order to survive. Accordingly, arms are manufactured and sold and, with that, the balance sheets of economies that sacrifice man at the feet of the idol of money are clearly rendered healthy. And no thought is given to hungry children in refugee camps; no thought is given to the forcibly displaced; no thought is given to destroyed homes; no thought is given, finally, to so many destroyed lives. How much suffering, how much destruction, how much grief. Today, dear brothers and sisters, in all parts of the earth, in all nations, in every heart and in grassroots movements, the cry wells up for peace: war no more!

[. . .]

We talk about land, work, housing . . . we talk about working for peace and taking care of nature. Why are we accustomed to seeing decent work destroyed, countless families evicted, rural farmworkers driven off the land, war waged and nature abused? Because in this system man, the human person, has been removed from the center and replaced by something else. Because idolatrous worship is devoted to money. Because indifference has been globalized: "Why should I care what happens to others as long as I can defend what's mine?" Because the world has forgotten God, who is Father; and by setting God aside, it has made itself an orphan.

[. . .]

Grassroots movements express the urgent need to revitalize our democracies, so often hijacked by innumerable factors. It is impossible to imagine a future for society without the active participation of great majorities as protagonists, and such proactive participation overflows the logical procedures of formal democracy. Moving toward a world of lasting peace and justice calls us to go beyond paternalistic forms of assistance; it calls us to create new forms of participation that include popular movements and invigorate local, national and international governing structures with that torrent of moral energy that springs from including the excluded in the building of a common destiny. And all this with a constructive spirit, without resentment, with love.

[. . .]

Address of Pope Francis to Participants in the Pilgrimage of the Poor, Accompanied by Cardinal Barbarin, Paul VI Audience Hall, The Vatican

(July 6, 2016)

Dear Friends,

I am delighted to welcome you. Whatever your state, your story and your burden might be, it is Jesus who brings us together around himself. [. . .]. He welcomes each person as they are. In Him we are brothers, and I would like you to feel how welcome you really are; your presence is important to me, and it is also important that you feel at home.

Together with the caregivers who are accompanying you, you offer a beautiful testimony of evangelical fraternity in walking together on the pilgrimage. You have indeed come accompanying one another. The caregivers have generously helped you, by providing resources and time to enable you to come; and, by giving to them, you give to us, you give to me, Jesus himself.

Since Jesus wanted to share in your condition, out of love He became one of you: despised by men, forgotten, one who does not count for much. When you happen to experience all of this, do not forget that Jesus also experienced it like you. It is proof that you are precious in His eyes, and that He is near to you. You are *in the heart of the Church* [. . .]

And in the Church [. . .] cannot rest until she has reached all those who experience rejection, exclusion, and feel that they do not matter to anyone. *In the heart of the Church,* you allow us to meet Jesus, because you speak to us about him, not so much with words, but with your whole life. And you bear witness to the importance of the small gestures, within everyone's reach, that help to build peace, reminding us that we are brothers and sisters, and that God is the Father of us all.

I try to imagine what people must have thought when they saw Mary, Joseph and Jesus along the roads, fleeing to Egypt. They were poor, they were afflicted by persecution: but God was there.

Dear caregivers, I want to thank you for everything that you do, you who are faithful to the insight of Father Giuseppe Wresinski, who wanted to start practically *with a shared life,* not with abstract theories. Abstract theories lead us to ideologies and ideologies lead us to deny that God became flesh, he became one of us! It is *a life shared* with the poor that transforms and converts us. Really think about this! Not only do you go to encounter them [. . .], not only do you walk with them, strive to understand their suffering and enter into their disposition [of mind]; but you make an effort to enter into their desperation. In addition, you *create a community around them,* and, in this way, you restore to them life, identity and dignity. [. . .]

Beloved brothers, I ask you above all to maintain the courage and to keep the joy of hope right in the midst of your anguish. That flame that lives in you must not go out: for we believe in a God who remedies all injustices, who consoles all pain and who knows how to reward those who maintain trust in him. While awaiting that day of peace and light, your contribution is essential to the Church and to the world: you are witnesses of Christ, you are intercessors before God who hears your prayers in a special way. [. . .] And, lastly, I would like to ask you for a favor, [. . .] to give you a mission: a mission that you alone, in your poverty, will be able to carry out. Allow me to explain: Jesus, at times, was very strict and strongly reprimanded people who were not ready to welcome the Father's message. Just as He said the beautiful word "blessed" to the poor, the hungry, those who weep, those who are hated and persecuted, He also said another word that, spoken by Him, is frightening! He said, "Woe!" He said it to the rich, the well sated, those who laugh now, those who enjoy flattery,[15] and hypocrites.[16] I give you the mission to pray for them, that the Lord may change their hearts. I ask you also to pray for the perpetrators of your poverty, that they may convert! Pray for the many wealthy people who dress in purple and fine linen and celebrate with large banquets, without realizing that there are many people like Lazarus at their door, eager to be fed the leftovers from their table.[17] Pray also for the priests, the

Levites, who — upon seeing the man beaten and left for dead — pass him by, looking the other way, because they have no compassion.[18]

To all of these people [. . .] smile at them from your heart, wish them well and ask Jesus to see to it that they convert. I assure you that, if you do this, there will be great joy in the Church, in your hearts and also in beloved France. Now, all together, under the gaze of our Heavenly Father, I entrust you to the protection of the Mother of Jesus and Saint Joseph, and I wholeheartedly impart my Apostolic Blessing to you.

■ ■ ■ ■

6

"MERCY IS A
JOURNEY FROM
THE HEART TO
THE HAND."

■ ■ ■ ■

Driving through Rome, whatever the time of day or the season, is always a wonder. All the more since we are staying at the convent of the Canons Regular of the Lateran, in the general house near the Basilica of San Pietro in Vincoli, which houses Michelangelo's majestic sculpture of Moses. Attending matins in these surroundings is an exceptional experience, whether one is a believer or not. Something magical absorbs us in Rome. The buildings, the atmosphere, the umbrella pines, history, the sky, daily life, eternity. And the approach to Saint Peter's always prompts the same emotion. This is the West, and a far from negligible part of the culture and greatness, in spite of upheavals, wars and changing rulers. What a vast, silent and almost eternal coexistence! And still the same gap between the modesty of the Holy Father and the immensity of everything around us. How does he do it? History, its depth and its immensity, is a constant presence. Everything that escapes our hurried, immediate world, which has become so much smaller, armed with high-performing "communication" technologies, and which grapples with its double, un-communication, a-communication. We are trying, through dialogue, to gain some understanding of something else, particularly not to turn into either an inquisitor or an apologist. How to imagine "the new scales of existence," identities, the relationship with the Other, the new definition of the individual, community, society and the upheaval in interpersonal relationships? Debate the chaos of values, aspirations, models of interpersonal relationships, morals and utopias? At the end of each of our discussions, very often, as we part, with that lovely smile in the chink of the door, gently, he repeats, "Pray for me . . ."

DOMINIQUE WOLTON: You speak a lot about the people. The people: in Europe, these days, we barely use this word, with its hints of fascism and communism. But you come from Latin America; you don't have the same experiences or the same references. You want to embrace the people. That's very different.

I think people feel it, when you are traveling around the world, in the youngest churches. Yes, you have a style that isn't traditional. Far from it. And that's good.

POPE FRANCIS: For you.

DOMINIQUE WOLTON: Yes, of course. And for the global Church too.

POPE FRANCIS: But here in Europe there have been all kinds of difficulties. It's true that history weighs heavily. It's never easy; in the winemaking process, aging doesn't always turn out well.

DOMINIQUE WOLTON: The Jesuits. What have they given you? Why are you a Jesuit and not a Franciscan?

POPE FRANCIS: Yesterday, I had a debate with some Dominicans, and, in the afternoon, I went to Assisi with the Franciscans, but, for me, the day, like today, can be described and defined as being that of a Jesuit among his brothers. The prime contribution of the Society of Jesus is the lofty *Spiritual Exercises,* it's the spirituality of the *exercises.* And out of them comes "mission-ality"[1] and everything that follows from it, but which isn't an original contribution. Obedience to the Pope is probably more original. The spiritual exercise, with the method of discernment, is probably what has frightened a lot of theologians. Think of Father Ricci,[2] in China. He had chosen a path of authentic inculturation, and he wasn't understood, the road was closed off to him. Think of Father Nobili,[3] in India. It's the same thing: he frightened people.

DOMINIQUE WOLTON: Yes, the trajectory of Ricci in China and Nobili in India is incredible. Could you have been Franciscan? Or Dominican?

POPE FRANCIS: I hesitated. Franciscan, no. But Dominican . . . I hesitated, then I chose the Jesuits.

DOMINIQUE WOLTON: When the battle was raging around "liberation theology," you preferred the term "theology of the people."

POPE FRANCIS: The theology of the people is that of the exhortation *Evangelii Gaudium,* which deals with the Church as the people of God. The Church is the people of God. Liberation theology has a partial aspect, in the good sense, but also in the bad sense. What is partial is the principle of the light of Jesus Christ which liberates us, taking as its model the liberation from Egypt of the people of Israel. But, at that time, after the French movement of May 1968, there were different interpretations of "liberation theology." One of those interpretations adopted the Marxist analysis of reality. What is called the "theology of the people" takes Jesus Christ as the subject of salvation, but in his people. The people of the Church, as the holy people of God.

I think those two tasks that Pope Ratzinger performed when he was Prefect of the Congregation for the Doctrine of Faith clearly led, first, to the condemnation of Marxist analysis, then to an account of the positive contribution of the movement. There is always a relation with politics. Because pastoral work cannot help but be political, but it can have a relationship with "big" politics: the Church, in fact, must do politics, but big politics, as I have said before. And, within liberation theology, some components have gone missing, let's put it that way, along partisan paths, with far-left parties or with Marxist analysis. In the 1980s, Father Pedro Arrupe wrote a letter against the Marxist analysis of reality, saying that it couldn't be done in the name of Jesus. A very fine letter. That's why there is a difference, and what is called the theology of the people — although I don't like that term either — was the alternative, proposed by certain theologians of turning the people of God into a protagonist. And that's what Vatican II achieved.

DOMINIQUE WOLTON: What you are saying here is important, because in Europe people don't always understand, there is a tendency to oversimplify. Liberation theology was "good," and the Church was opposed to it because it was "reactionary." It's a binary way of looking at things. Coming from Argentina, you can explain the different situations and nuances to avoid falling into dichotomies.

POPE FRANCIS: The danger in theology lies in making things over-ideological. Here in Europe, when we speak of the people, the connection is immediately made with populism. Populism is a political and ideological word. "This head of state is a populist, this party is populist" — it has a negative sense.

DOMINIQUE WOLTON: You come from Latin America, and the term doesn't have the same meaning here as it does there. Here, as I have said, it has much more negative connotations; it conjures up the authoritarian regimes that have stressed a certain demagogical vision of the people. It is used a little too easily. In Europe, as soon as there is an antielitist reaction, or the people revolt against the well-trodden paths, people speak, often wrongly, of populism. In any case, John Paul II didn't talk about it, Benedict XVI didn't talk about it.

POPE FRANCIS: Yes, I think I've said that. The word "people" isn't a logical category, it's a mythical category. In Europe, the use of the people in the ideological sense lies at the origin of the great dictatorial movements . . .

DOMINIQUE WOLTON: In what way do you feel Argentinian? What, in your view, constitutes the Argentinian identity?

POPE FRANCIS: In Argentina, there are natives. We have indigenous peoples. Argentinian identity is mixed. Most of the Argentine people come from mixed backgrounds. They are a mixed people. Because waves of immigration have mixed, mixed and mixed . . . I think the same thing happened in the United States, where waves of immigration mixed the peoples. The two countries have considerable similarities. For us, it was absolutely normal to have different religions together at school.

DOMINIQUE WOLTON: But there's the same mixture in Brazil, mainly with people of African origin. And what about your Italian roots?

POPE FRANCIS: I'm one of five, and my mother had her second child when I was eleven months old. My Piedmontese grandparents lived just nearby, just a few meters away. My grandmother came to get me in the morning, I spent the day with them and she brought me back in the afternoon. That was how I learned to speak Piedmontese as my first language.

DOMINIQUE WOLTON: So this is a homecoming. The ways of God . . .

POPE FRANCIS: I remember, when I was a child, at the age when children start touching everything, my grandmother said to me, *"Toca nen, toca nen!"* "Don't touch, don't touch!" And I remember that I understood Piedmontese perfectly. Now, I don't speak it anymore. But I understand it. Today, I called three cousins, and it was a long time since I'd called them to say hello. They lived in Turin. Cousins of my father. There are seven who still speak Piedmontese.

DOMINIQUE WOLTON: It's Europe via Italy, and the new continent via Latin America.

POPE FRANCIS: Argentina, with its waves of migration . . . When people wanted to invest there, and went there, there was work, there was money: it could be done.

DOMINIQUE WOLTON: Why are the next World Youth Days in Panama in 2018?

POPE FRANCIS: There were two options: Seoul or Panama. In the end, I chose Panama because it will make it possible to bring the whole of Central America together. That's why it's hard for me to tell you how I feel about my Italian roots. Argentina's like that. The blood of the Argentinians is *criollo* (Creole) for those who have their origins here, but now it's a mixed blood: Arab, Italian, French, Polish, Spanish, Jewish, Russian, Ukrainian . . . all of those things all at once. The two wars accentuated that, but the first wave of migration from Piedmont dates from 1884.

DOMINIQUE WOLTON: Your parents arrived from Italy in 1926?

POPE FRANCIS: No, my grandparents went with my father, who then got married in Argentina. They arrived in 1929.

DOMINIQUE WOLTON: But, you know, this double identity that you symbolize, Europe and Latin America, is a first in the history of the Church.

POPE FRANCIS: Yes.

DOMINIQUE WOLTON: And it's an advantage, in the age of globalization.

POPE FRANCIS: Yes, but it's not the same thing.

DOMINIQUE WOLTON: Is that why you're free, much more free than others?

POPE FRANCIS: But it isn't the same phenomenon for all the countries in Latin America. This true mixing happened in Argentina, partially in Chile, in southern Brazil, completely in the south of São Paulo . . . And in Uruguay.

DOMINIQUE WOLTON: All the way to Porto Alegre.

POPE FRANCIS: In Porto Alegre, they speak German, Italian . . . The big waves . . .

DOMINIQUE WOLTON: And in the north, it's the black population . . .

POPE FRANCIS: And then there's Central America. Mexico has a very separate culture. Argentina is very different. The Southern Cone is very specific. In Bolivia, 85 percent of the inhabitants are Indians. That's why we Argentinians are so proud. And that's not a good thing. It's why you get jokes about Argentinians. You know how an Argentinian commits suicide?

DOMINIQUE WOLTON: No.

POPE FRANCIS: He climbs to the top of his ego and jumps off. Another funny story about me: "But look how humble the Pope is! Even though he's Argentinian, he chose to call himself Francis and not Jesus II!" That's how we are! And you know the best way of making yourself rich? Buy an Argentinian at his true value, and sell him for the value he thinks he has!

DOMINIQUE WOLTON: *(laughter)* The two biggest fairs I've been to for translations of my books were in Tehran, ten years ago, and in Buenos Aires. The Buenos Aires book fair is even bigger than the one in Mexico. When you see the pride of the French . . . The Argentinians might be proud, but we are too!

One other question: what still surprises you about the Church?

POPE FRANCIS: The faith of the holy people of God. The courage of so many men, young people, in putting their lives at the service of others. There's so much holiness. It's a word I want to use in the Church today, but in the sense of everyday holiness, in families . . . And that's a personal experience. When I talk of this *ordinary holiness,* which the other day I called the "middle class" of holiness . . . you know what that conjures up for me? Millet's *Angelus.*[4] That's what comes to mind. The simplicity of those two peasants, praying. A people praying, a people sinning and then repenting of their sins.

There is a form of hidden holiness in the Church. There are heroes who set off on missions. You, the French, have done a lot, some have sacrificed their lives. That's what strikes me most in the Church: fruitful, ordinary holiness. That capacity to become a saint without even making oneself noticed.

DOMINIQUE WOLTON: But the first anarchists, the utopian socialists, and the communists, before Stalinism, were *also saints*! Those militants did some extraordinarily generous things between 1820 and communism. And, even in communism, particularly at the start, there was also that great solidarity, that generosity. You also find that in libertarian socialism!

POPE FRANCIS: Let's consider the authority of a pope. Think of an iceberg. You see papal authority, but the truth of the universal Church is the foundation. Let's invert the iceberg: the pope's service is at the top. That's why the conception of authority in the Gospel of Jesus is the service: the pope must serve everyone. One of the pope's titles is *"Servus servorum Dei."*[5]

DOMINIQUE WOLTON: That perspective isn't known, isn't understood. We see the tip, but not the inversion. Because we're used to power, to hierarchy.

POPE FRANCIS: Things change too. The

fact that the pope lives in a boarding-house . . . those are small signs.

DOMINIQUE WOLTON: (*laughter*) Yes, I agree, but what if, by some misfortune, your successor wanted to go back to the pontifical apartments?

POPE FRANCIS: I don't know.

DOMINIQUE WOLTON: And if he wanted to put on golden shoes?

POPE FRANCIS: But God is greater!

DOMINIQUE WOLTON: Yes. Having said that, you fight symbolic battles, like the one we just talked about.

POPE FRANCIS: Yes, that seemed natural to me. I couldn't live in there, all by myself.

DOMINIQUE WOLTON: Of course, you're freer here.

What worries you most, and what reassures you most, about globalization?

POPE FRANCIS: You speak of globalization? Because there's another term, and I prefer to talk about "globality."

DOMINIQUE WOLTON: In fact, to refer to the world process of economic openness, we should really talk about globalization.

POPE FRANCIS: There is something I think I haven't said yet. I think we need unity among all peoples, just as Europe, for example, needs unity. But not a unity that would mean uniformity. The example I give is that of the sphere. It represents unity, but all its points are at the same distance from the center, they are all identical. In fact, it is the image of uniformity, and that is what kills cultures. And that's also what kills people. On the other hand, true globalization, for me, would be the figure of the polyhedron, as I've already explained, a form in which everyone exists. That is, all together, but everyone with their own personality or culture. And it's all the more important with Brexit, because we have this problem: what is Europe going to do? It needs to be creative. It needs to stress, to highlight the difference between countries and, starting with those differences, unite again. Perhaps the sin — "sin," in inverted commas — the error is to believe that unity could be attained by making things uniform, by Brussels saying, "We have to do this and that . . ."

301

DOMINIQUE WOLTON: Praying is communicating?

POPE FRANCIS: Communicating in the sense of communicating with others, yes. Jesus says that in the Gospel: praying isn't repeating words, words, words. It's talking to a person, to the Father. That's communicating. "Who do you pray to?" "God." "But 'God,' like that?"

" 'God,' like that," isn't a person. God is three people: the Father, the Son, the Holy Spirit. Or all three. But praying must always be personal. Otherwise, it's a monologue, it's talking to oneself. And that's why in prayer silence is very important. That is, waiting, expressing oneself, waiting, letting oneself be looked at by the Lord. Very often, when I'm with a friend, we talk but we can also be silent. It's a real communication of friendship. Even in love, in love between married couples, silence is very important. Because, with silence between a husband and wife, it's a silence of love that is communicating.

DOMINIQUE WOLTON: How do we hear silence, today?

POPE FRANCIS: We're afraid of silence.

We're afraid, and we prefer to reduce it to rigidity. I'm going to use two images as examples. Let's return to Millet's *Angelus.* They are praying in silence, but there is a communication between them and with God: that's obvious. And the other image is of soldiers processing in silence. There, there is no communication. There is discipline, order, rigidity — which is necessary in this case. There is always something chaotic in communication; basically, it makes spontaneity grow. And silence too.

On the other hand rigidity is only order. When I arrive in a country, with all those soldiers waiting for me by the exit of the airplane, there is no communication . . . But when children approach with flowers, and they kiss me, as has become habitual, it's done in silence, but, in this case, there is communication. I would like to return to this theme of rigidity. Remember that. I have to think about it.

DOMINIQUE WOLTON: All right. It's interesting to talk about rigidity. Today, people believe, particularly thanks to new technologies and direct expression, that there is no rigidity anymore. Sadly, there is a lot of it. Particularly with emails and texts, which rigidify exchanges and interpretation.

There's a lot of uncommunication on the internet. My research is into the relationships between communication, uncommunication and a-communication. I criticize the technical hold of the internet and social media, and more generally the excessive importance of technologies, because everyone thinks that using them will finally mean there will be communication! Sadly, it's a lot more complicated . . . As if all it took for better mutual understanding was 7.5 billion internet users . . .

POPE FRANCIS: You mentioned "a-communication"?

DOMINIQUE WOLTON: Absolutely. That's what I've been trying to say for twenty years . . . Help me! I'll pray for you, and you, you help me, OK? (*laughter*) This encounter is incredible. In the end, you have the same humanistic and political philosophy as I do. That's quite rare. When you speak of "rigidity," it's the same thing as the "a-communication" that I speak about. The internet, contrary to appearances, is rigidity. Of course, one can say something on it, often lots of things, but it gets rid of the "human" risk. First of all, because we're far apart. There is no vision, there is no touch, there is no body. We are faced with a form of schizophrenic communication. Then communication is often reduced to expression. All young people on the internet have huge generosity. And, besides, young people are generous and often utopian. But, in general, that generosity is oriented toward the network, and the network is everyone, but it's also no one. In any case, it's the "same," leaving aside the "other." So I don't understand the Church. It may be the institution with the greatest experience of all forms of communication, which has constructed, experienced, betrayed them. A real patrimony. All the more so since communication is love, which is itself a Christian word. The Church should contextualize advances in technology and highlight the ways in which it differs from human communication. Furthermore, the clergy is multicultural, in all the churches in the world! So they are sensitive to the extraordinary cultural complexity of the different forms of human communication. The Church could serve as a reminder that "in communication the simplest thing is technology, the most complicated is mankind and societies!" So why this silence for half a century? And you, personally, since you belong to two cultures, you can deepen this research into the complexity of the human and cultural situations of communication. At any rate moving away from technical performance and rediscovering the riches and uncertainties of human communication. If the Europeans "invented" communication, they are also lost in technologies, like the whole world, or most of it.

What can a pope do? What's the limit of your freedom?

POPE FRANCIS: The main one: leaving the Vatican by myself.

DOMINIQUE WOLTON: I want to go with you, leave with you. One day we'll go out. We'll go out for a walk.

POPE FRANCIS: But it's a political problem for the Italian state, and one that I can understand. If I go out on to Italian territory, without an escort, and something happens, I put the state in an embarrassing situation. I can see that. But sometimes, when I have to go to Rome, when you leave here to go just over there (*gestures*), I go there alone with my driver. The windows are tinted, I go back, no one sees me, no one knows. There are things I miss. But that's what reality is like.

DOMINIQUE WOLTON: I understand.

POPE FRANCIS: It's understandable . . . But you can live here . . . There are people who have no gardens . . . but all these lovely things around me: I can live well here.

DOMINIQUE WOLTON: Yes, but it's not the same. Freedom means going out. Did you realize that, before? That you wouldn't have that freedom?

POPE FRANCIS: I was always out and about, I went to the parishes . . .

DOMINIQUE WOLTON: Of course, but when you were elected pope, did you understand? Not straight away?

POPE FRANCIS: I realized, and straight away things happened quite naturally. For example I don't live at the palace, I've gone on living here, in Saint Martha's House. It's things like that that keep me close to people.

DOMINIQUE WOLTON: And your successor, after you, I don't know if he'll be able to go back to the apartments?

POPE FRANCIS: I don't know.

DOMINIQUE WOLTON: (*laughter*) Very good.

POPE FRANCIS: Castel Gandolfo . . .

DOMINIQUE WOLTON: Yes, and why don't you go there?

POPE FRANCIS: Because it was a bit . . . psychologically . . . the pontifical court, moving to Castel Gandolfo. And now the gardens, the ground floor and the first floor, which is the pope's floor, have become museums. If my successor wants to go back to Castel Gandolfo, there are two big buildings that he can occupy. But the main building, the historic one, is becoming a museum. For example, the pope's dormitory: thirty-eight children were born in that bed, most of them Jewish, during the war. Pius XII had hidden them there. It's going to become a museum. So, if I want to get some air, there are these gardens. There's enough air here.

DOMINIQUE WOLTON: What are the key words for you, the words that you'd want to see preserved from your pontificate?

POPE FRANCIS: I realized afterwards, the

word I use most is "joy." The three texts that I wrote: *Evangelii Gaudium,* "The Joy of the Gospel," *Laudato Si',* which is a song of joy, *Amoris Laetitia,* "The Joy of Love . . ." But why did I start with that? I couldn't say . . . The Gospel gives us very great joy. There is also the cross, which allows us to experience difficult moments peacefully, which is the most intimate, the deepest level of joy.

DOMINIQUE WOLTON: Another word?

POPE FRANCIS: I often use "tenderness," "closeness." I say to the priests, "Please be close to people." To the bishops I say, "Don't be princes; be close to people, to the priests." "Closeness" is a word I use often. There is also prayer. Praying, but praying in the sense of being before God. In the sense we talked about.

DOMINIQUE WOLTON: How can you be Catholic and reactionary, when you read the Gospel?

POPE FRANCIS: There's an indispensable key to reading it. *One must read the Gospel with an open soul, without prejudice, without preconceived ideas.* Why? Because the

Gospel is an announcement. It must be received the way one receives something completely new. If we receive the Gospel in a sanitized way, like an ideology or a prejudice, the Gospel won't enter us. The Gospel must touch us. And what is the proof that the Gospel must be read like that, directly? It's astonishment. Wonder. A reactionary, whatever side they are on — there are also left-wing reactionaries, to use a "classic" left-right terminology — is someone who goes against the Gospel, who approaches it while wanting to make it conform to their ideological preconception. And they appropriate the Gospel. They might praise the Gospel, and say, "How lovely the Gospel is!" but they never feel the marvel of someone who reads it and feels it without . . . (*a gesture accompanies the idea*). What the reactionary feels might be as if he was talking through the intermediary of an interpreter. A painful experience — I can do that with you, because I understand, more or less, and we're looking each other in the eye, and the interpreter isn't really an interpreter. When I have to talk in a language with an interpreter, what a palaver! *But there you are, the reactionary is reactionary because he has an inner interpreter: his own ideology.*

DOMINIQUE WOLTON: So a reactionary doesn't read. He doesn't receive the novelty of the text, he annexes the text to his idea. You often say, "We need more synodality in the Church." Isn't it simply more collegiality?

POPE FRANCIS: The synod is one of the tools of collegiality. No one questions the fact that all the bishops in the world work in a collegial way, but when that collegiality has to go into action, it needs instruments. And one of the chief of these is synodality. I delivered an address about that at the last synod, when there was the commemorative act for the fiftieth anniversary of the Second Vatican Council. I talked about synodality, which is an instrument. While communion is reality. It's an instrument for maintaining and extending collegiality or communion. You can use "collegiality" and "communion" interchangeably. They aren't synonyms, because collegiality is used mostly among bishops and communion among the faithful as a whole.

DOMINIQUE WOLTON: Is there something that you, or that a pope can change?

POPE FRANCIS: We can change lots of things.

DOMINIQUE WOLTON: Yes, of course! (*laughter*)

POPE FRANCIS: I think the Church has survived very different cultures. Think of the period before 1870, the time of the pontifical states, the king pope going to war . . . That did me good, I loved reading the thirty volumes of the masterwork by Ludwig von Pastor.[6] Pastor was a Lutheran, very, very rigorous, who was authorized to consult all the archives. And, in the end, he converted to Catholicism, saying, "You can't understand, if God isn't there." Because he is so closely intertwined with all circumstances, good most of the time, but also in the bad times, the sinful episodes . . . Think of the launch of the Crusades, the hunts for witches, who were burned alive, the Inquisition . . . Think of the saints who ended up in prison, Saint John of the Cross, your Joan of Arc . . . How can we understand that? Because there was that holiness that was there, that soil that is the holy believing people of God . . . When people say to me, "The Church has to change in this way or that," who are they talking about? Priests?

Bishops? No, the Church is all of us. But the history of the Church is a history that can't be understood without God.

DOMINIQUE WOLTON: A purely institutional history doesn't actually allow us to understand. As an institution, the Church should have disappeared a long time ago . . . That's the limit of a sociopolitical analysis of the Church. Certainly, the Church has all the shortcomings of humanity, but it constantly starts over, there's something else. You say, "There is no communication without humility."

POPE FRANCIS: Yes, because you need humanity to listen.

DOMINIQUE WOLTON: But all the young people, with all those technologies? There may be humility, of course, but they think it's easy. How do we tell them that they have to leave their technologies or at least regain humility? Your definition of communication, like mine, presupposes a search for authenticity.

POPE FRANCIS: Every media has its dangers. It's possible to do good things, but there's the danger of creating barriers.

Technology is a mediation of communication. But if the protagonist of the communication becomes a mediator, there is no communication. It's the mediator who issues the commands and becomes a dictator. Provoking addiction and everything else, that's it ...

DOMINIQUE WOLTON: And not many people are saying it, at the moment. Certainly not Google, Apple, Facebook or Amazon (the GAFA). No one is saying anything. Because there is so much individual pleasure and political silence, for the moment, about all the issues.

It's a difficult question: where was God in Auschwitz?

POPE FRANCIS: In Auschwitz, I saw how man is without God. And when I talked in Jerusalem, at the commemoration of the Shoah, I started with the word from Genesis when, after the sin, God looks for Adam. "Adam, where are you?" The question is really, "Where is man?" The man who is capable of acting like Adam, like Cain. "You aren't the man I created, you're too far away and you're a monster." A man without God is capable of doing that.

I turn the question around. Perhaps to

have a better understanding of my thought, you can read what I said in Jerusalem at the Shoah monument. And, in Auschwitz, quite simply: who did that? Human beings who had forgotten to be in God's image.

DOMINIQUE WOLTON: Yes, but in the course of history, there have been lots of massacres with God.

POPE FRANCIS: More in the name of God . . .

DOMINIQUE WOLTON: Fine, but the Church has committed many, many massacres . . .

POPE FRANCIS: I should have talked to you about that passage from *The Song of Roland*. The passage in which the infidels had the choice between baptism and the sword . . .

DOMINIQUE WOLTON: You say, "That's what mankind does without God." How can an atheist understand that? He can't understand. And yet an atheist man or woman is as intelligent and just as a believer.

POPE FRANCIS: No, no, I just mean what

man is capable of. Full stop. You can ask the question, you can experience it. Man did that. And you think. Try. That was done by a man who thought he was God.

DOMINIQUE WOLTON: An idea to fight against the idolatry of money? An idea, or a rage, or an intuition?

POPE FRANCIS: Work. Work with both hands. The concrete aspect of work. Because the idolatry of money eases in rituals. What ceases is liquidity. The remedy is work, concrete work.

DOMINIQUE WOLTON: Why is the theme of mercy so important to you? Mercy is a word that is not easy to understand.

POPE FRANCIS: But it's one of the names of God. In the Bible, in our narrative, there is mercy. In paganism, for example, in the pagan traditions, there is cruelty, the evil god. In the Bible, God is revealed with mercy. If I, as an individual, do not accept that God is merciful, I am not a believer. I am making a God in my image.

DOMINIQUE WOLTON: Why are you not

keen on the expression "the Christian roots of Europe"?

POPE FRANCIS: I think Europe has Christian roots, but they aren't the only ones. It has other ones that mustn't be denied. And yet I think it was a mistake not wanting to say "Christian roots" in the European Union document about the first constitution, and that was also down to the governments. It was a mistake not to see the reality. That doesn't mean that Europe has to be entirely Christian. But it is a heritage, a cultural heritage, which we have received.

DOMINIQUE WOLTON: Yes, because there is Judaism and Islam, but there is also socialism and free thinking. There are several different cultural roots. There is no monopoly.

After the murder of Father Hamel[7] in France on July 26, 2016, there has been a powerful movement of solidarity between Christians and Muslims. There are Muslims who have come to Mass. For now, Christians don't go to mosques very much. Could one take advantage of this tragedy to reinforce interreligious dialogue, and ensure that Christians can go to mosques more easily?

POPE FRANCIS: That's true. The Christian people didn't go there. Some Christian rulers went there. I went there, in Africa, in Bangui, and in Asia, in Azerbaijan, to a mosque. But it's true, people don't yet go . . . In some African countries, where that coexistence is normal and peaceful, that exists. They give each other gifts. At Christmas, Muslims give Christians presents. And, for the end of Ramadan, Christians give them to Muslims. There are good relations where there is coexistence; the problem is when ideology comes into play. But let me come back to your first point, which is a reality. Muslims went to church, and Christians aren't yet going to greet them at the mosque. They should go there on feast days, greet them, pray with them a little. It would be a good thing.

DOMINIQUE WOLTON: Yes, because, for now, in the world, with battles against fundamentalists, Islam is often stigmatized. And also, we should construct more links, more "bridges," between them and us.

POPE FRANCIS: Yes, I agree. I did it and I will do it again. I agree.

DOMINIQUE WOLTON: In difficulties involving interreligious dialogue with Islam, isn't one of the causes that dialogue between Christians and Jews has occupied too much room for fifty years, compared to dialogue with Islam?

POPE FRANCIS: No, I don't think so. In Buenos Aires, I sat with Jews and Muslims at the same table . . .

DOMINIQUE WOLTON: Yes, in Buenos Aires, but what about in Europe? And the Middle East?

POPE FRANCIS: Doesn't that happen here? I don't know. We did it in Buenos Aires.

DOMINIQUE WOLTON: The Eastern Christians, who have been fought against and massacred on a large scale — couldn't they forge the connection between Judaism and Islam?

POPE FRANCIS: They could do it more. There are the beginnings of bridges. Some priests are making the beginnings of bridges. The best place to do it at the moment, in the East, is Jordan. Because it is a Muslim country, but it has good relations with Jews and with Christians. The King of Jordan is very close.

DOMINIQUE WOLTON: Has the Church given enough support to the Eastern Christians for the last thirty to forty years?

POPE FRANCIS: The Holy See has helped them a lot. It has been very close to them.

DOMINIQUE WOLTON: Yes, but Europe?

POPE FRANCIS: As to Europe, I don't know.

DOMINIQUE WOLTON: The West?

POPE FRANCIS: There's a problem there that goes much further. I still can't understand the Gulf War. Because the West wanted to export a democratic model to a country that had a different model, saying, "This isn't a democracy, it's a dictatorship." But it was a dictatorship with a system of agreements, because it was about "tribes" who could only be governed in that way. Libya is the same, even if Gaddafi wasn't Saint Augustine. Today, the Libyans are wondering, "Why did the Westerners come and tell us what democracy has to be? We had one Gaddafi, now we've got fifty." In the Middle East, the responsibility is that of the West, which wanted to implant its ideas there.

DOMINIQUE WOLTON: Of course. Sadly, I agree. There are four words that you use: more brotherhood with Muslims, more mutual tolerance, more separation of church and state, and a common quest for humanism. *In what order do you put those four words: brotherhood, tolerance, secularism, humanism?*

POPE FRANCIS: They need to be nuanced. They are all looking for the same things, with different attitudes, but with the same goal.

DOMINIQUE WOLTON: If I talk about the separation of church and state (*laïcité*), couldn't the Church say that we need a model in which separation is central, meaning a respect for all religions, mutual tolerance and the separation of politics and religion?

POPE FRANCIS: Yes, I've already said that. The state is secular. What does that mean? That it is open to all values, and one of those values is transcendence. And when it is open to transcendence, it is open to all religions. The word I don't like is "tolerance." Because tolerance means putting up with something that doesn't suit you, but which you put up with. Tolerance is an outmoded word.

DOMINIQUE WOLTON: Ah, you mean "equality," not "tolerance"?

POPE FRANCIS: Yes, equality. Everyone equal. Because tolerance is when I carry the cross myself and I tolerate someone else's cross . . . I carry the cross of one religion, but I tolerate this other one . . . If you trace it back to its etymological root, "tolerate" means allowing something that shouldn't exist. When, in reality, they are things that are equal. The separation of church and state is the secular state. That means it is open to all values. One of those values is transcendence. That's why I'll go back a little bit: the state cannot consider religions like a subculture. Because, by doing that, it denies transcendence. A state of "healthy secularism" admits transcendence. One woman can wear a crucifix, the other a veil . . . But everyone expresses their own way of transcending with respect, not with "tolerance." With respect. With equal rights.

DOMINIQUE WOLTON: So you prefer the words "equality," "brotherhood," "humanism" and "secularism"?

POPE FRANCIS: A healthy separation of church and state. Because there is a different separation of church and state that is misunderstood: the one that comes down to denying the possibility of religion. What does neutral mean? It means "healthy separation of church and state." I like that term, "healthy separation of church and state." A separation in which transcendence can be expressed according to each culture.

DOMINIQUE WOLTON: That's a new theoretical and political position. Perhaps it should be said more? In fact, there is a risk of more and more cultural and religious conflicts, implicating states and making them wary of that separation . . .

POPE FRANCIS: But that's in *Gaudium et Spes*[8] . . .

DOMINIQUE WOLTON: That was more than fifty years ago. And who reads that text? Not many people, sadly. And besides, the context has changed. Today, conflicts involving culture, religion and politics are becoming

323

increasingly violent. If even the Catholic Church, which has faced a combative secularism in France, says that there can be a "healthy secularism" — to pick up your vocabulary — which would enable us to establish more peaceful relations between states and religions, that constitutes progress.

POPE FRANCIS: I think we have to make ourselves better understood. I agree.

DOMINIQUE WOLTON: For fifty years, cultural and religious conflicts have been becoming more violent, particularly in terms of various forms of fundamentalism.

Fifty years ago, no one would have thought that religion would be a factor of war as much as it is today . . .

POPE FRANCIS: But that isn't all that new. The wars of religion . . .

DOMINIQUE WOLTON: Of course, but I mean that it's starting over again with fundamentalism. And, more than that, more than that, it's the first time in the history of humanity that, thanks to the revolution in information, everyone is informed simultaneously!

POPE FRANCIS: Yes, there is a crisis, which has been growing. There is a crisis, a moment of crisis. But it has to be treated as a crisis. We need to take the measures that are taken when there is a crisis. There is a crisis of violence that emerges from religious fundamentalisms, but that's nothing new. It's something that has always existed, but which is now manifested more strongly. There is also something else: with communication almost in real time, we can see what we used not to see. In the face of this crisis, the Church must repeat and emphasize its position. And, in that sense, I agree with you.

DOMINIQUE WOLTON: Yes, because it's better to put across the position of the Church, even if it means discussing it.

POPE FRANCIS: Yes. Where the wars of religion are concerned, I would say that I'm not sure these wars are historically inspired by the zeal for God, the love of God, in order to save God from all forms of blasphemy. It's God being used for political ends, for reasons of power . . . The victim of those wars is always God. God is "reified." He is turned into a thing. It is the reification of God.

DOMINIQUE WOLTON: I agree. It's the same thing with Islam, the jihadists today use God against Islam.

As regards the World Youth Days, what can be done with the extraordinary capital that they represent? Because they also represent an experience of physical communication. People meet one another and live together. What connection do you make with the Year of Mercy?

POPE FRANCIS: I saw something new in those World Youth Days. New for me — perhaps it existed before, but it's the first time I've seen it. There were World Youth Day Centrals, including the ones organized in other towns in Poland by catechism groups. Then I saw that certain countries, such as Cuba, organized their own World Youth Days. Why? Because a lot of young people couldn't go to Krakow, they decided to do something there. Other countries did the same thing: "little World Youth Days." And that's very important. It represents a potential.

DOMINIQUE WOLTON: Decentralize the World Youth Days?

POPE FRANCIS: No, go on organizing them

as before. But increase the number of places. There are places where young people can't go, because they can't afford to.

DOMINIQUE WOLTON: Is it the same as when you said, "I don't care if Christians don't come to Rome for the Year of Mercy; I'd rather they did the Year of Mercy somewhere else"?

POPE FRANCIS: Yes, but there is one small difference. This is the Vatican, we organize things. But perhaps the World Youth Day Centrals are more important, stronger than the Year of Mercy in the Vatican. That's the difference. Decentralization is one of the criteria I set out in *Evangelii Gaudium*. The Church needs a healthy decentralization. What should we do with young people? Follow them while guiding them. Accompany them in their growth. Many marriages are formed that way. They met there, and then they continued via "chat," then they got engaged, then, because these are our times, they lived together, and then in the end they got married.

DOMINIQUE WOLTON: You have done a lot to mobilize young people and encourage their commitment. You said, "Get committed, get committed." And you also said, "Don't confuse happiness with a sofa." You really are a good communicator . . . You also said to young people: "Refugees are our brothers, the Christian excludes no one." And you said, in Krakow: "Watch out, don't take early retirement." John Paul II said to young people, "Evangelize." Benedict XVI said, "Find your interiority." You say, "Commit yourselves." But what difference is there between commitment and evangelization?

POPE FRANCIS: Commitment is the more human part. The raw material for evangelizing.

DOMINIQUE WOLTON: It's what comes first.

POPE FRANCIS: Commitment, but also through values, through a lifestyle.

DOMINIQUE WOLTON: Sure, but isn't that inevitably political commitment?

POPE FRANCIS: Yes, perhaps.

DOMINIQUE WOLTON: Do you mean that commitment is the prerequisite to evangelization?

POPE FRANCIS: Politics may be one of the greatest acts of charity. Because engaging in politics means carrying peoples. One of Plato's dialogues deals with true politics and bad politics, and, back then, there were bad politicians: sophists. In the *Gorgias,* Plato said of sophists: "Words, speeches . . ."

DOMINIQUE WOLTON: Demagogy . . .

POPE FRANCIS: No, he didn't use that disparaging term. "Words, speeches are to politics what makeup is to health." And that's true. True politics isn't "blah blah blah" and then you close the door and do something else. The best definition that I have heard is the following: "Eight or nine politicians come together, each with different points of view, to reach an agreement. And, after hours of discussion, they reach that agreement. But, at the moment of signing, some of them are already under the table, reaching another one . . ."

Address by the Holy Father
at the Welcoming Ceremony
by the Young People of WYD
on the Occasion of the
XXXI World Youth Day
(July 27–31, 2016),
Jordan Park, Błonia,
Kraków, Poland

(July 28, 2016)

Dear Young Friends, good evening!

At last we are together! Thank you for your warm welcome! I thank Cardinal Dziwisz, the bishops, priests, religious people, the seminarians, lay faithful, and those who have accompanied you. I am also grateful to all those who made it possible for us to be here today, who "went the extra mile" so that we could celebrate our faith. Today, all of us together are celebrating our faith!

In this, the land of his birth, I especially want to thank Saint John Paul II (loud applause) — louder, louder — who first came up with the idea of these meetings and gave them such momentum. From his place in heaven, he is with us and he sees all of you: so many young people from such a variety of nations, cultures and languages but with one aim, that of celebrating Jesus, who is living in our midst.

[. . .]

Knowing your enthusiasm for mission, I repeat: mercy always has a youthful face! Because a merciful heart is motivated to move beyond its comfort zone. A merciful heart can go out and meet others; it is ready to embrace everyone. A merciful heart is able to be a place of refuge for those who are without a home or have lost their home; it is able to build a home and a family for those forced to emigrate; it knows the meaning of tenderness and compassion. A merciful heart can share its bread with the hungry and welcome refugees and migrants. To say the word "mercy" along with you is to speak of opportunity, future, commitment, trust, openness, hospitality, compassion and dreams. [. . .]

Let me tell you another thing I have learned over these years. I do not want to offend anyone, but it pains me to meet young people who seem to have opted for "early retirement." This pains me. Young people who seem to retire at twenty-three, twenty-four, twenty-five years of age. This pains me. I worry when I see young people who have "thrown in the towel" before the game has even begun, who are defeated even before they begin to play. I am saddened to see young people who walk around glumly as if life had no meaning. Deep down, young people like this are bored . . . and boring, who bore others, and this upsets me. But it is also hard, and troubling, to see young people who waste their lives looking for thrills or a feeling of being alive by taking dark paths and in the end having to pay for it . . . and pay dearly. Think of so many young people you know, who have chosen this path. It is disturbing to see young people squandering some of the best years of their lives, wasting their energies running after peddlers of false illusions, and they do exist (where I come from, we call them "vendors of smoke"), who rob you of what is best in you. This pains me. I am sure that among you there are no such persons, but I want to tell you: there are young people that have gone into retirement, who have thrown in the towel before the game has even begun, there are young people who are enthralled by false illusions and end up in nothingness.

We are gathered here to help one another, because we do not want to be robbed of the best of ourselves. We don't want to be robbed of our energy, our joy, our dreams by false hopes.

So I ask you: are you looking for empty thrills in life, or do you want to feel a power that can give you a lasting sense of life and fulfillment? Empty thrills or the power of grace? [. . .]

In these days, Jesus wants to stop and enter our home: your home, my home, enter into our hearts; Jesus will look at us hurrying about with all our concerns, as He did with Martha . . . and He will wait for us to listen to him, like Mary, to make space for him amid the bustle. May these be days given over to Jesus and to listening to one another. May they help us welcome Jesus in all those with whom we share our homes, our neighborhoods, our groups and our schools.

Whoever welcomes Jesus, learns to love as Jesus does. So He asks us if we want a full life. And in His name, I ask you: do you want a full life? Start right this moment by letting yourself be open and attentive! Because happiness is sown and blossoms in mercy. That is His answer, His offer, His challenge, His adventure: mercy. Mercy always has a youthful face. Like that of Mary of Bethany, who sat as a disciple at the feet of Jesus and joyfully listened to His words, since she knew that there she would find peace. Like that of Mary of Nazareth, whose daring "Yes" launched her on the adventure of mercy. All generations would call her blessed; to all of us she is the "Mother of Mercy." Let us call upon her together: Mary, Mother of Mercy. All of us: Mary, Mother of Mercy.

All together, let us ask the Lord, each repeating in the silence of his or her heart: Lord, launch us on the adventure of mercy! Launch us on the adventure of building bridges and tearing down walls, be they barriers or barbed wire. Launch us on the adventure of helping the poor, those who feel lonely and abandoned, or no longer find meaning in their lives. Launch us on the journey of accompanying those who do not know You, and telling them carefully and respectfully Your Name, the reason for our faith. Send us, like Mary of Bethany, to listen attentively to those we do not understand, those of other cultures and peoples, even those we are afraid of because we consider them a threat. Make us attentive to our elders, to our grandparents, as Mary of Nazareth was to Elizabeth, in order to learn from their wisdom. [. . .]

Address by His Holiness Pope Francis at the prayer vigil with young people on the occasion of the XXXI World Youth Day (July 27–31, 2016), Campus Misericordiae, Kraków, Poland

(July 30, 2016)

Dear Young Friends,
[. . .]
We have no desire to conquer hatred with more hatred, violence with more violence, terror with more terror. We are here today because the Lord has called us together. Our response to a world at war has a name: its name is fraternity, its name is brotherhood, its name is communion, its name is family. We celebrate the fact, that coming from different cultures, we have come together to pray. Let our best word, our best argument, be our unity in prayer. [. . .]

As we were praying, I thought of the Apostles on the day of Pentecost. Picturing them can help us come to appreciate all that God dreams of accomplishing in our lives, in us and with us. That day, the disciples were together behind locked doors, out of fear. They felt threatened, surrounded by an atmosphere of persecution that had cornered them in a little room and left them silent and paralyzed. Fear had taken hold of them. Then, in that situation, something spectacular, something grandiose, occurred. The Holy Spirit and tongues as of fire came to rest upon each of them, propelling them toward an undreamed-of adventure. [. . .]

The fear and anguish born of knowing that leaving home might mean never again seeing their loved ones, the fear of not feeling appreciated or loved, the fear of having no choices. They shared with us the same experience the disciples had; they felt the kind of fear that only leads to one thing. Where does fear lead us? The feeling of being closed in on oneself, trapped. Once we feel that way, our fear starts to fester and is inevitably joined by its "twin sister," paralysis: the feeling of being paralyzed. Thinking that, in this world, in our cities and our communities, there is no longer any room to grow, to dream, to create, to gaze at new horizons — in a word, to live — is one of the worst things that can happen to us in life, and especially at a younger age. When we are paralyzed, we miss the magic of encountering others, making friends, sharing dreams, walking side by side with others. [. . .]

In life there is another, even more dangerous, kind of paralysis. It is not easy to put our finger on it. I like to describe it as the paralysis that comes from confusing happiness with a sofa. In other words, to think that, in order to be happy, all we need is a good sofa. A sofa that makes us feel comfortable, calm, safe. A sofa like one of those we have nowadays with a built-in massage unit to put us to sleep. A sofa that promises us hours of comfort so we can escape to the world of video games and spend all kinds of time in front of a computer screen. A sofa that keeps us safe from any kind of pain and fear. A sofa that allows us to stay home without needing to work at, or worry about, anything. [. . .]

This is itself a great form of paralysis,

whenever we start thinking that happiness is the same as comfort and convenience, that being happy means going through life asleep or on tranquilizers, that the only way to be happy is to live in a haze. Certainly, drugs are bad, but there are plenty of other socially acceptable drugs that can end up enslaving us just the same. One way or the other, they rob us of our greatest treasure: our freedom. They strip us of our freedom.

My friends, Jesus is the Lord of risk. He is the Lord of the eternal "more." Jesus is not the Lord of comfort, security and ease. Following Jesus demands a good dose of courage, a readiness to trade in the sofa for a pair of walking shoes and to set out on new and uncharted paths. To blaze trails that open up new horizons capable of spreading joy, the joy that is born of God's love and wells up in your hearts with every act of mercy. To take the path of the "craziness" of our God, who teaches us to encounter Him in the hungry, the thirsty, the naked, the sick, the friend in trouble, the prisoner, the refugee and the migrant, and our neighbors who feel abandoned.

[. . .]

That is the secret, dear friends, and all of us are called to share in it. God expects something from you. Have you understood this? God expects something from you, God wants something from you. God hopes in you. God comes to break down all our fences. He comes to open the doors of our lives, our dreams, our ways of seeing things. God comes to break open everything that keeps you closed in. He is encouraging you to dream. He wants to make you see that, with you, the world can be different. For the fact is, unless you offer the best of yourselves, the world will never be different. [. . .]

The times we live in do not call for young "couch potatoes," but for young people with shoes — or, better, boots — laced. The times we live in require only active players on the field, and there is no room for those who sit on the bench. Today's world demands that you be a protagonist of history because life is always beautiful when we choose to live it fully, when we choose to leave a mark. [. . .]

So today, my friends, Jesus is inviting you, calling you, to leave your mark on life, to leave a mark on history, your own and that of many others as well. [. . .]

■ ■ ■ ■

7
"TRADITION IS A MOVEMENT."

■ ■ ■ ■

Rome is crushed by heat. Not so many people around. Everything is there, still and permanent. I know the way. Enter the Vatican on foot, walk around Saint Peter's, past security. Cross the courtyards. Listen to the turtle doves in the morning silence. A combination of time and space that makes the head spin. The Holy Father is still just as direct, and still a little absent. The miracle of dialogue and communication resumes quite naturally. Where am I? Small talk, somehow remote from the world . . . Particularly since we are dealing with relations between tradition and modernity, globalization, and new evangelizations. How are we to think of the different kinds of spirituality of the future, ecumenism and interreligious dialogue? In these exchanges everything seems calm, honest, often joyful, and yet how are we to understand one another, in spite of the huge distances, of all kinds, between us? The miracle of human communication. Everything, or nearly every-thing, seems possible. And yet I already know that these exchanges, this encounter, will have a limit, will come to an end. I've read and worked a lot to understand the Pope's history, every dimension of it. The whole problem in the miracle of this meeting lies in being able to locate and preserve the high level of the dialogue in these discussions. They succeed one another without any prees-tablished schedule on the part of either of us.

POPE FRANCIS: Before we start, I would like to define the meaning of tradition. Tradition isn't an immovable bank account. Tradition is the doctrine that's moving, ad-vancing.

And you French have a lovely phrase from the fifth century — it's from Vincent de Lérins,[1] a French monk and theologian — which says that "tradition is a movement." I'm sorry. He says that in Latin: *"Ut annis scilicet consolidetur, dilatetur tempore, subli-metur aetate"* "Even the dogma of the Church must follow these laws, consolidat-ing over the years, developing over time, deepening with age." Tradition moves for-ward, but in what ways? So that, over the years, it consolidates itself to grow over time and be sublimated with age. The principles of tradition don't change, the essence doesn't change, but it grows, it evolves.

For example, about the death penalty. We bishops decreed the death penalty in the Middle Ages. The Church says more or less — and we are working to change the catechism on this point — that the death penalty is immoral. Does that mean tradition has changed? No, but conscience evolves, the moral conscience evolves. It's the same with slavery. There are slaves, but it's immoral. On the other hand, when Saint Peter Claver,[2] in Colombia, was working with slaves, he was reprimanded because some people doubted that they had a soul. In the dynamic tradition, the essence remains: it doesn't change, it grows. It grows in explanation and in understanding. Those three phrases of Vincent de Lérins are important. How does tradition grow? It grows as a person grows: through dialogue, which is like suckling for a child. Dialogue with the world around us. Dialogue makes us grow. If we don't engage in dialogue we can't grow, we remain closed, small. I can't just walk with blinkers on, I have to watch and engage in dialogue. Dialogue makes things grow, it makes tradition grow. In engaging in dialogue and listening to another opinion, I can, as in the case of the death penalty, torture, slavery, change my point of view. Without changing doctrine. Doctrine has grown with understanding. That's the basis of tradition.

DOMINIQUE WOLTON: This conception of tradition that you are developing would be accepted more easily today than fifty years ago, because modernity is in crisis. Modernity was progress. Then it became ideology. And now it's in crisis. People used to say that tradition was conservatism, the past, and now we are very slowly coming to understand that tradition is something else, as you say, a movement. And if you say that clearly, it rehabilitates and relegitimizes tradition and also modernity.

POPE FRANCIS: Yes.

DOMINIQUE WOLTON: A century of systematic devaluation of tradition has done a great deal of damage. Of course, tradition was often synonymous with conservatism. Today, tradition isn't necessarily conservatism. It's something else.

POPE FRANCIS: It's something else. That doesn't change the doctrine, the true doctrine. But it makes the conscience grow, it gives you a better understanding of it, it's dialogue according to the principles of Vincent de Lérins, again in *Commonitorium* . . .

DOMINIQUE WOLTON: Let me return to my question: the Church, with its experience and its mistakes, can contribute something to modernity, specifically by returning our attention to tradition, which has been devalued for a hundred years. There was a conflict between modernity and tradition, which we can now go beyond. As you say, through dialogue . . . . but it isn't yet accepted. Perhaps because Vatican II was identified with modernity? But, in the end, it was both modernity AND tradition.

POPE FRANCIS: Pope Benedict said something very clear: the changes in the Church must be carried out with the hermeneutic of continuity. A lovely phrase.

Hermeneutic means growth: some things change, but there is always continuity. It doesn't betray its roots, it clarifies them, making them easier to understand.

DOMINIQUE WOLTON: Yes. The very principle of modernity is not continuity, it is rupture. And it's the strength of the Church, compared to a century ago, to remind us of that. Tradition has often been identified with conservatism and modernity with progress. Today, we understand that modernity, as such, is nothing. The important thing is the tension between the two. The hermeneutic of continuity — as Benedict XVI puts it — may also be reacquiring an intellectual and even a spiritual force. A great boulevard is opening up in front of you, here. You're facing a "formidable business." (*laughter*)

POPE FRANCIS: As I said: growth. Tradition cannot under any circumstances be ideological.

DOMINIQUE WOLTON: For a hundred years, people have been saying that tradition is an ideology. Modernity has also become an ideology.

POPE FRANCIS: Tradition, when it becomes an ideology, is no longer tradition. It is no longer alive.

DOMINIQUE WOLTON: Exactly! Tradition is modern, in the end. Because it has not yet been understood, it hasn't been heard. In dichotomous visions of the world it is said that the Church is tradition and doesn't understand anything about modernity. That's not quite true. It would be useful if everyone could understand it. Even atheists. The Church could take a step toward the atheists. Not to "make them come to church," but to say, "We are both on the side of transcendence." To be atheist is to give an atheist response to the question of transcendence. In fact, the true change for the Church would be for it no longer to be perceived as a force for rejection and negation, but as a force of proposition. Even by atheists. That would be progress.

POPE FRANCIS: There is also a difference between modernity and worldliness. Neither must we confuse evolution and tradition, pastoral comprehension and confusion about the nature of things. What should we think about same-sex marriage? "Marriage" is a historical word. Forever, throughout humanity, and not only in the Church, it's between a man and a woman. You can't change it just like that. It's the nature of things. That's how they are. So let's call them "civil unions." Don't let's joke with the truths. It's true that, behind it, there is the ideology of gender. In books, too, children learn that they can choose their sex. Why gender, being a woman or a man, is a choice and not a fact of nature? That favors this error. But let's talk about things as they are; marriage is a man and a woman. That's the precise term. Let's call same-sex unions "civil unions."

DOMINIQUE WOLTON: The ideology of gender is a different problem. It's a sociological deviation. It consists of saying that the sexes are undifferentiated, and that it's solely society that distributes the male and female roles. That determinism is terrible. There is no nature, culture, fate or freedom; all that remains is social determination. And, if you're against those determinisms, you're called a reactionary. You're told that you're adopting the positions of the Church!

That ideological drift has occurred over twenty years.

POPE FRANCIS: That's a critical confusion right now. I said so, publicly, one day in Saint Peter's Square, talking about marriage. I said, "There are new ideas, and I wonder if these new ideas, like the ideology of gender, do not essentially rely on the fear of differences."

DOMINIQUE WOLTON: A denial of the

multiple forms of otherness?

POPE FRANCIS: I said it in the form of a question. And I encourage researchers to investigate the subject.

DOMINIQUE WOLTON: The ideology of gender is the risk of a denial of difference. Difference isn't only social. It's much more complicated.

It's a form of reverse determinism. Saying that there are no men, no women, that everything depends on society, in fact you create a form of social determinism.

POPE FRANCIS: I wouldn't like people to confuse my position on the attitude toward homosexual people with the subject of gender theory.

DOMINIQUE WOLTON: Yes, of course, because there's an essential difference! Perhaps a "civil union" would be enough. But at present there is an aspiration for legitimacy on the part of the homosexual community. A need to go beyond centuries of the condemnation and exclusion of homosexuals. Legitimizing them, in fact, even if that might look like an ideology of equality.

POPE FRANCIS: Yes, it's an ideology.

DOMINIQUE WOLTON: But we can understand where it comes from, after so many centuries of contempt, guilt and repression. Besides, many homosexuals aren't necessary favorable toward "marriage." Some prefer civil union. It's all complicated. Beyond the ideology of equality, there is also, in the word "marriage," a search for acknowledgment.

POPE FRANCIS: But it isn't a marriage, it's a civil union. "There is no other way" — let's put it like that . . .

DOMINIQUE WOLTON: What frightens you about secularization, which is between modernity and tradition?

POPE FRANCIS: It ends up with a dictatorship, with worldly principles, because that's when worldliness comes into play. Secularization is also linked to money. Good things, for our century, are the ones that are worth money. That's what underlies this attitude of worldliness, which weakens the individual.

DOMINIQUE WOLTON: Because it severs all roots?

POPE FRANCIS: It's a problem. You talk about roots, that's true. But there are also lifestyles which are completely relative, relative to circumstances. You let yourself be carried along by the current . . . But secularization also contains a denial of transcendence. Nothing to do with healthy secularism. The secular world has its own autonomy, that of governments, societies, laws. Secularization tells us to go forward to . . .

DOMINIQUE WOLTON: Could we say that secularization is secularism that has become an ideology?

POPE FRANCIS: I'd like to return to the healthy secularism that I've spoken about before, which consists of saying that created things have their own autonomy. For example, the state needs to be secular. Secular. We've already talked about that, about the French legacy of the Enlightenment. A secular country is one where there's room for everyone. It's transcendence for everyone. Anyone can practice a trade or a profession and at the same time be open to transcendence: the one doesn't rule out the other. That's a secular state that respects all human values. Secularization is a movement . . . I wouldn't want to use this word, which I don't generally use, but which I'm trying to explain: it's like a "sickness," closing off doors and windows to all kinds of transcendence. Then everything would be done within that. A bad secularism, an exaggerated secularism. Secularization only seeks values that are shut away within itself. And it rules out transcendence.

DOMINIQUE WOLTON: That's probably the reason why you say that, in secularism, religions have to be in the public space. But the French concept of *laïcité* advocates religions remaining in the private space.

POPE FRANCIS: That's *laïcisme.* A legacy of the Enlightenment. As for politics, Christians have to engage in politics. But not to create a "Christian party": you can have a party with Christian values that doesn't have to be Christian.

DOMINIQUE WOLTON: Last of all, coming from the New World, do you think it gives you a better understanding of the problems of the world or not?

POPE FRANCIS: It helps me, because I see things that I hadn't seen there. And it makes me think. Understand, seek ways of resolving issues . . . In this sense, it helps me. But that is a big principle: differences always help you grow. And, with that, we come back to the subject we were talking about a moment ago: being afraid of differences diminishes us.

DOMINIQUE WOLTON: I agree. Differences are an enriching factor, certainly. That's why highlighting cultural diversity is an apprenticeship in otherness and constitutes progress. If humanity doesn't respect cultural diversity, it means death. The Church could easily say this more forcefully, because it is its witness. But people don't always accept difference, for fear of communitarianism. There can be respect for cultural diversity and respect for universalism. That's the universalist message of the Church. It's the connection and the common good that exists between the Church and the UN.

POPE FRANCIS: Some countries have been able to integrate immigrants into their lives. But others, for two or three generations, have "objectified" them in ghettoes. Without integration.

DOMINIQUE WOLTON: Let me come back to one of your slogans: "The three Ls: land, lodging, labor." Why don't you write an encyclical about the three Ls?

POPE FRANCIS: A "mini-encyclical" was brought out for the second meeting of the popular movements, where I delivered a long address. The first meeting was held here at the Vatican, the second in Bolivia. The third meeting will be held in November, here at the Vatican. Because the poor, the workers, always have to be defended. I'm talking on the basis of my experience in Argentina with the trade unions, and, because of the corruption and a lot of other things, the poor are forgotten. And the poor begin to associate among themselves on other bases. They are the popular movements. They are very important in Asia, in the Philippines, in India, in Thailand. Very, very important. And they're trying to develop in Latin America. They're organizing well in Central America. In Argentina, when I was a bishop, I started working with them when I heard about them. Then that first meeting was organized, then the second, and now the third. But my intervention during the second meeting turned into a mini-encyclical on the three Ls.

DOMINIQUE WOLTON: Yes, but that isn't well known, not at all. People don't know what you've done to support popular movements, or about the three meetings you're referring to. It's your whole commitment in favor of the *cartoneros* [waste pickers], the poorest of the poor.

POPE FRANCIS: For Saint Gaetano, in Argentina, there's a big manifestation of faith that brings the population together, the poor people looking for work, the ones asking for work or the ones expressing gratitude for having work. After the religious celebration, there is always a march by grassroots organizations to the center of the city, which has nothing to do with the Church, to call for justice. The three Ls . . . Of the three Ls, labor is the most important because it is the one that gives dignity.

DOMINIQUE WOLTON: That's a "revolutionary" statement, precisely in terms of "the liquid economy of capitalism." And there is a great tradition in the Church from Leo XIII and his encyclical *Rerum Novarum*[3] denouncing the excesses of capitalism — a great tradition that goes sadly unacknowledged.

POPE FRANCIS: My encyclical *Laudato Si'* is not a green encyclical. It is a social encyclical.

DOMINIQUE WOLTON: Yes. There was a misinterpretation. You were labeled an ecologist.

POPE FRANCIS: There's ecology, but behind that there lie social problems.

DOMINIQUE WOLTON: The whole history of the Church has involved giving value to labor, but that has been forgotten. There are at least four or five subjects in which the Church has strong experience, including everything that pertains to work. You can agree or not, but it exists and it isn't acknowledged.

POPE FRANCIS: I say a lot of things in my morning homilies at Saint Martha's. You can find them on the site. There are eight volumes of morning homilies.

DOMINIQUE WOLTON: Eight, already? OK.

POPE FRANCIS: They're short. Eight minutes. They deal with all of these subjects. I prepare them, I think about them the day before, but without writing them down.

DOMINIQUE WOLTON: You know why we're seeing the misunderstanding of communication again? Because in most cases communication is a misunderstanding. It's not just the message; the main thing is the receiver and interaction. What if people don't understand? Humanity's worst enemy is the humanity that doesn't want to understand. The philosopher Raymond Aron had a phrase that I like a lot: "The main obstacle to press freedom is the reader." Because the reader only wants to find in newspapers, on the radio, on television or the internet that which confirms his ideas, his ideological choices. No communication without a higher value being assigned to the receiver, while, at the same time, the receiver resists everything that does not correspond to his or her own ideological and cultural choices . . .

POPE FRANCIS: That happens to me too. I read the paper and look for the things that interest me.

DOMINIQUE WOLTON: That means we are the obstacles to our own openness . . . It makes me think of another problem that we've touched upon: the connections between tradition and conservatism. Often, the Church is accused of being traditional. Is it the same with conservatism? What can we say to remind people that the question of tradition isn't the same as the question of conservatism?

POPE FRANCIS: Simply that tradition is carried forward by the Holy Spirit. Ideologies carry it too, but without the Holy Spirit. Ideologies are based on a political position. In the Church, what carries the life of the Church forward is the Holy Spirit. That doesn't mean that I'm falling into Joachimism[4] . . . And, yes, there's a very fine study of Joachimism by Father Henri du Lubac, called *La Postérité spirituelle de Joachim de Flore.*[5] You'll find all kinds of things in there, even your George Sand!

DOMINIQUE WOLTON: By the way, did you win the battle against the "fifteen Curial diseases"?[6] They aren't only Curial diseases, in the end they're universal diseases (*laughter*).

362

POPE FRANCIS: Yes, yes. I'm preparing my address to the cardinals for Christmas. And that will be about reform. Yes, it's made considerable progress, not only the organic reform of the organization, but the reform of attitudes.

DOMINIQUE WOLTON: If you succeed, it will be because the Holy Spirit has acted . . .

POPE FRANCIS: Yes, of course . . .

DOMINIQUE WOLTON: In your view, have relations between the Church and political power changed since Vatican II?

POPE FRANCIS: Yes.

DOMINIQUE WOLTON: In what sense?

POPE FRANCIS: Autonomy and collaboration for the good of the people. Collaboration when it's necessary.

DOMINIQUE WOLTON: Everywhere in the world?

POPE FRANCIS: No, that would be too much to hope for.

DOMINIQUE WOLTON: How could you popularize the four principles you set out in *Amoris Laetitia,* namely welcoming, accompanying, discerning, integrating?

POPE FRANCIS: Of course, priests and bishops are working on these subjects and on ways of rendering them concrete. I define the line, and, in each situation, everyone must take these four principles and bring them forward. These are principles for real life. If I chose another way and started saying, "To welcome people we have to do this or that, to integrate you have to do that and that . . ." I would fall into the trap of casuistry.

When a young person in the pastoral ministry in Buenos Aires came to talk about his problems, I asked him, "You're doing that? And you've thought of another option for your life? Because it isn't enough to act like that, and then go running to the dry cleaner to get the stain out. Think. Think about other ways." You can't erase a sin like that. A sin fades slowly, very slowly . . . as you move toward goodness. It's God who attracts you, to take you away from sin. But if God isn't there, you can't erase it.

DOMINIQUE WOLTON: That makes me

think about a contradiction: Catholicism is a religion of love, and yet it is full of prohibitions, full of "whips hanging in the sacristy." You aren't allowed to do this thing or that . . .

POPE FRANCIS: I think that has a little to do with casuistic morality.

DOMINIQUE WOLTON: Casuistic morality? When you have a religion of love on one side and a sequence of prohibitions on the other? While the strength of the Catholic discourse lies in love and freedom . . .

Last question about the articulation between tradition and modernity. What we call the young churches, in the Catholic world — Africa, Asia, Latin America — what more can they bring?

POPE FRANCIS: Many things, many things. The vitality of the churches. And awareness as against rigid absolutism. They bring us the awareness of inculturation. A faith that does not become culture is not a true faith. And a culture which is not capable of expressing faith in its own culture is not an open culture. There is the relationship between faith and culture. The inculturation of faith and the evangelization of culture are essential.

There is a great openness today . . . What Ricci and Nobili didn't have in their day. The doors were closed in their faces, and today, since the Council, they have been opened. *Inculturation is more current than ever.* If you go to Africa, a Mass lasts three or four hours. Why? Because they can't conceive of a Mass without dance. And isn't that sacred? Yes, it's sacred. Because dance is sacred. And they have great piety. Because the faith is inculturated. On the other hand, the traditionalist ideology has a faith like this (*he gestures to indicate a pair of blinkers):* the blessing must be given like that, the fingers must be like that during Mass, with gloves, as used to be the case . . . What Vatican II did to the liturgy was really a very big thing. Because it opened the worship of God to the people. Now, the people participate.

DOMINIQUE WOLTON: Jean-Marie Lustiger said that Vatican II was a revolution for the liturgy. But secularists and atheists don't see it that way. They don't see that the liturgy, after Vatican II, was opening up to participation.

POPE FRANCIS: But maybe in France? If

you go to a liturgy by Philippe Barbarin you'll see that. Why? Because he has lived as a missionary, and he proposes a new experience of the Church. Other bishops didn't understand Vatican II as well.

DOMINIQUE WOLTON: I know the Bishop of Oran, in Algeria, a little. He replaced Monsignor Claverie, the Dominican bishop assassinated in 1996. He is at a meeting point between several different cultures. He told me he was in the synod on the family. He is warm and open.

POPE FRANCIS: Open.

DOMINIQUE WOLTON: He's rebuilding the big cross of Santa Cruz, in Oran. A symbol for everyone! A bit like the Christ of Rio de Janeiro.

I've nearly finished for today. The torture is over! (*laughter*)

POPE FRANCIS: But torture is a sin.

DOMINIQUE WOLTON: You're going to go to Georgia and Azerbaijan. You've been in the poor countries of Latin America. It's rare for a pope. You always choose new or small churches. Georgia is tiny, and it's very conflict-ridden! Why these small countries, forgotten by everybody except you? Are they the *cartoneros* [waste pickers] of globalization?

POPE FRANCIS: When I was coming back from Albania in 2014, on the plane, the journalists said to me, "But the first country you visited in Europe is a country that isn't part of the European Union. Why?" It's the same question. Because it's a signal. The first country I visited in the European Union was Greece. Lesbos. Because Strasbourg wasn't France; I went there for the European Union, not for France. The second was Poland. The first were Albania and Bosnia-Herzegovina . . . Now, I'm thinking about Macedonia, about the Balkans.

DOMINIQUE WOLTON: The Balkans . . .

POPE FRANCIS: Yes, these are signals. I'm going to Africa; I'd like to go to both Congos.

DOMINIQUE WOLTON: When?

POPE FRANCIS: I don't know. And, at the end of 2016, to Sweden, for the Catholic-Lutheran commemoration.

DOMINIQUE WOLTON: Yes, for ecumenism.

POPE FRANCIS: And then Georgia and Azerbaijan.

DOMINIQUE WOLTON: There was also your trip to Lampedusa.

POPE FRANCIS: Yes, the first trip. But that just occurred to me like that. I had to go to Lampedusa.

DW: Yes, it's like Lesbos.

POPE FRANCIS: Yes, the same thing. "I have to go to Lesbos." I talked to Bartholomew I about it. There had to be a doctor there as well, and I talked to the Greek ambassador. And then I brought Muslim families on the plane. At first, I took in two families, in the two parishes of the Vatican, then nine more arrived. One of these days, we're going to have lunch here with the families that came with me. Most of them are Muslim and the others are Christian.

DOMINIQUE WOLTON: Weren't the Eastern Christians offended?

POPE FRANCIS: No, no. No, because they

come here too. The choice was made by drawing lots. The families who had their papers ready, fifty or sixty of them, with a lawyer. We drew lots the night before. It was good . . . Prime Minister Tsipras was a great help to me.

DOMINIQUE WOLTON: Yes, Tsipras is brave. But he has limited room for maneuver.

POPE FRANCIS: He's a good man. He helped me a lot. What we planned was that at the end of the visit, after a private discussion with him, we were to go to the airport to greet the refugees. But they made a mistake, and they put them on the airplane before us, those thirteen people, those families. When Tsipras arrived, he asked where those people were, so that he could greet them. They were already on the plane! We went to see them to ask them to get off the plane, but they didn't want to. (*laughter*) They were frightened. And so Tsipras greeted the Pope . . . And the people got off the plane.

DOMINIQUE WOLTON: Are you going to organize a World Day of the Poor?

POPE FRANCIS: Yes, I'll explain to you how

the idea came about. There were those days of meetings with the poor, in November 2016. After one of them, and then the Mass with the homeless, when I was going to leave the sacristy, the young man who had organized the day with Monsignor Barbarin said, "Holy Father, why wouldn't we have a day of the poor today?" That has stayed with me. My heart was touched, I felt it. And I thought of a phrase that was a little like "throwing a pebble and seeing what happens." I said, "I'd like today to be the day of the poor." I threw that into the air. When I went back to the sacristy, Barbarin and the others were there, and they said, "Thank you, the day of the poor, the day of the poor!" The people adopted it.

DOMINIQUE WOLTON: So you're going to be able to do it?

POPE FRANCIS: We'll see, we'll see. But we don't want it to be just one day a year. We want that day to inspire the place that the poor occupy within the Church.

DOMINIQUE WOLTON: What's the hardest thing, at ground level?

POPE FRANCIS: In my experience, I would

say that interreligious dialogue was easier than ecumenism. I've done a lot of ecumenical dialogues; I like that a lot. But, comparing the two, I would say that interreligious dialogue was easier for me. Because it involves talking more about humanity . . .

DOMINIQUE WOLTON: Differences bring you closer together?

POPE FRANCIS: Yes. It's dialectics.

DOMINIQUE WOLTON: When you're close, everything is difficult. When you're further away, it's easier. It's strange. Is there anything you'd like to add?

POPE FRANCIS: No, I've talked enough already!

DOMINIQUE WOLTON: What was your objective in the consistory of November 19, 2016, when you appointed seventeen new cardinals from all over the world? What were you trying to do?

POPE FRANCIS: Stress the universality of the Church. The first cardinal I appointed — the first one is always the most important — was a nuncio. Nuncios are hardly ever appointed cardinal. It happened four hundred years ago, when it was the Syrian nuncio. This appointment is a message for that martyred people.

ADDRESS OF HIS HOLINESS POPE FRANCIS ON THE OCCASION OF THE PRESENTATION OF THE CHRISTMAS GREETINGS TO THE ROMAN CURIA, CLEMENTINE HALL, THE VATICAN

(December 22, 2014)

Dear Brothers and Sisters,
[. . .]
I would like this meeting and the reflections which I will now share with you to be [. . .] a stimulus to a true examination of conscience, in order to prepare our hearts for the holy feast of Christmas.
[. . .]
The Roman Curia is a complex body
[. . .]
And yet, like any body, like any human body, it is also exposed to diseases, malfunctioning, infirmity. Here I would like to mention some of these probable diseases, "Curial diseases." [. . .]

1. The disease of thinking we are [. . .] "indispensable." [. . .] A Curia which is not *self-critical,* [. . .] which does not seek to be more fit, is a sick body. A simple visit to the cemetery might help us see the names of many people who thought they were immortal, immune and indispensable! [. . .]

2. Another disease is the "Martha complex," excessive busyness. It is found in those who immerse themselves in work [. . .] Neglecting needed rest leads to stress and agitation. A time of rest [. . .] is necessary, obligatory and should be taken seriously [. . .]

3. Then too there is the disease of mental and spiritual "petrification." It is found in those who have a heart of stone [. . .], in those who in the course of time lose their interior serenity, alertness and daring, and hide under a pile of papers, turning into *paper pushers* and not *men of God.* [. . .]

4. The disease of excessive planning and bureaucracy. When the apostle plans everything down to the last detail [. . .], he becomes an

accountant or an office manager. Things need to be prepared well, but without ever falling into the temptation of trying to contain and direct the freedom of the Holy Spirit [. . .]

5. The disease of poor coordination. Once the body's members lose communion [. . .] it then becomes an orchestra which produces noise: its members do not work together and lose the spirit of fellowship and teamwork. [. . .]

6. There is also a "spiritual Alzheimer's disease." It consists of losing the memory of our [. . .] past history with the Lord and our "first love."[7] It involves a progressive decline in the spiritual faculties which [. . .] greatly handicaps a person [. . .]. We see it in those who [. . .] are caught up completely in the present moment, in their passions, whims and obsessions [. . .]

7. The disease of rivalry and vanity. When appearance, the color of our clothes and our titles of honor become the primary object in life [. . .]

376

8. The disease of existential schizophrenia. This is the disease of those who live a double life [. . .] It [. . .] often strikes those who abandon personal service and restrict themselves to bureaucratic matters, thus losing contact with reality, with concrete people. [. . .]

9. The disease of gossiping, grumbling and backbiting. [. . .] It is a grave illness which [. . .] takes over a person, making him become a "sower of weeds" [. . .] and, in many cases, a cold-blooded killer of the good name of our colleagues and confrères. [. . .]

10. The disease of idolizing superiors: This is the disease of those who court their superiors [. . .] in order to obtain their submission, loyalty and psychological dependency [. . .].

11. The disease of indifference to others. This is where each individual thinks only of himself and loses the sincerity and warmth of human relationships. [. . .] When out of jealousy or deceit we take joy in seeing others fall instead of

helping them up and encouraging them.

12. The disease of a lugubrious face. Those glum and dour persons who think that, to be serious, we have to put on a face of melancholy and severity, and treat others — especially those we consider our inferiors — with rigor, brusqueness and arrogance. [. . .]

13. The disease of hoarding. When an apostle tries to fill an existential void in his heart by accumulating material goods, not out of need, but only in order to feel secure. [. . .]

14. The disease of closed circles, where belonging to a clique becomes more powerful than belonging to the Body and, in certain circumstances, to Christ himself. [. . .]

15. Lastly, the disease of worldly profit, of forms of self-exhibition. When an apostle turns his service into power, and his power into a commodity in order to gain worldly profit or even greater power. [. . .]

[. . .] These diseases and these temptations are a danger for every Christian and for every [. . .] community [. . .] [and] parish [. . .]

We need to be clear that it is only the Holy Spirit who can heal [. . .] who sustains every sincere effort at purification and every effort at conversion. [. . .]

Healing also comes about through an awareness of our sickness and of a personal and communal decision to be cured by patiently and perseveringly accepting the remedy. [. . .]

I offer cordial good wishes for a holy Christmas to all of you. [. . .]

Address of His Holiness Pope Francis on the Occasion of the Presentation of the Christmas Greetings to the Roman Curia, Clementine Hall, The Vatican

(December 22, 2016)

Dear Brothers and Sisters,

[. . .]

Christmas is [. . .] the feast of the loving humility of God.

[. . .]

The logic of Christmas is the reversal of worldly logic, the logic of power and might.

[. . .]

In this [. . .] light [. . .] I have chosen as the theme of this, our yearly meeting, the reform of the Roman Curia.

[. . .]

Reform is first and foremost a sign of life, of a Church advancing on her pilgrim way, [. . .] in need of form because she is alive.

[. . .]

Reform will be effective only if it is carried out by men and women who are "renewed" and not simply "new."

[. . .]

In this process, it is normal, and indeed healthy, to encounter difficulties, which [. . .] might present themselves as different types of resistance. [. . .] Open resistance, [. . .] hidden resistance, [. . .] malicious resistance [. . .]. This last kind of resistance hides behind words of [. . .] accusation; it takes refuge in traditions, appearances, formalities [. . .]

The absence of reaction is a sign of death! Consequently, the good cases of resistance [. . .] are necessary and deserve to be listened to, welcomed and their expression encouraged. It is a sign that the body is alive.

[. . .]

Some Guiding Principles of the Reform

There are principally twelve [. . .]

1. **Individual responsibility** (personal conversion)

   Once again I reaffirm the importance of individual conversion,

381

without which all structural change would prove useless. The true soul of the reform lies in the men and women who are part of it and make it possible.

[. . .]

2. **Pastoral concern** (pastoral conversion)

[. . .] That [. . .] we may feel, cultivate and practice a sound pastoral sense, especially toward the people whom we meet each day. May no one feel overlooked or mistreated, but everyone experience, here first of all, the care and concern of the Good Shepherd. Behind every paper is a person.

[. . .]

3. **Missionary spirit** (Christocentrism)

[. . .] It is the chief aim of all forms of service in the Church to bring the Good News to the ends of the earth. [. . .] Without new life and an authentic evangelical spirit [. . .] any new structure will soon prove ineffective.

4. **Organizational clarity**

[. . .] A clearer organization of the offices of the Roman Curia is needed to bring out the fact that each Dicastery[8] has its own areas of competence. These areas of competence must be respected, but they must also be distributed in a reasonable, efficient and productive way. [. . .]

5. Improved functioning

The eventual merging of two or more Dicasteries competent in similar or closely connected matters to create a single Dicastery serves on the one hand to give the latter greater importance (even externally). On the other hand, the closeness and interaction of individual bodies within a single Dicastery contributes to improved functioning.
[. . .]

6. Modernization (updating)

This involves an ability to read and listen to the "signs of the times" [. . .] as requested by the Second Vatican Council: "the departments of the Roman Curia should be reorganized in a manner more appropriate to the needs of our time and of different regions and rites, especially in regard to their number, their titles, their competence [. . .] and how they coordinate their activities."

7. **Sobriety**

Here, what is called for is a simplification and streamlining of the Curia. This involves [. . .] the possible suppression of offices that no longer correspond to contingent needs, [. . .] the reduction of Commissions, Academies, Committees, etc. [. . .]

8. **Subsidiarity**

This involves the reordering of areas of competence specific to the various Dicasteries, transferring them if necessary from one Dicastery to another, in order to achieve [. . .] subsidiarity in areas of competence and effective interaction in service.
[. . .]

9. **Synodality**

The work of the Curia must be synodal [. . .]

Synodality must also be evident in the work of each Dicastery. [. . .]

10. **Catholicity**

[. . .] The Curia must reflect the catholicity of the Church in the hiring of personnel from all over the world [. . .]. Also of great importance is an enhanced role for women and lay people in the life of the Church and their integration into roles of leadership in the Dicasteries, with particularly attention paid to multiculturalism.

11. **Professionalism**

Each Dicastery must adopt a policy of continuing formation for its personnel, to avoid their falling into a rut or becoming stuck in a bureaucratic routine. Equally essential is the definitive abolition of the practice of *promoveatur ut amoveatur.* This is a cancer.

12. **Gradualism** (discernment)

Gradualism has to do with the necessary discernment entailed by historical processes, [. . .] assessment, correction, experimentation, and approvals *ad experimentum.* In these cases, then, it is not a matter of indecisiveness [. . .] but of the flexibility needed to achieve a true reform.

■ ■ ■ ■

8
A DESTINY

■ ■ ■ ■

8

A DESTINY

Meeting up twice during the day . . . suspended time. Everything is possible and yet the distance is still here. How does the Pope avoid being crushed by his responsibilities, his many activities, not to mention the unstinting relationships of internal forces, connected to the reality of an institution that is so human, so eternal? For once I try to speak directly about the man himself. But the preservation of modesty and respect for private life are so indispensable in an age that is drunk on self-expression and voyeurism. What is a destiny so close to Europe and at the same time so profoundly inscribed in the history of Argentina, one of the most magical symbols of this "New World," which, in the end, is so different? Here, there is no theater in the simple commentary on a few events and a few connections. How does the banality of a life story, which is ordinary although deeply marked by immigration, coexist with the encounter with God? What can be said on the subject in a dialogue, inevitably limited in time, with a French intellectual? Isn't silence, mentioned so often in our exchanges, enough? The Pope has always been marked — I would almost say it is embedded in him — by what he calls "big politics," politics with a capital P, the kind that is a match for the Gospel and for history. With his share of indignation. And, at the same time, all of this can only be understood in the light of faith, which has a different logic of dialogue than the one that exists between us. Always bearing in mind the diversity of the contexts in which our exchanges will be received, by many readers on different continents . . .

INTERVIEW — OCTOBER AND DECEMBER 2016

In October, Rome is mild once again and everything is calmer. In December, the climate reminds me of the atmosphere of my first trip, in February 2016. The Romans are there, peacefully, in their city. Everything is gentler than in Paris. We bring everything full circle, the circle of this experience, this encounter with the Holy Father, whose charity and open-ness of mind are a constant presence, along with a great will and an indignation, no less real, in response to the world. Yes, he is happy, but he is nobody's fool, and he is entirely enveloped in the faith that has barely anything to do with our dialogue.

Two new meetings to finish this dialogue, to reply to certain points, not to reach a conclusion, but to locate the ellipses. We will meet up again in January and February 2017 to talk about the manuscript.

The Vatican is still there, vast and tiny in the face of time and history, peaceful and almost silent compared to Saint Peter's Square, which is still so close by and so noisy. And still there are these men, not many of them now, walking in silence through this little space. They cross the courtyards, they go in and out of the buildings, barely speaking to one another . . . And I don't yet fully understand how the conditions of this meeting, so authentic, just, honest, natural and respectful, have come about. Such a human dialogue, spread over the months of a year. The fragility and grandeur, in the end, of humanity — isn't that also what lies at the heart of the Church? And in most religions, after all? And in all forms of secular universalism?

INTERVIEW — JANUARY
AND FEBRUARY 2017

Winter has returned. It is almost cold. Wind and drizzle over Rome. The vegetation and the stones have engaged in another dialogue, with subtler lights. There are not so many people in front of Saint Peter's now. The rain on the square changes the atmosphere, as do the pilgrims and visitors in their cagoules. I can't wait to meet up with the Pope to collect his observations on the manuscript. He is grateful to me for coming all the way here to talk to him again.

He arrived with the text under his arm, like a university colleague. We sit down around this impractical low table, and spend a long time turning all the pages to evaluate what we have said. We agree about almost all of his suggestions. There is no censorship on his part, just a wish to be as close as possible to what he said during our conversations. There is a lot of laughter about some of the things we have said. We delete a few passages in which people might recognize themselves. He is serene and contented. And so am I! Everything, from our first encounter to today's, has been conducted with exceptional understanding, sympathy and grace. I have no words, and no desire to try to find them.

The project, a considerable amount of work over more than two years, was fair, honest, human and free. A genuinely exceptional encounter. We talk about publications in several languages, about titles and planning. He says, "You're the only author, because you've done everything." Humor, always that humor. He compliments me on having grasped his thought and captured his personality, and on allowing our exchanges to flow. He is happy, and I am very touched by this meeting, by the prevailing atmosphere and by the result. A simple and accessible book in which the Pope speaks freely about his relationship with history, with society, with people. I am filled with nostalgia as soon as I walk across Saint Peter's Square. It is already dark, only a few people around at this time of the evening. The almost-silence reflects to my own. Time goes on.

DOMINIQUE WOLTON: What is the personal or collective event that has marked you most in your life?

POPE FRANCIS: A personal event is one thing; a collective event is something else.

DOMINIQUE WOLTON: Yes. For you personally, and in the world.

POPE FRANCIS: There is something which always caused me pain, even when I was a child. It's hatred and war. And the hatred of others. When I became aware of that hatred that some people feel for others, it caused me pain. On the world scale, it's hatred and war. But the joy I felt the day when the Second World War ended . . . Have I told you about that?

DOMINIQUE WOLTON: Yes.

POPE FRANCIS: You know, when my mother and neighbor used to talk over the wall, climbing on a chair . . . I remember that day as if it were yesterday; that lady called my mother while I was in the courtyard: "The war is over, the war is over!" And I felt joy, such joy . . . I was born in 1936, and the war ended in 1945. I don't know if that's the most important event, but it was an experience that I will never forget. When there is hatred, I suffer. Including the hatred that I myself, as a sinner, have felt many times for other people.

DW: What do you feel about murdered priests, or about the Eastern Christians, or about Father Hamel, in France, in the summer of 2016?

POPE FRANCIS: Grief.

DOMINIQUE WOLTON: What moves you most in life?

POPE FRANCIS: Acts of tenderness always make me feel good; understanding, forgiveness . . . But not only in the field of religion. Everywhere. When I was a child and I saw people arguing, it caused me pain. On the other hand, tenderness . . . Tenderness is something that brings me a lot of peace.

DOMINIQUE WOLTON: What makes you most angry?

POPE FRANCIS: Injustice. Selfish people. And myself, when I'm in that situation. And always injustice. Whenever I commit an act of injustice against anyone, it takes me a lot of time to convince myself that the Lord has punished me, and then to ask forgiveness of the person and do something to repair that injustice. But there are injustices that can't be repaired in life. And they are terrible.

DOMINIQUE WOLTON: You're greatest shortcoming?

POPE FRANCIS: I don't know how to put it . . . but it's a bit like the opposite of what people see in me. I have a certain tendency to laziness and taking the easy way. People think the opposite.

DOMINIQUE WOLTON: And your most important quality?

POPE FRANCIS: Quality . . . I would simply say that I like listening to other people. Because I discover that every life is different. And that each person has his or her own path. Listening. Not to gossip, to judge, but to open oneself up to different lifestyles or different kinds of success . . . There is also patience — for example, listening to certain old people who seem to be saying the same thing over and over again. That's a patience that comes naturally to me.

DOMINIQUE WOLTON: Yes, but you say that your shortcoming is laziness?

POPE FRANCIS: A tendency.

DOMINIQUE WOLTON: When have you been lazy in your life?

POPE FRANCIS: I don't know, but . . .

DOMINIQUE WOLTON: In my opinion, never. (*laughter*)

POPE FRANCIS: . . . since I was a child, probably, since I was very young: if I could pass an exam or a college test by studying as little as possible . . .

DOMINIQUE WOLTON: Yes, like all children. But today? What shortcoming today?

POPE FRANCIS: Oh, but I have so many!

DOMINIQUE WOLTON: Yes, I know, that's for your confessor. But just one.

POPE FRANCIS: It's this tendency that's part of my temperament, and I have to fight against it.

DOMINIQUE WOLTON: But that's quite a Latin American thing . . .

POPE FRANCIS: Yes, that's quite possible. I've never thought about it, but it's possible. But I can't say that, because they'd tear my eyes out!

DOMINIQUE WOLTON: We Europeans are always quick and anxious. I know Latin America a little, and what always strikes me about it straight away is the joy. Even in Argentina there's a joy, and a kind of tranquility in life. In Europe, there's no tranquility in life. There are those two World Wars, which are the background to everything, then those fifty years of East-West confrontation. A European is always someone anxious. And you Latinos are incredibly lucky, there have been small wars, but no big wars, so there is a kind of carefree attitude. And I think that's great. You bring that as a style to the pontificate, and you don't realize it. John Paul II is tragic, so is Benedict XVI, but you, a Latino, are "lighter," more "relaxed." What's more, it's obvious, and some traditionalist Catholics don't appreciate it . . . You laugh more easily, one can see that you have time to listen to people, you're not in a European psychological paradigm. I think millions of people perceive that difference.

POPE FRANCIS: I don't think that comes only from me, or from the Latin-American peoples. It's also bound up with the fact that there are younger churches. It's the young churches that have a freer attitude. In Africa, for example, where there's an inculturation of the liturgy, with dance, for example, where it wouldn't occur to anyone to have a Mass less than three hours long! The young churches are like that. In Europe, the churches are old. You have a Christianity that is 2,000 years old. I don't mean an aged Christianity, or rather, I do, but aged in the good sense of the word. I'll give you an example so that you can understand what I mean. Good wine, when it ages, becomes excellent. Bad wine, as it ages, turns to vinegar. Europe is good wine. It has become *añeja,* as we say in Spanish, meaning that it's better. But it may be that it takes away a little of its spontaneity and freshness.

DOMINIQUE WOLTON: I liked it when you said to the bishops, on September 16, 2016, "The world is weary of lying charmers, and, if I may be so bold, of fashionable priests and bishops." You remember? That was you, on September 16, talking to the new bishops! And you also spoke of "emotional illiteracy." You have some astonishing phrases. Perhaps fewer friends afterward, and a lot more enemies, but your phrases are remarkable. Where does it come from, this talent of yours to express yourself clearly, simply, making yourself understood by everyone with the right words? Has it always been like that? Did it come with age?

POPE FRANCIS: I've always talked like that. I don't really know why . . . . It doesn't come from my studies . . . .

DOMINIQUE WOLTON: Really? Always? Even when you were young?

POPE FRANCIS: It's how I am . . . It comes from the family. We're a big family, and on Sunday, around the table, with the grandparents, there were thirty-six, forty of us, and we talked a lot! It might come from that, I don't know.

DOMINIQUE WOLTON: The advantage is that, everywhere in the world, everyone understands you. It's short and very clear. Even John Paul II was more complicated.

POPE FRANCIS: He was a philosopher, and a university professor. But there was also something very good: because he was chaplain to the students, he had that simplicity . . .

DOMINIQUE WOLTON: But, in order to attain that simplicity, didn't it mean enduring a lot of personal suffering?

POPE FRANCIS: I've suffered, yes. At the age of twenty or twenty-one, I came close to death. They opened me up, from there to there, they took out part of my lungs. That was a time of terrible suffering. And then there has been "normal" suffering, like everyone has. Nothing extraordinary.

DOMINIQUE WOLTON: Usually, historically, popes don't talk a lot; they talk officially. You talk a lot. You're very media-friendly, and very popular too. My question is: isn't there a risk of a gap between what you say personally and your official statements? Or do you do that voluntarily to create another kind of communication that is more direct and beyond institutions?

POPE FRANCIS: I think prudence is necessary. Not a "cold" prudence, but one that allows us to understand the extent to which we can say things, and where we mustn't go. There are reactions, and I myself have made mistakes. I have made two or three mistakes in my way of saying things.

DOMINIQUE WOLTON: Since you've been Pope?

POPE FRANCIS: Yes, yes, since then. On the plane. Two or three times I've made mistakes.

DOMINIQUE WOLTON: The plane is a dangerous thing. The journalists are there, right in front of you. They are looking for anything that's forbidden. They like that. But, at the same time, it's brave of you to do it. There must be a limit, because your credibility is at stake. Journalists start by devouring, and then they throw it back. And for a pope, as for the president of a republic, that can be dangerous. They like you because you're very direct, but the day will come when they will say, *"Basta."* The question is, when?

POPE FRANCIS: There are some things that I can't say. Because I know it would be rude or imprudent. Or a breach of a secret that I'm supposed to keep. But I say what I can

403

say. And some people are shocked, that's true.

DOMINIQUE WOLTON: Do you think that, with that direct and human style, you can take things further more easily?

POPE FRANCIS: I think that's the pastoral style. I try not to talk like a professor, but like a pastor.

DOMINIQUE WOLTON: Good answer. Listening to you, looking at you, one can see this great freedom, a real revolt: you're angry. Or at least I perceive you as someone who's angry. Angry, not conformist. How have you managed to reconcile that freedom, that critical spirit, that irony, with all the constraints of the institutions that you've been through? How did you manage those contradictions?

POPE FRANCIS: There have been many occasions when I haven't succeeded in managing all of that.

DOMINIQUE WOLTON: Are you happy?

POPE FRANCIS: Yes, I'm happy. I'm happy. Not about being Pope, but the Lord gave me that and I pray not to do anything silly . . . And I do silly things!

DOMINIQUE WOLTON: (*laughter*) Careful, not too many silly things! The main thing that's made you happy since you've been Pope?

POPE FRANCIS: Meeting people.

DOMINIQUE WOLTON: As ever!

POPE FRANCIS: When I'm out and about.

DOMINIQUE WOLTON: Or, in other words, when you leave the "prison." (*laughter*) You're one of the few figures in the world who has such considerable symbolic responsibility. When the Pope says something, it's global. Don't you occasionally feel anxiety about your symbolic power?

POPE FRANCIS: I've never felt anxious, but when I get on to the plane with the journalists, I feel I'm going into the lions' den. And there I begin by praying, then I try to be very precise. There's a lot of pressure. But there have been a few slip-ups.

DOMINIQUE WOLTON: Never mind, it doesn't matter.

POPE FRANCIS: But no anxiety.

DOMINIQUE WOLTON: There have been many events in your life where one has sensed your conflicts with institutions, the "orders." When you were sent to Germany by the Jesuits, to finish your thesis, or when you spent so long in Córdoba[1] . . .

POPE FRANCIS: I don't know if I've told you this already, but, when I was a student, an old Jesuit gave me this advice: "Listen, if you want to get ahead, well, think clearly and speak obscurely." But I make an effort to speak clearly.

DOMINIQUE WOLTON: So you must have encountered a lot of difficulties . . .

POPE FRANCIS: Oh yes! But I hate hypocrisy. If I can't say something, I don't say it. But I'm not being hypocritical. Hypocrisy is something that revolts me.

DOMINIQUE WOLTON: And always has done?

POPE FRANCIS: It's in my temperament. And it's one of the insults that I used most when I was young: "Hypocrite!" "Hypocrite," said in a subtle way, but the word "hypocrite" has so many synonyms that mean the same thing. When you're young, you don't speak academically. You use those synonyms that we can't repeat here (*laughter*).

DOMINIQUE WOLTON: On the evening of March 13, 2013, the day of your election, when you first appeared on the balcony of Saint Peter's, you said, "Brothers and sisters, good evening!" It was so simple! It wasn't traditional.

POPE FRANCIS: What happened that day happened in a completely natural way. Because I wasn't thinking about it. At noon that day, I wasn't thinking of that possibility, and then all of a sudden . . . *pfft!* Everything happened with so much peace, a peace that has never left me, of course. I never thought about what I was going to say. I saw all those people in front of me . . . I was a little frightened. "Good evening" is what you say when you're greeting someone politely.

DOMINIQUE WOLTON: Yes, but it was completely unfamiliar. Because it was equality, equality between you and the people.

POPE FRANCIS: Yes, but that "good evening" was a normal greeting. I couldn't think of what else to say at that moment.

DOMINIQUE WOLTON: Why is Saint Matthew so important in your life?

POPE FRANCIS: Because I heard my calling, my vocation, on September 21, Saint Matthew's day. It was a powerful experience, which I've related several times. And then there is the office of readings on Saint Matthew's Day, the homily by the Venerable Bede. When I was in Rome, I lived at Paul VI House, Via della Scrofa. As I wasn't far away, I liked going to the Church of Saint Louis of the French to see Caravaggio's *Calling of Saint Matthew.*

DOMINIQUE WOLTON: You have said to me, "One must read the Gospel with an open mind, without prejudice, without preconceived ideas." Can you explain that?

POPE FRANCIS: It means that the Gospel has a power, which is the Word of God. And in the Word of God, in the Gospel, there is the Lord. That's what the Council [Vatican II] says. It's the Lord calling you. If I read the Gospel with a preconceived ideology, or with prejudice, I don't allow the Gospel in, I resist that Word.

It isn't a matter of reading literature: I can read the Gospel scientifically, analyzing the text: "This Greek word means this, and that means that." But I can also read the Gospel as a Christian, with an open mind and without preconceived ideas.

But I also told you that I wanted to add two things.

The first is the following: you asked me, "Where was God in Auschwitz?" and I told you that I hadn't seen God, I had only seen the work of man without God. That's what I said the other day. At the time, that was all I could see: what man without God is capable of. I've thought since then, and there's one thing that I didn't see at the time, but which I can say after having thought about it, even if the answer isn't spontaneous: it's that God was in the Christians who have been killed and beaten. God is always manifested in the flesh. That was the first thing, but it's a later reflection.

The other thing, which I think I said, but I'm not sure . . . . How does God communicate? It's curious, because he is a master of communication. God communicates by lowering himself. He communicates by tracing a path with his people. With the people of Israel, the slavery in Egypt . . . But always by humbling himself. He humbles himself in Christ. That's what theologians call "condescension," *syncatabasis, "kenosis,"* as the Church Fathers put it. But it's astonishing. God communicates by humbling himself. And thus every human communication, because man is in the image of God, must humble itself if it is to be a true communication. Putting oneself on the other person's level. Lowering oneself, not because the other person is inferior to me, but out of an act of humility, of freedom . . .

Thus — as I think I said before — the parents, the father and the mother, when they want to communicate with the child, they imitate the child's voice! They humble themselves. And they don't speak very correctly, they speak the language of children — "ba be bi." They humble themselves. I think I've said that before, but, if I haven't said it, it's important. It's a rule: if I don't go out of myself to go and look for the other person by abasing myself, no communication is possible! Communicating, to put it in a slightly more sophisticated way, is an act of humility. One cannot communicate without humility. It would be very interesting to analyze the speeches of the great dictators to see if one can find traces of humility in them. The language of the great dictators is . . . I don't know how to say it in Italian or in French. In Spanish, I would say, *"Yo, me, mi, conmigo y para mi."* ["I, me, myself, with me and for me."] In their speeches, the powerful dictators communicate with this confidence, they seem to be divine.

It's interesting. The language of smugness, of self-deification. On the other hand, the humble language that accompanies the other always humbles itself.

DOMINIQUE WOLTON: Yes, the phrase "self-humbling" is always a term that evokes hierarchy, relationships from the higher toward the lower. You are using it in a more human dimension. Self-abasement means going toward the other. With humility. It is an unusual concept. On the other hand, in the democratic vision, we speak of equality, and I don't know to what extent equality can contain humbling.

POPE FRANCIS: I think that, to be equal,

you have to put yourself on the level of the other person. And, in principle, I have to bring myself down to the level of the other, even if the other is superior to me. But it's always an act that consists of "going to the house of the other." I'm the one who has to go there. I have to take the first step. I must tell the other, as a first step to come into my way of seeing things, my way of thinking.

DOMINIQUE WOLTON: True equality consists precisely of being capable of being able to perform that act of abasement to go toward the other. And, we might say, there is theoretical equality and real equality.

POPE FRANCIS: Yes, theoretically everyone is equal. But in everyday life . . . It's a way of life geared toward service. It's a Christian way of life; Christian communication is service. "I came not to be served, but to serve," Jesus says in the Gospel.

DOMINIQUE WOLTON: Today, in globalization, with "democratic" ideology, the idea of humbling oneself to go and find the Other does not exist. We imagine that equality solves problems. But it isn't true. And you, when you say that "to communicate is to humble oneself," you introduce a new dimension which doesn't currently exist in democratic culture. In fact, you go beyond equality, you say that equality isn't enough. If you really want to communicate with the other, you have to go and find them where they are, and, most of the time, you have to humble yourself. In saying, "I humble myself," you are really going toward others. What you are saying is that communication is a movement "toward" and that one mustn't be afraid of humbling oneself.

POPE FRANCIS: Those are the two things I wanted to stress.

DOMINIQUE WOLTON: And I've forgotten one question. It's banal, and very important. What role do women play in your life?

POPE FRANCIS: Personally, I thank God that I have known some real women in my life. My two grandmothers were very different, but they were both real women. They were mothers, they worked, they were brave, they spent time with their grandchildren . . . But always with that womanly dimension . . . I remember it clearly. I still talk about my paternal grandmother, Rose, the one who took me to her house every morning when my mother gave birth. But there was also the other grandmother, Maria. For example, I remember the day of Prokofiev's death. I was at her house, with my grandfather as well, because, thank God, I had all four grandparents until I was quite old. The first one died when I was sixteen. A blessing. And Prokofiev died, and I loved music. During the year, we often spent three or four days in our grandparents' house, one set or the other, me and my brothers . . . During the holidays, three of us went to stay with those grandparents, and two with the others. That way, my mother and father were left in peace. After that, we swapped. They had two months without the children; they only saw us on Sundays or at the sports stadium, when we all went there together. So, one day, Prokofiev died, when I was sixteen, I think. I don't remember the date exactly.[2] And I started talking about music. I was fifteen or sixteen . . . Then I started dreaming about how much I would like to be a conductor . . . all those things that young people dream of. My grandmother listened to me patiently, and she said, "To do that, you have to study. And to study, you have to make an effort, you don't get there easily." She taught me quite naturally what work was, the role of work, of effort.

It was a blessing to have those two grandmothers. Then there was my mother. My mother . . . I saw my mother suffering, after having her last child — there were five — when she contracted an infection that left her unable to walk for a year. I saw her in pain. And I saw how careful she was not to waste anything. My father had a good job, he was an accountant, but his salary just enabled us to get to the end of the month. And I saw this mother, the way she faced problems, one after the other . . . And then a lovely image: every Saturday, my mother's family, who loved opera, would listen to the national Argentinian radio station, which broadcast an opera at two o'clock. My mother knew a lot about opera, because her father was a carpenter and he always sang operatic arias while he worked. And she passed them on to us, the four older children . . .

DOMINIQUE WOLTON: Italian operas?

POPE FRANCIS: Yes, Italian. Some French ones, too. I remember one she taught me *Mignon*,[3] and also *Manon*.[4] She explained the story to us, and then, at certain points, she said to us, "Listen to this passage, how lovely it is." It was all in the art. She was a wife, a mother. And then my sisters ... It's important for a man to have sisters, very important. Then there were my teenage friends, the "little girlfriends . . ." I've been enriched by the relationships I've always had with women. Even as an adult, I learned that women see things differently from men. Because when you have a decision that needs to be taken, when you face a problem, it's important to listen to both.

DOMINIQUE WOLTON: But how can you enhance the role of women in the Church, with a view to enriching dialogue between men and women?

POPE FRANCIS: It's very important. With the reform of the Curia, there will be a lot of women with the power to make decisions, not just advise. Because you don't have to be a priest to run an education department . . . There's already a woman vice-director at the Curia, in the Vatican press office . . .

DOMINIQUE WOLTON: I see very clearly what you're talking about, but there's still an imbalance.
It's true that men and women don't see reality in the same way. From a personal

point of view, have you met women, after your childhood and adolescence, who have made a mark on you?

POPE FRANCIS: Yes. There's one who taught me to think about political reality. She was a communist.

DOMINIQUE WOLTON: Is she still alive?

POPE FRANCIS: No . . . During the dictatorship, she was . . . *pfftt* . . . killed. She was captured in the same group as two French nuns, they were together. She was a chemist, the head of the department where I worked in the food science lab. She was a communist from Paraguay, from the party there that's called the Febreristas.[5] I remember she made me read the Rosenbergs' death sentence![6] She showed me what lay behind that sentence. She gave me books, all communist books, but she taught me to think about politics. I owe that woman a lot.

DOMINIQUE WOLTON: A terrible thing, the Rosenberg case.

POPE FRANCIS: Were they really guilty? I remember she said to me, "You know that when they gave them permission to say their goodbyes, before going to the electric chair, they held hands, and they were in handcuffs?" Inhuman. That was when she taught me the inhuman logic of that policy. I owe that woman so much. To the extent that, when the persecution began, she invited me over; I was already a priest, but not yet a superior. And she called me to say, "Jorge, my mother-in-law (who was very Catholic) isn't very well. I don't suppose you could come and give her extreme unction?" When she was a communist. "Yes, I'll come." I knew her mother-in-law. "Then come with the pickup, the truck; it'll be easier to get to our district that way." I worked out that she wanted to move something. That was it. We took away her books, because she was afraid they would go to her house and find communist books. She would have been arrested. I saw her often, and I always found her very respectful of my choice in life. I owe that woman a lot, because she was the woman who taught me to think. I met up with her children . . .

DOMINIQUE WOLTON: What was her name?

POPE FRANCIS: Esther Ballestrino De Careaga.[7]

DOMINIQUE WOLTON: Esther, an Old Testament name.

POPE FRANCIS: Yes. She had three children. One lives in Sweden, the other two live in Argentina, but they went to Asunción, in Paraguay, to meet up with me when I went there. They told me again and again how much their mother loved me. That woman really taught me to think.

DOMINIQUE WOLTON: And today, in spite of your responsibilities, do you manage to have friendly relations with women?

POPE FRANCIS: No, really friendly, friendly, I wouldn't say that, but good relations, yes. My two women friends died when I was in Buenos Aires, very beautiful people, they died. But, yes, there are women I have very good contact with, women I discuss things with . . .

DOMINIQUE WOLTON: Do you think you will succeed in reforming the Curia to give more room to women?

POPE FRANCIS: Yes, yes, I think so. Because there isn't as much misogyny as that. That's not the problem, there are others.

DOMINIQUE WOLTON: Is it more a question of otherness, of a lack of familiarity? And shyness, too? Men's shyness with women? Particularly when they're priests? After a while . . . it isn't necessarily misogynist, it becomes uncommunication.

POPE FRANCIS: Yes. When they see how much better women are at doing things, there's no problem. That's not where the problem lies, it's something else . . .

DOMINIQUE WOLTON: What will the problem be?

POPE FRANCIS: The problem of power. We're working on it. But I think that today, here, among sensible people, there is no problem. But it's going to be difficult.

DOMINIQUE WOLTON: Reform of the Curia is a difficult task. Will you succeed with that?

POPE FRANCIS: Yes . . . An old cardinal said to me: "Don't be discouraged, because the road to Curial reform is difficult. And the Curia doesn't need to be reformed, it needs to be got rid of!" (*laughter*) Joking, obviously!

DOMINIQUE WOLTON: At the same time, it's an image. Sometimes you have to be radical. But it's difficult.

POPE FRANCIS: But he said that as a joke. It's unthinkable; the Curia is indispensable. And there have been so many fine men, so many! There have been a few saints, men of God. You know what they say, a falling tree makes more noise than a growing forest.

DOMINIQUE WOLTON: That's nice. The other day, I saw Cardinal Tauran.[8]

POPE FRANCIS: He's from Bordeaux.

DOMINIQUE WOLTON: Yes. What a marvel of speed and intelligence.

POPE FRANCIS: I see him as a friend.

DOMINIQUE WOLTON: He's very fond of you too. Monsignor Tauran has been at the heart of all the political communication of the Church for half a century.

POPE FRANCIS: He knows how to find the ways. He is a man who communicates. And he is good at communicating. Because he engages in dialogue with everyone. I see him talking to nonbelievers, Buddhists, Muslims, with everybody. He talks. And even when he doesn't agree, he says so. But he knows the wisdom of dialogue.

DOMINIQUE WOLTON: I agree. Let's return to the topic of interreligious dialogue. I think you wanted to add something about rigorism[9] . . .

POPE FRANCIS: Behind every form of rigidity, there is an inability to communicate. And I've always found . . . Take those rigid priests who are afraid of communication, take rigid politicians . . . It's a form of fundamentalism, which is a rigidity. When I come across a rigid person, particularly a young one, I immediately say to myself that they're sick. The danger is that they're looking for security.

While we're on that subject, I can tell you an anecdote. When I was master of novices, in 1972, for a year or two, we accompanied the candidates who wanted to join the Society. They studied at university and, on Saturdays and Sundays, they came to us. They played sport at the novitiate, they talked to their spiritual director, but they had no direct relationship with me; they didn't even look at me, I wasn't anyone important. They were given interviews, and they also had to sit for some quite advanced examinations, such as Rorschach tests, with a good team including a believing Catholic psychiatrist who studied there. I accompanied those young men to the tests. I remember one of them, who was visibly a bit rigid, but who had great intellectual qualities, and who I thought was of a very high standard. There were others, much less brilliant, who I wasn't sure would pass. I thought they would be rejected because they were having difficulties, but in the end they were allowed through because they had that ability to grow, to succeed. And when that first student's test came in they said no straight away. "But why? He's so intelligent, he has plenty of positive qualities." "There's a problem," they explained. "He's a bit stiff, a bit artificial about certain things, a bit rigid." "And why's he like that? Because he isn't sure of himself."

One senses that these men are unconsciously aware that they are "psychologically ill." But they don't know it, they feel it. It's unconscious, they don't know. So they look for strong structures that protect them in life. They become policemen, they join the army or the Church. Strong institutions, to protect themselves. They do their work well, but once they feel they're in safety, unconsciously, the sickness manifests itself. And that's when the problems arise. And I asked, "But, doctor, how can you explain that? I don't really understand." And she said this: "Have you never wondered why there are policemen who are torturers? Those young men, when they arrived, were decent young men, they were good, but sick. Then they became sure of themselves, and the sickness manifested itself."

I'm afraid of rigidity. I'd rather have a chaotic young man, with normal problems, who gets annoyed about things . . . because all those contradictions will help him to grow. We've already talked about the differences between the Argentinians and the French . . . The Argentinians are very much attached to psychoanalysis, that's true. In Buenos Aires, there's a very smart neighborhood, a neighborhood called Villa Freud. That's the district where all the psychoanalysts are.

DOMINIQUE WOLTON: But that's a disaster. You should never put several psychoanalysts together, because they'll become pretentious. That isn't to say that psychoanalysis isn't one of the greatest intellectual and cultural revolutions of the twentieth century!

POPE FRANCIS: But they aren't all the same. Some of them are like that. But I've also known some who were very human, very open to humanism and to dialogue with other sciences as well, with medicine . . .

DOMINIQUE WOLTON: Yes, of course! When they're doctors, they're often better, because they know about the art of healing. I've known that for a long time, through my immediate entourage. When they're intellectuals, on the other hand . . .

POPE FRANCIS: But when they engage with science . . . I know one, for example, who is very clever, a fine woman, in her fifties, more or less. She works in Buenos Aires, but she comes three times a year and gives classes, a week in Spain and a week in Germany. She has found a good form of dialogue with medicine and physics. It's interesting; she's found a way of enriching psychoanalytic analysis with homeopathy and a lot of other sciences.

But the ones I've known helped me a lot at a time in my life when I needed to consult someone. I consulted a Jewish psychoanalyst. For six months, I went to her once a week to clear up certain things. She was very good. Very professional as a doctor and as a psychoanalyst, but she always stayed where she was. And then, one day, when she was on the brink of death, she called me. Not for the sacraments, because she was Jewish, but for a spiritual dialogue. A very good person. She helped me a lot for six months; I was already forty-two at the time.

DOMINIQUE WOLTON: We may all need a dialogue of this kind, with a psychiatrist or a psychoanalyst, to get some distance when we're unhappy. When the profession is practiced well, it's like the priest's. The comparison with the priest exists, and, besides, a good psychiatrist is often a person who takes on other people's pain. The psychiatrist heals other people and "absorbs" their diseases. They take on other people's sorrow, just as a priest does. Psychical closeness . . .

POPE FRANCIS: Accompaniment is a difficult process.

426

DOMINIQUE WOLTON: Do you miss Argentina?

POPE FRANCIS: No, no. It's a curious thing. I came here with a little suitcase and a return ticket, because there was no chance for me, I didn't even think about it, there were three or four "big" names. According to the bookmakers in London, I was at number forty-two or forty-six. They said I was just a *kingmaker.*

DOMINIQUE WOLTON: Ah, *you speak English?*

POPE FRANCIS: *So-so . . .* The bookmakers thought that this man Bergoglio would bring a different vision from Latin America, which would help them to choose the next pope, to say, "This one's better than that one . . ." When things changed from one hour to the next, I felt a great peace. And that peace hasn't left me, even today. I think that peace is a gift from the Lord. I think that's why I haven't missed Argentina.

DOMINIQUE WOLTON: Why do you always ask people to pray for you?

POPE FRANCIS: Because I need it . . . I

need it. Because I am supported by the prayer of the people. Really.

ADDRESS OF HIS HOLINESS POPE FRANCIS ON THE OCCASION OF HIS VISIT TO THE UNITED NATIONS OFFICE AT NAIROBI (UNON), KENYA

(November 26, 2015)

[. . .]

In a few days an important meeting on climate change will be held in Paris, where the international community as such will once again confront these issues. It would be sad, and I dare say even catastrophic, were particular interests to prevail over the common good and lead to manipulating information to protect their own plans and projects.

[. . .]

The Paris Agreement can give a clear signal in this direction, provided that, as I stated before the UN General Assembly, we avoid "every temptation to fall into a declarationist nominalism which would assuage our consciences. We need to ensure that our institutions are truly effective."[10] For this reason I express my hope that COP21 will achieve a global and "transformational" agreement based on the principles of solidarity, justice, equality and participation; an agreement which targets three complex and interdependent goals: lessening the impact of climate change, fighting poverty and ensuring respect for human dignity.

For all the difficulties involved, there is a growing "conviction that our planet is a homeland and that humanity is one people living in a common home."[11] No country "can act independently of a common responsibility. If we truly desire positive change, we have to humbly accept our interdependence."[12] The problem arises whenever we think of interdependence as a synonym for domination, or the subjection of some to the interest of others, of the powerless to the powerful.

[. . .]

We need to be alert to one sad sign of the "globalization of indifference": the fact that we are gradually growing accustomed to the suffering of others, as if it were something normal,[13] or, even worse, becoming resigned to such extreme and scandalous kinds of "using and discarding" and social exclusion as new forms of slavery, human trafficking, forced labor, prostitution and trafficking in organs. "There has been a tragic rise in the number of migrants seeking to flee from the growing poverty aggravated by environmental degradation. They are not recognized by international conventions as refugees; they bear the loss of the lives they have left behind without enjoying any legal protection whatsoever."[14] Many lives, many stories, many dreams have been shipwrecked in our day. We cannot remain indifferent in the face of this. We have no right.

Together with neglect of the environment, we have witnessed for some time now a rapid process of urbanization, which in many cases has unfortunately led to a "disproportionate and unruly growth of many cities which have become unhealthy to live in [and] efficient."[15] [. . .]

Here, I would offer a word of encouragement to all those working on the local and international levels to ensure that the process of urbanization becomes an effective means for development and integration. This means working to guarantee for everyone, especially those living in outlying neighborhoods, the basic rights to dignified living conditions and to land, lodging and labor. [. . .] The forthcoming Habitat-III Conference, planned for Quito in October 2016, could be a significant occasion for identifying ways of responding to these issues.

In a few days, Nairobi will host the tenth Ministerial Conference of the World Trade Organization. In 1967, my predecessor, Pope Paul VI, contemplating an increasingly interdependent world and foreseeing the current reality of globalization, reflected on how commercial relationships between states could prove a fundamental element for the development of peoples or, on the other hand, a cause of extreme poverty and exclusion.[16] [. . .]

It is my hope that the deliberations of the forthcoming Nairobi Conference will not be a simple balancing of conflicting interests, but a genuine service to care for our common home and the integral development of persons, especially those in greatest need. I would especially like to echo the concern of all those groups engaged in projects of development and health care — including those religious congregations which serve the poor and those most excluded — with regard to agreements on intellectual property and access to medicines and essential health care. Regional free-trade treaties dealing with the protection of intellectual property, particularly in the areas of pharmaceuticals and biotechnology, should not only maintain intact the powers already granted to states by multilateral agreements, but should also be a means for ensuring a minimum of health care and access to basic treatment for all. Multilateral discussions, for their part, should allow poorer countries the time, the flexibility and the exceptions needed for them to comply with trade regulations in an orderly and relatively smooth manner. [. . .]

In the context of economic relationships between states and between peoples, we cannot be silent about forms of illegal trafficking which arise in situations of poverty and in turn lead to greater poverty and exclusion. Illegal trade in diamonds and precious stones, rare metals or those of great strategic value, wood, biological material and animal products, such as ivory trafficking and the related killing of elephants, fuels political instability, organized crime and terrorism. This situation too is a cry rising up from humanity and the earth itself, one which needs to be heard by the international community.

[. . .]

Once again, I express the support of the Catholic community, and my own, to continue to pray and work so that the fruits of regional cooperation, expressed today in the African Union and the many African agreements on commerce, cooperation and development, may be vigorously pursued and always take into account the common good of the sons and daughters of this land.

May the blessing of the Most High be with each of you and your peoples. Thank you!

ADDRESS OF HIS HOLINESS POPE FRANCIS TO THE PARTICIPANTS IN THE INTERNATIONAL PEACE CONFERENCE, AL-AZHAR CONFERENCE CENTER, CAIRO, EGYPT

(April 28, 2017)

As-salamu alaykum!

I consider it a great gift to be able to begin my visit to Egypt here, and to address you in the context of this International Peace Conference. I thank my brother, the Grand Imam, for having planned and organized this Conference, and for kindly inviting me to take part. I would like to offer you a few thoughts, drawing on the glorious history of this land, which over the ages has appeared to the world as *a land of civilizations* and *a land of covenants.*

A land of civilizations.

From ancient times, the culture that arose along the banks of the Nile was

435

synonymous with civilization. Egypt lifted the lamp of knowledge, giving birth to an inestimable cultural heritage, made up of wisdom and ingenuity, mathematical and astronomical discoveries, and remarkable forms of architecture and figurative art. The quest for knowledge and the value placed on education were the result of conscious decisions on the part of the ancient inhabitants of this land, and were to bear much fruit for the future. Similar decisions are needed for our own future, decisions of peace and for peace, for there will be no peace without the proper education of coming generations. Nor can young people today be properly educated unless the training they receive corresponds to the nature of man as an open and relational being.

[. . .]

Three basic areas, if properly linked to one another, can assist in this dialogue: *the duty to respect one's own identity and that of others, the courage to accept differences,* and *sincerity of intentions.*

The duty to respect one's own identity and that of others, because true dialogue cannot be built on ambiguity or a willingness to sacrifice some good for the sake of pleasing others. *The courage to accept differences,* because those who are different, either culturally or religiously, should not be seen or treated as enemies, but rather welcomed as fellow-travelers, in the genuine conviction that the good of each resides in the good of all. *Sincerity of intentions,* because dialogue, as an authentic expression of our humanity, is not a strategy for achieving specific goals, but rather a path to truth, one that deserves to be undertaken patiently, in order to transform competition into cooperation.

[. . .]

May the sun of a renewed fraternity in the name of God rise in this sun-drenched land, to be the dawn of a *civilization of peace and encounter.* May Saint Francis of Assisi, who eight centuries ago came to Egypt and met Sultan Malik al Kamil, intercede for this intention!

A land of covenants

In Egypt, not only did the sun of wisdom rise, but also the variegated light of the religions shone in this land. Here, down the centuries, differences of religion constituted "a form of mutual enrichment in the service of the one national community."[17] Different faiths met and a variety of cultures blended without being confused, while acknowledging the importance of *working together for the common good.* Such "covenants" are urgently needed today. Here, I would take as a symbol the "Mount of the Covenant" which rises up in this land. Sinai reminds us above all that authentic covenants on earth cannot ignore heaven, that human beings cannot attempt to encounter one another in peace by eliminating God from the horizon, nor can they climb the mountain to appropriate God for themselves.[18]

[. . .]

Our world has seen the globalization of many useful technical instruments, but also a globalization of indifference and negligence, and it moves at a frenetic pace that is difficult to sustain. As a result, there is renewed interest in the great questions about the meaning of life. These are the questions that the religions bring to the fore, reminding us of our origins and ultimate calling. We are not meant to spend all our energies on the uncertain and shifting affairs of this world, but to journey toward the

Absolute that is our goal. For all these reasons, especially today, religion is not a problem but a part of the solution: against the temptation to settle into a banal and uninspired life, where everything begins and ends here below, religion reminds us of the need to lift our hearts to the Most High in order to learn how to build the city of man.

To return to the image of Mount Sinai, I would like to mention the commandments that were promulgated there, even before they were sculpted on tablets of stone. At the center of this "Decalogue," there resounds, addressed to each individual and to people of all ages, the commandment, "Thou shalt not kill."[19]

[. . .]

Together, in the land where heaven and earth meet, this land of covenants between peoples and believers, let us say once more a firm and clear "No!" to every form of violence, vengeance and hatred carried out in the name of religion or in the name of God. Together let us affirm the incompatibility of violence and faith, belief and hatred. Together let us declare the sacredness of every human life against every form of violence, whether physical, social, educational or psychological. [. . .]

Religion, however, is not meant only to unmask evil; it has an intrinsic vocation to promote peace, today perhaps more than ever. Without giving in to forms of facile syncretism, our task is that of praying for one another, imploring from God the gift of peace, encountering one another, engaging in dialogue and promoting harmony in the spirit of cooperation and friendship.

[. . .]

In order to prevent conflicts and build peace, it is essential that we spare no effort in eliminating situations of poverty and exploitation where extremism more easily takes root, and in blocking the flow of money and weapons destined to those who provoke violence. Even more radically, an end must be put to the proliferation of arms; if they are produced and sold, sooner or later they will be used. Only by bringing into the light of day the murky maneuverings that feed the cancer of war can its real causes be prevented. National leaders, institutions and the media are obliged to undertake this urgent and grave task. So too are all of us who play a leading role in culture; each in his or her own area, we are charged by God, by history and by the future to initiate processes of peace, seeking to lay a solid basis for agreements between peoples and states. It is my hope that this noble and beloved land of Egypt, with God's help, may continue to respond to the calling it has received to be a land of civilization and covenant, and thus to contribute to the development of processes of peace for its beloved people and for the entire region of the Middle East.

As-salamu alaykum![20]

ACKNOWLEDGMENTS

I have wanted to write this book for two and a half years. With this in mind, I wrote to Pope Francis personally, setting out the tenor of the project and telling him the plan for the book. My publications over many years, as well as the three books of interviews, illustrated the seriousness of my proposition. I acted without knowing his entourage. The two French Cardinals, Monsignor Philippe Barbarin and Monsignor André Vingt-Trois, confirmed the interest of such a project. I thank them warmly. I worked alone, to avoid the problem of being overwhelmed by information, documentation and testimonies concerning this "unexpected" pope.

The positive reply arrived quite quickly. Father Louis de Romanet, whom I know, agreed to accompany me on this adventure, to translate and because he knows the Vatican from having worked at the State

Secretariat. Thanks also to the canons of the Lateran who put me up when necessary, near the basilica of Saint Peter in Chains. Thanks also to Cardinal Jean-Louis Tauran, and to the Pope's personal secretariat for their discretion and efficiency. Stéphane Martin also helped me with institutional relations with the Vatican.

I would like to thank Fulvia Musolino for her translation and Laure Hinckel for the help she gave me in the preparation of this book. Last of all, the team at the international journal *Hermès,* at CNRS, Sophie Bied-Charreton, David Rochefort and Émilie Silvoz helped me with this work, which was inevitably long, unfamiliar and somewhat complicated. I thank them all, as I thank the few people with whom I have been able to discuss this project which, in the end, goes beyond the writing of a book.

SOME QUOTES FROM
POPE FRANCIS

During our conversations, the Pope, who has the gift of expressing himself simply, directly and sometimes provocatively, came out with some surprising phrases. Some of them are in the book, others not. I've chosen a few that I quote, here, at random:

"The only key that opens the door of communication is humility."

"Four evils of the press: disinformation, slander, defamation, coprophilia."

"My favorite words? Joy, tenderness, closeness, amazement, wonder."

"Communicating means humbling oneself as Christ did with man."

"Tradition is doctrine on the move. It is a movement."

"Secularization includes a denial of transcendence."

"Differences always help us to grow."

"Where is God in Auschwitz? I haven't seen

God, I have only seen the work of man without God."

"God communicates by humbling himself."

" 'Downloading': the best link is the link of the heart."

"Jesus doesn't like paths half traveled, doors left half open, having it both ways."

"Don't confuse happiness with a sofa."

"Our answer to this world at war has a name: fraternity."

"Beware of the temptation to take 'early retirement.' "

"Refugees are our brothers. The Christian excludes no one."

"Terrorism is not a religion. But how many young people have we Europeans left empty of ideals?"

"The world is weary of lying charmers. And, I would even say, 'fashionable priests' or 'fashionable bishops.' "

"Preach — make our ministry an *icon of modernity.*"

"Pay attention to 'emotional illiteracy.' "

"What should we do with young people? Follow them while guiding them."

"Politics may be one of the greatest acts of charity. Because to engage with politics is to engage with the needs of the people."

"It's a rule: if I don't go out of myself to go in search of the other by humbling myself, no communication is possible!"

"It's a Christian way of life: Christian communication is service. 'I didn't come to be served, but to serve,' Jesus says in the Gospel."

"The Bible tells us that God hears the cry of His people, and I wish to join my voice to yours in calling for the three Ls for all our brothers and sisters: land, lodging and labor. I have said it before and I say it again: these are sacred rights."

"Make bridges, not walls, because walls fall."

BIOGRAPHY OF POPE FRANCIS

The first pope from the Americas is the Argentinian Jesuit Jorge Mario Bergoglio, seventy-six, Archbishop of Buenos Aires. He is a leading light for the whole continent, and a simple and well-loved pastor in his diocese, which he visited from end to end, not least by metro and bus, during the fifteen years of his episcopal ministry. "My people are poor, and I am one of them," he has said on a number of occasions, to explain his choice of living in an apartment and preparing his own meals. He has always recommended that his priests show mercy and apostolic courage, and that they open the doors to everyone. The worst thing that can happen in the Church, he has explained several times, "is what De Lubac calls spiritual worldliness," which means "putting oneself at the center." And when he cites social justice, he first of all invites us to pick up the catechism again, and to rediscover the Ten Commandments and the Beatitudes. His project is a simple one: if one follows Christ, one understands that "trampling on a person's dignity is a grave sin."

In spite of his discreet character — his official biography is only a few lines long, at least until his nomination as Archbishop of Buenos Aires — he has become a point of reference because of his strong positions during the dramatic economic crisis that afflicted his country in 2001.

He was born in the Argentinian capital on December 17, 1936, the son of Piedmontese immigrants: his father, Mario, was an accountant, while his mother, Regina Sivori, took care of the house and brought up her five children.

Graduating as a chemical technician, he then chose the path of the priesthood and entered the diocesan seminary of Villa Devoto. On March 11, 1956, he moved on to the novitiate of the Society of Jesus. On May 11, 1958 he completed his studies in literature in Chile and, in 1961, returned to Argentina, where he obtained a master's in philosophy at the Colegio de San José in San Miguel. Between 1964 and 1965 he was professor of literature and psychology at the Colegio de la Inmaculada Concepción in

Santa Fé, and, in 1966, he taught the same subjects at the Colegio del Salvador in Buenos Aires. Between 1967 and 1970 he studied theology, obtaining a master's degree, again at the Colegio de San José.

He was ordained as a priest on December 13, 1969, by Archbishop Ramón José Castellano. He underwent preparatory training between 1970 and 1971 in Alcalá de Henares in Spain, and, on April 22, 1974, he took perpetual profession as a Jesuit. Back in Argentina, he was master of novices at the Colegio de San José in San Miguel, professor at the faculty of theology, provincial consultor of the Society of Jesus and rector of the college.

On July 31, 1973, he was elected a provincial (the superior of a Catholic province) of the Jesuits of Argentina, a post that he occupied for six years. He then resumed his work in universities and, between 1980 and 1986, he was once again appointed rector of the Colegio de San José, and priest in San Miguel. In March 1986, he went to Germany to finish his doctoral thesis; his superiors then sent him to the Colegio del Salvador in Buenos Aires and then to the Jesuit Church in the city of Córdoba, as spiritual director and confessor.

It was Cardinal Antonio Quarracino who

wanted him as his close collaborator in Buenos Aires. So, on May 20, 1992, John Paul II appointed him Titular Bishop of Auca and Auxiliary Bishop of Buenos Aires. On June 27, in the cathedral, he received episcopal ordination from the hands of the cardinal himself. He chose as his motto *Miserando atque eligendo* ("By showing mercy and by choosing"), and included in his coat of arms the Christogram IHS, the symbol of the Society of Jesus. He gave his first interview as bishop to a small parish newspaper, *Estrellita de Belém*. He was immediately appointed episcopal vicar of the district of Flores and, on December 21, 1993, he also received the position of Vicar General of the Archdiocese. So it was no surprise when, on June 3, 1997, he was made Coadjutor Archbishop of Buenos Aires. Less than nine months later, with the death of Cardinal Quarracino, he succeeded him, on February 28, 1998, as Archbishop, Primate of Argentina and Ordinary for the faithful of the Eastern Rite who were resident in the country and without an ordinary of their own rite.

Three years later, at the consistory on February 21, 2001, John Paul II appointed him cardinal, assigning him the title of Cardinal Priest of San Roberto Bellarmino. He invited the faithful not to go to Rome to celebrate his cardinalship, and instead to give the money for the trip to the poor. Grand Chancellor of the Catholic University of Argentina, he was the author of the books *Meditaciones para Religiosos* (Meditations for the Religious) (1982), *Reflexiones sobre la Vida Apostólica* (Reflections on the Apostolic Life) (1986) and *Reflexiones de Esperanza* (Reflections of Hope) (1992).

In October 2001, he was appointed relator (recording secretary) at the tenth Ordinary General Assembly of the Synod of Bishops, devoted to the episcopal ministry, a post passed to him at the last moment, replacing Cardinal Edward Michael Egan, Archbishop of New York, who was obliged to stay in his own country after the terrorist attacks on September 11. At the synod, he placed particular emphasis on the "prophetic mission of the bishop," his identity as a "prophet of justice," his duty to "preach ceaselessly" the Church's social doctrine, but also to "express an authentic judgment on matters of faith and morals."

Meanwhile, in Latin America, he became an increasingly popular figure. However he did not lose the sobriety of his character and his rigorous lifestyle, which some people call almost "ascetic." It was in this spirit that, in 2002, he refused to be appointed President of the Argentinian Episcopal Conference, but three years later he was elected and then reconfirmed for a new three-year period in 2008. In the meantime, in April 2005, he took part in the conclave that saw the election of Benedict XVI.

As Archbishop of Buenos Aires — a diocese of more than 3 million inhabitants — he initiated a missionary project based on communion and evangelization. The four main goals were: open and fraternal communities; active participation of a laity with the missionary spirit; evangelization addressed to all the inhabitants of the city; visits to the poor and the sick. He aimed to re-evangelize Buenos Aires, "taking into account those who live there, its configuration, its history." He invited priests and laypeople to work together. In September 2009, he launched a solidarity campaign to celebrate the bicentenary of the country's independence: two hundred works of charity to be performed between then and 2016. And, on the continental level, he continued to nurture powerful hopes in the wake of the message of the Aparecida Conference in 2007, which he went so far as to name the "*Evangelii Nuntiandi* of Latin America."

Until the start of the Vacancy of the Holy See, he was a member of the Congregations for Divine Worship and the Discipline of the Sacraments, for the Clergy, for the Institutes of the Consecrated Life and the Societies of Apostolic Life, of the Pontifical Council for the Family and of the Pontifical Commission for Latin America.[1]

SELECT BIBLIOGRAPHY OF POPE FRANCIS

1. Encyclicals

Laudato Si' (Praise Be to You), encyclical letter on care for our common home, May 24, 2015.

Lumen Fidei (The Light of Faith), encyclical letter to the bishops, priests and deacons, consecrated persons and the lay faithful, on faith, June 29, 2013.

2. Apostolic Exhortations

Amoris Laetitia (The Joy of Love), on love in the family, March 19, 2016.

Evangelii Gaudium (The Joy of the Gospel), exhortation to bishops, priests and deacons, consecrated persons and the lay faithful, on the proclamation of the Gospel in today's world, November 24, 2013.

3. Apostolic Letters

Apostolic letter *Misericordia et Misera,* November 20, 2016.

Apostolic letter *Motu Proprio,* instituting the dicastery for promoting integral human development, August 17, 2016.

Apostolic letter *Motu Proprio,* instituting the dicastery for the laity, the family and life, August 15, 2016.

Apostolic letter *Motu Proprio, I Beni Temporali,* regarding certain competencies in economic and financial matters, July 4, 2016.

Apostolic letter *Motu Proprio, As a Loving Mother,* June 4, 2016.

Misericordiae vultus. Bull of Induction of the Extraordinary Jubilee of Mercy, April 11, 2015.

Apostolic letter *Motu Proprio, Fidelis Dispensator et Prudens,* February 24, 2014.

4. Books
Before his pontificate:

Corrupción y Pecado (Corruption and Sin), Buenos Aires, Claretiana, 2006.

Sobre la Acusación de Sí Mismo (On Self-Accusation), Buenos Aires, Claretiana, 2006.

El Verdadero Poder es el Servicio (*The True Power Is Service*), Buenos Aires, Claretiana, 2007.

Mente Abierta, Corazón Creyente (*Open Mind, Believing Heart*), Buenos Aires, Claretiana, 2012.

During his pontificate:

Dieu Rit — L'Humor et la Joie à Travers la Foi, Paris, Michel Lafon, 2017.

Les Peuples, les Murs et les Ponts, interviews with Antono Caño and Pablo Ordaz, Éditions du Cerf, 2017.

À la Jeunesse, Éditions des Équateurs, 2016.

Le Nom de Dieu est Miséricorde, interviews with Andrea Tornielli, Robert Laffont/ Presses de la Renaissance, 2016.

Guérir de la Corruption, Éditions Embrasure, 2014.

5. Website

http://w2.vatican.va/content/vatican/fr.html

BIBLIOGRAPHY OF DOMINIQUE WOLTON

Communiquer, C'est Vivre, Cherche midi, 2016.

Avis à la Pub, Cherche midi, 2015.

Indiscipliné, Odile Jacob, 2012; *La Communication, Les Hommes et La Politique,* CNRS Éditions, coll. "Biblis," 2015.

Informer n'est pas Communiquer, CNRS Éditions, 2009.

McLuhan Ne Répond Plus. Communiquer, C'est Cohabiter, interviews with Stéphane Paoli and Jean Viard, Éditions de l'Aube, 2009.

Demain la Francophonie. Pour Une Autre Mondialisation, Flammarion, 2006.

Mondes Francophones: Auteurs et Livres de Langue Française Depuis 1990 (Ed.), ADPF, ministère des Affaires étrangères, 2006.

Sauver la Communication, Flammarion, 2005; Champs Flammarion, 2007.

Télévision et Civilisations, interviews with

Hugues Le Paige, Bruxelles, Belgium, Labor, 2004.

La Télévision au Pouvoir: Omniprésente, Irritante, Irremplaçable (Ed.), Universalis, coll. "Le tour du sujet," 2004.

"Francophonie et Mondialisation," *Hermès,* no. 40, CNRS Éditions, 2004.

L'Autre Mondialisation, Flammarion, 2003; Champs Flammarion, 2004.

"La France et les Outre-mers. L'enjeu multiculturel," *Hermès,* no. 32–3, CNRS Éditions, 2002.

Internet. Petit Manuel de Survie, interviews with Olivier Jay, Flammarion, 2000.

Internet et Après? Une Théorie Critique des Nouveaux Médias, Flammarion, 1999, prix Georges Pompidou; Champs Flammarion, 2000.

Penser la Communication, Flammarion, 1997; Champs Flammarion, 1998.

L'Unité d'un Homme, interviews with Jacques Delors, Odile Jacob, 1994.

Naissance de l'Europe Démocratique, Flammarion, 1993; Champs Flammarion, 1997.

War Game. L'Information et la Guerre, Flammarion, 1991.

Éloge du Grand Public. Une Théorie Critique de la Télévision, Flammarion, 1990; Champs, Flammarion, 1993.

Le Choix de Dieu, interviews with Jean-Marie Lustiger and J.-L. Missika, Éditions B. de Fallois, 1987; Le Livre de poche, 1989.

Terrorisme à la Une. Média, Terrorisme et Démocratie, with M. Wieviorka, Gallimard, 1987, prix Radio France, 1988.

La Folle du Logis. La Télévision dans les Sociétés Démocratiques, with J.-L. Missika, Gallimard, 1983.

Le Spectateur Engagé, interviews with Raymond Aron and J.-L. Missika, Julliard, 1981, prix Aujourd'hui, 1981.

Le Tertiaire Éclaté. Le Travail sans Modèle, with the CFDT, J.-Ph. Faivret, J.-L. Missika, Éditions du Seuil, 1980.

L'Illusion Écologique, with J.-Ph. Faivret and J.-L. Missika, Éditions du Seuil, 1980.

L'Information Demain de la Presse Écrite aux Nouveaux Médias, with J.-L. Lepigeon, La Documentation française, 1979, prix AFIN 1979 (Associations des informaticiens français).

Les Réseaux Pensants. Télécommunications et Société, with A. Giraud and J.-L. Missika, Masson, October 1978.

Les Dégâts du Progrès. Les Travailleurs Face au Changement Technique, with the CFDT, Éditions du Seuil, 1977, prix futuribles 1977.

Le Nouvel Ordre Sexuel, Éditions du Seuil, 1974.

Co-screenwriter of the film *Mais Ou et Donc Ornicar.* Directed by B. V. Effenterre with Jean-François Stévenin, Brigitte Fossey, Géraldine Chaplin, 1979.

NOTES

Epigraphs

1. Extract from the address to participants in the World Meeting of Popular Movements on October 28, 2014.
2. Extract from the address delivered at the award of the Charlemagne Prize on May 6, 2016.

Introduction

1. The Frankfurt School was set up by a group of Marxist intellectuals in 1923, concerned with social theory and philosophy in the face of rising fascism.

1. Peace and War

1. This modern building, built during the pontificate of John Paul II and finished in 1996, serves as hotel accommodation for

the cardinals during the conclaves. After his election, Pope Francis, feeling more at ease and less alone among the other members of the clergy, decided to stay there "for the time being."

2. EU–Turkey Agreement of March 18, 2016. This text decrees the return to Turkey of people who arrived irregularly in Greece after 20 March 2016 and who did not request or receive asylum.

3. Press conference during the return flight from Mexico, February 17, 2016.

4. *"L'incommunication,"* as expressed in the original French text, is not simply incommunication, which suggests a lack of communication. Rather, "uncommunication" or "a-communication" is where information is being communicated but not understood, and no dialogue exists to build a mutual understanding.

5. A polyhedron is a solid bounded by polygonal faces whose intersections form edges, and the meeting points of which form vertices. "That is why I like the image of the polyhedron, a geometric figure with many different facets. The polyhedron reflects the confluence of all the partialities that still retain their integrity. Nothing is dissolved, nothing is destroyed, nothing is dominated, everything is inte-

grated. Nowadays you too are looking for that synthesis between the local and the global," the Holy Father explained in an address on October 28, 2014.

6. Romano Guardini (1885–1968), Catholic priest, philosopher and theologian.

7. Israeli statesman, born August 2, 1923, died September 28, 2016.

8. Born in 1935, the President of the Palestinian state since 2005.

9. Pastoral visit to Caserta, Italy, July 26, 2014.

10. Pre-Protestant Christian movement, founded around 1173.

11. *Dans un monde qui change, retrouver le sens du politique,* Permanent Council of the Conference of Bishops in France, Bayard-Marne-Éditions du Cerf, 2016.

12. The theory according to which the emperor and the head of the religion are one and the same.

13. *Laïcité* is the French form of secularism, based on the separation of church and state. It is not opposed to religion as such, but seeks to prevent religion from enjoying special privileges.

14. Last day of the trip to Mexico, Wednesday, February 17, 2016. Meeting with the world of work, Colegio de Bachilleres del Estado de Chihuahua, Juárez. This part of

the discussion took place February 25, 2017.

15. Homily of Benedict XVI, known as the "Aparecida Document," delivered on the esplanade of the Sanctuary of Our Lady of Aparecida, the patron saint of Brazil, during his Apostolic Trip to Brazil to coincide with the General Conference of the Bishops of Latin America and the Caribbean, on May 13, 2007.

16. *Evangelii Gaudium* (The Joy of the Gospel), November 24, 2013.

17. *Laudato Si'* ("Praise be to You"), June 18, 2015.

18. A movement, originating in Latin America, which seeks to address issues of poverty and social inequality as well as spiritual matters. The term was first used by the Peruvian priest Gustavo Gutiérrez in his work of the same name, published in 1972. The work is an attack on capitalism, and uses Marxist methods of analysis and argues for the liberation of the people in order to reestablish the Christian tradition of solidarity.

19. Günter Rodolfo Kusch (1922–79), anthropologist and philosopher. His work *Indigenous and Popular Thinking in America* has appeared in English translation (Duke University Press, 2010).

20. The document produced at the end of the Aparecida Conference of Latin American Bishops in 2007, and written by the then Cardinal Bergoglio, now Pope Francis. It emphasizes the power of prayer and concern for the environment, and is often quoted because of its influence on the life of the Church in Latin America.

21. In Christianity, inculturation refers to the way in which Church teachings are presented to non-Christian cultures, and the influence of those cultures on the teachings.

22. Visit to the European Parliament November 25, 2014.

23. The International Charlemagne Prize is an award founded in 1949 and given since 1950 by the city of Aachen in Germany to remarkable individuals who have committed themselves to European unification. It was awarded to Pope Francis on 6 May 2016.

24. Robert Schuman (1886–1963), a Luxembourg-born French statesman, and Konrad Adenauer (1876–1967) were both among the founding fathers of the European Union.

25. The religion of the ruler is the religion of the people. The principle was accepted at the Peace of Augsburg 1555.

26. Interreligious meeting for peace, organized by the Community of Sant'Egidio in the Italian city of Assisi, set up by John Paul II in October 1986.

27. The Beatitudes: Blessed are the poor in spirit,/ for theirs is the kingdom of heaven./ Blessed are those who mourn,/ for they will be comforted./ Blessed are the meek,/ for they will inherit the earth./ Blessed are those who hunger and thirst for righteousness,/ for they will be filled./ Blessed are the merciful,/ for they will be shown mercy./ Blessed are the pure in heart,/ for they will see God./ Blessed are the peacemakers,/ for they will be called children of God./ Blessed are those who are persecuted because of righteousness,/ for theirs is the kingdom of heaven./ Blessed are you when people insult you, persecute you and falsely say all kinds of evil against you because of me./ Rejoice and be glad,/ because great is your reward in heaven. Matthew 5, 3–12.

28. The Gospel According to Matthew, 25.

2. Religions and Politics

1. The Portuguese António Guterres was elected Secretary General of the United Nations on October 13, 2016.

2. Doctrine according to which general ideas or concepts have no existence outside the words used to express them.

3. *Gorgias* 465: "So cookery is the counterpart within flattery of medicine, ornamentation is the counterpart of exercise [. . .] As ornamentation is to exercise, so sophistry is to the legislative process, and as cookery is to medicine, so rhetoric is to the administration of justice." Translated by Robin Waterfield, Oxford, 1994.

4. Basil the Great (329–379), Bishop of Caesarea, Doctor of the Church, author of treatises on the Holy Spirit.

5. For Christians, compassion for the suffering of others is a kindness that encourages indulgence and forgiveness for a person who is guilty of an error and repents of it. Divine mercy is the kindness of God through which he forgives man's errors. When God shows mercy to men and women, he does not give them what they desired (his anger), but instead he grants them his grace, eternal life. He is merciful.

6. David wanted to know the exact number of people in his kingdom, and was punished for this act of pride by a plague. Analogously, drawing up a precise balance here is to hold a census and commit the

sin of pride.

7. These sins are the profanation of the consecrated host (or sacred host, or Eucharistic host, the bread and wine changed into the body of Christ), the absolution of his own accomplice, episcopal consecration without a pontifical mandate, the direct violation of the secret of confession and violence against the person of the Pope.

8. Marcel Lefebvre (1905–91), Superior General of the Fathers of the Holy Spirit, opposed to the Second Vatican Council, he founded the priestly fraternity of Saint Pius X and the Seminary of Écône. He was excommunicated in 1988.

9. Catechesis: in the Catholic Church, religious instruction

10. There are fourteen works of mercy: seven corporal and seven spiritual. The first represent the instructions of the Gospels, notably Matthew 25: "Feed the hungry, give drink to the thirsty, clothe the naked, bury the dead, shelter the homeless, visit the sick and imprisoned." The spiritual works form a list of very concrete and ordinary gestures which touch every area of friendship, family, professional and ecclesiastical life: "Counsel the doubtful, instruct the ignorant,

admonish sinners, comfort the afflicted, forgive offenses willingly, bear wrongs patiently, pray for the living and the dead."

11. *God Rich in Mercy,* the second encyclical, written by John Paul II in 1980 and published on November 30, of the same year.

12. Saint Maria Faustina Kowalska of the Blessed Sacrament (1905–38), canonized by John Paul II in 2000.

13. The Longobardi (Lombards), a Germanic people originally from Scandinavia, who settled on the Italian peninsula in the sixth century; they gave their name to present-day Lombardy.

14. Christian feast celebrating the coming of the Holy Spirit, fifty days after Easter, to the Apostles and the people present with them, and reported in the Acts of the Apostles. Officially concluding the period of Easter, it gives the Church the founding principles of its mission: announcing the good news of the resurrection of Christ to all nations.

15. Acts 8, 26–40.

16. Matteo Ricci (1552–1610), an Italian Jesuit who died in Peking, was the first European to absorb Chinese culture. He invented the transcription of Mandarin into Roman letters.

17. Roberto de Nobili (1577–1656), an Italian Jesuit, a missionary in Southern India and precursor of Indianist studies, worried the Church with his method of the inculturation of the Christian faith.

18. Matthew 23, 22–6.

19. Matthew 6, 24–34.

20. The application of formal, Church-based rules to religious leadership.

21. Jean-Marie Lustiger (1926–2007), French cardinal of Jewish origin, Archbishop of Paris between 1981 and 2005. *See also* Jean-Marie Lustiger, *Le Choix de Dieu, entretiens avec Dominique Wolton,* B. de Fallois, 1987.

22. Byzantine-Rite Christians from Middle Eastern countries.

23. The Council of Chalcedony (AD 451) reaffirmed the dogma of the Holy Trinity, establishing Christ's double nature, divine and human, in a perfect fusion. But the information was passed on to the Armenians in a confused way, leading them to condemn the doctrine of Chalcedony and, consequently, to prefer monophysitism, the doctrine of the "single nature" of Christ.

24. Nerses died on June 25, 2015.

25. Trip between June 24 and 26, 2016.

26. Ahmed el-Taleb, senior Egyptian Sunni

Islamic cleric.

27. The extraction and processing of natural resources — for example through farming, fishing and mining.

28. The Epistle to Diognetus is a letter from an anonymous Christian author to a high-ranking pagan named Diognetus which dates from the end of the second century AD. It is an apologia demonstrating the radical novelty of Christianity as compared to paganism and Judaism.

29. Charles Péguy (1873–1914), writer, poet and essayist.

30. *Quadragesimo Anno,* May 15, 1931, paragraph 109.

31. *Octogesima Adveniens,* May 14, 1971, paragraph 44.

32. Address in the Moria Refugee Camp, Lesbos, April 16, 2016.

3. Europe and Cultural Diversity

1. The role of deaconess is understood as a stepping stone toward the priesthood.

2. In May 1968, there was a period of civil unrest in France, sparked by anti-capitalist protests. The impact of the upheaval is widely considered to be a pivotal moment in the history of the country.

3. Joseph Malègue (1876–1940), *Augustin*

ou Le Maître est là, Spes, 1933.

4. Action Française is a right-wing French political movement originally established in 1899. Monarchist and counterrevolutionary, the movement supported the Vichy regime in the Second World War, and was closely connected with the Catholic Church.

5. Louis Billot (1846–1931) was appointed cardinal in 1911 by Pius X. His disagreement with the condemnation of Action Française by Rome in 1926 led him to resign the following year.

6. Jean-Marie Vianney (1786–1859), curé of the parish of Ars, venerated by the Catholic Church.

7. Pierre Fourier (1565–1640), Augustinian canon, curé of Mattaincourt, was closely attached to the ducal family of Lorraine. His commitment to the renewal of educational pastoral made him a pioneer of Catholic reform.

8. The movement founded by Archbishop Marcel Lefebvre which rejected many of the reforms of the Second Vatican Council and notably continued to serve the Latin Mass.

9. The Society of Jesus, the Jesuit Order.

10. Alcide de Gasperi (1881–1954), Italian statesman who was, along with Schuman

and Adenauer, one of the founding fathers of the European Union.

11. Address to the European Parliament, Strasbourg, November 25, 2014.

12. Ibid.

13. Apostolic Exhortation *Evangelii Gaudium,* paragraph 223.

14. Declaration of May 9, 1950, Salon de l'Horloge, Quai d'Orsay, Paris.

15. Ibid.

16. *Evangelii Gaudium,* paragraph 239.

17. Konrad Adenauer, Chancellor of the Federal Republic of Germany, "Address delivered on the occasion of the signature of the Treaties of Rome," March 25, 1957.

18. Address at the Conferral of the Charlemagne Prize, May 6, 2016, *L'Osservatore Romano* May 12, 2016.

4. Culture and Communication

1. "La voie des sens," *Hermès,* No. 74, CNRS Éditions, March 2016. *Hermès,* an international journal devoted to communication as a scientific and political issue, was set up in 1988 by Dominique Wolton, who remains its editor in chief.

2. Luke 2, 22–38.

3. 13 November 2016.

4. Philippe Barberin, b. 1950, Cardinal

477

Archbishop of Lyon.

5. According to the 2015 report by Twiplomacy, Pope Francis is the most influential leader on Twitter. He has 32 million followers, especially in Spanish (12.5 million), English (10.2 million) and Italian (4.2 million). Below the million figure are Polish (751,000), Latin (735,000), German (412,000) and Arabic (350,000).

6. Translation © libreria editrice Vaticana.

5. Otherness, Time and Joy

1. A formal written defense of one's belief or conduct.

2. "I ask you to be shepherds with God's tenderness, to leave the 'whip' hanging in the sacristy and be shepherds with tenderness." Homily delivered for the third world retreat of priests, Basilica of St. John Lateran, Friday June 12, 2015.

3. Cardinal Barbarin was accused of covering up for a pedophile priest in his Church. The investigation was eventually dropped by prosecutors.

4. *Gaudete in Domino (Rejoice in the Lord),* May 9, 1975.

5. Google, Apple, Facebook and Amazon

6. Heinrich Joseph Dominicus Denzinger (1819–1883), 19th-century German Cath-

olic theologian. His major work, *Enchiridion* (1854), is a collection of official doctrinal texts.

7. "Langues romanes: un milliard de locuteurs." *Hermès,* no. 75, CNRS Éditions, 2016.

8. Italian singer, born in 1940.

9. Center Nationale de la Recherche Scientifique, France's National Center for Scientific Research.

10. "La voie des sens," (The Way of the Senses) *Hermès,* no. 74, CNRS éditions, 2016.

11. A former French Army officer who became a priest and then a hermit in the Algerian Sahara, Charles de Foucauld (1858–1916) devoted his life to the poorest of the poor. He was murdered at the door of his hermitage on 1 December 1916. He was beatified by Benedict XVI in 2005.

12. Angelism: taken here to mean the desire to live as disembodied creatures when we are embodied.

13. Doctrine of Pelagius, 5th-century Breton monk, concerning grace and original sin, which maintained that man could ensure his salvation by merit alone. By extension, a doctrine placing excessive emphasis on man's natural goodness.

14. "L'Univers religieux de Dostoïevski," Editions du Seuil, 1963. Italian Edition: Dostojevskij. Il mondo religioso, Brescia, 1920.
15. Luke 6, 24–6.
16. Matthew 23, 15.
17. Luke 16, 19.
18. Luke 10, 30–2.

6. "Mercy Is a Journey From the Heart to the Hand."

1. A belief in the importance of mission: bringing the Church's message to those who do not know it.
2. Matteo Ricci (1552–1610), Jesuit missionary to China.
3. Roberto de Nobili (1577–1656), Italian Jesuit missionary in India. He kept those aspects of Indian culture and religion that were not at odds with Catholic teaching.
4. Jean-Francois Millet painted The Angelus between 1857 and 1859. It depicts two peasants in a field with heads bowed in prayer, a basket of freshly dug potatoes between them.
5. Servant of the servants of God. This ancient title refers indirectly to the message delivered by Christ as he washed Peter's feet at the Last Supper. The pre-

ferred title of Paul VI, who had it added to the official list after the Second Vatican Council.

6. Ludwig von Pastor (1854–1928), Austrian historian and diplomat, the author of a history of the popes from the end of the Middle Ages. A book written on the basis of a large number of unpublished documents taken from the secret archives of the Vatican and others. All forty volumes of the *History of the Popes,* published between 1899 and 1953, are available on the internet archive.

7. Jacques Hamel (1930–2016), Catholic priest in the archdiocese of Rouen, killed in the church of Saint-Étienne in Saint-Étienne-du-Rouvray by two Islamist terrorists during the attack on the place of worship on July 26, 2016.

8. *Gaudium et Spes* (Joy and hope) is one of the main documents to emerge from the Vatican II ecumenical council (1965).

7. "Tradition Is a Movement."

1. Vincent, a monk at Lérins (died before 450), author of the Commonitorium (Tradition and Progress) under the pseudonym of Peregrinus.

2. Peter Claver (1580–1654), Catalan Jesuit

priest, missionary in South America, principally with African slaves, was sanctified by the Catholic Church.

3. *Rerum novarum* (New things), encyclical published on May 15, 1891 by Pope Leo XIII (1810–1903) setting out the foundations of the social teaching of the Catholic Church.

4. Joachim of Flore (ca. 1132–ca. 1202), Calabrian Franciscan monk, Catholic theologian, divided the history of mankind into three ages (of the Father, of the Son, of the Holy Spirit), the last of which began, in his view, in the Middle Ages. This theory had a millenarian aspect, and later exerted a strong influence on utopian theories and certain revolutionary movements.

5. Editions du Cerf, 2014.

6. A reference to the address delivered at the presentation of Christmas greetings at the Roman Curia, Clementine Hall, December 22, 2014, known as the "Address of the Fifteen Curial Diseases." On the occasion of the presentation of Christmas Greetings at the Roman Curia, December 22, 2016, "some guiding principles for the conduct of reform" were announced: Individuality, Pastoral sense, Missionary sense, Rationality, Functionality, Moder-

nity, Sobriety, Subsidiarity, Synodality, Catholicity, Professionalism, Graduality.

7. Revelation 2, 4.
8. A department of the Roman Curia through which the Pope governs the Church.

8. A Destiny

1. A city in the North of Argentina.
2. March 5, 1953, which was also the date of Stalin's death.
3. Opera by Ambroise Thomas (1866).
4. Comic opera by Jules Massenet (1884).
5. Revolutionary Febrerista Party, founded in Buenos Aires.
6. Members of the American Communist Party, Julius and Ethel Rosenberg were accused of giving the Soviet Union the secret of the atom bomb. They died in the electric chair on June 19, 1953.
7. Esther Balestrino De Careaga (1918–1977). A Paraguayan who was close to the communists, and who became one of the founders of the Mothers of Plaza de Mayo after the disappearance of one of her daughters and a son-in-law. Arrested in December 1977 with two French nuns, she was tortured and murdered, then thrown in the sea from an airplane.

8. French cardinal born in 1953, appointed Camerlengo of the Holy Roman Church in 2014, Jean-Louis Tauran presides over the Pontifical Council on Interreligious Dialogue.
9. In Catholic doctrine, the belief that the strict course is always the right one to follow in doubtful cases.
10. Address to the United Nations, September 25, 2015.
11. *Laudato Sí,* paragraph 164.
12. Address to Popular Movements, July 9, 2015.
13. Message for World Food Day, October 16, 2013.
14. *Laudato Sí,* paragraph 25.
15. Ibid., paragraph 44.
16. *Populorum Progressio,* paragraphs 56–62.
17. John Paul II, Address at the Arrival Ceremony, Cairo, February 24, 2000.
18. Exodus 19, 12.
19. Exodus 20, 13.
20. © Libreria Editrice Vaticana.

Biography Of Pope Francis

1. © Libreria Editrice Vaticana.

ABOUT THE AUTHORS

Jorge Mario Bergoglio, cardinal-archbishop of Buenos Aires, was elected pope under the name of Francis on March 13, 2013. He is the first Jesuit and Latin American pope in the history of the Catholic Church.

Dominique Wolton is a research director at the CNRS. He is the founder and director of the international journal Hermès (CNRS Éditions) since 1988. He is interested in the connections between people and politics and technology and the economy. He is the author of thirty books, translated into twenty languages.

The employees of Thorndike Press hope you have enjoyed this Large Print book. All our Thorndike, Wheeler, and Kennebec Large Print titles are designed for easy reading, and all our books are made to last. Other Thorndike Press Large Print books are available at your library, through selected bookstores, or directly from us.

For information about titles, please call:
(800) 223-1244

or visit our website at:
gale.com/thorndike

To share your comments, please write:

Publisher
Thorndike Press
10 Water St., Suite 310
Waterville, ME 04901